# ACT® Math Mastery Level 1

(2014-15 Edition)

The ultimate workbook to help you succeed on the ACT Math test

Craig Gehring

MasteryPrep

ACT® is the registered trademark of ACT, Inc. MasteryPrep, LLC has no affiliation with ACT, Inc., and the ACT Mastery program is not approved or endorsed by ACT, Inc.

Copyright © 2014 by Craig Gehring.

All Rights Reserved. No part of this publication may be reproduced or transmitted in any form or by any means, electronic or mechanical, including photocopy, recording, or any information storage or retrieval, without permission in writing from Craig Gehring.

This publication, its author, and its publisher, are in no way affiliated with or authorized by ACT, Inc. or by College Board. ACT and SAT are copyrights and/or trademarks of ACT, Inc. and College Board, respectively.

Inquiries concerning this publication should be mailed to:

MasteryPrep
7117 Florida Blvd.
Baton Rouge, LA 70806

Printed in the United States of America.

ISBN-10: 1500693472
ISBN-13: 978-1500693473

LR-120414

# Contents

How to Use This Book .................................................................................................. 5
Lesson 1: Division ........................................................................................................ 6
Lesson 2: Averages ..................................................................................................... 17
Lesson 3: Probability .................................................................................................. 29
Lesson 4: Combinations ............................................................................................. 41
Lesson 5: Review ........................................................................................................ 53
Lesson 6: Combinations With Removal ..................................................................... 65
Lesson 7: Multiplication ............................................................................................. 77
Lesson 8: Algebra ....................................................................................................... 89
Lesson 9: Multiplication Using FOIL ....................................................................... 101
Lesson 10: Review .................................................................................................... 113
Lesson 11: Working Backwards ................................................................................ 125
Lesson 12: Sequences & Patterns ............................................................................. 137
Lesson 13: Perimeter ................................................................................................ 149
Lesson 14: Angles ..................................................................................................... 161
Lesson 15: Review .................................................................................................... 173
Lesson 16: Pythagorean Theorem ............................................................................ 185
Lesson 17: Area ........................................................................................................ 197
Lesson 18: Y-Intercepts ............................................................................................ 209
Lesson 19: Rates ....................................................................................................... 221
Lesson 20: Review .................................................................................................... 233
Lesson 21: Slope ....................................................................................................... 245
Lesson 22: Systems of Equations ............................................................................. 257
Lesson 23: Review of Lessons 1 - 10 ........................................................................ 269
Lesson 24: Review of Lessons 11 - 20 ...................................................................... 281
Lesson 25: Final Review ........................................................................................... 293
Math Mini-Practice Tests ......................................................................................... 305
Math Glossary .......................................................................................................... 379
About the Author / More Information ..................................................................... 396

# 🛑 Have You Registered Your Book Yet?

With your purchase of *ACT Math Mastery, Level 1*, you have gained access to a special series of videos on prepping for the ACT Math test by the workbook's author, Craig Gehring, who made perfect scores on both the ACT and the SAT. These videos are not available anywhere. You'll also have the option to receive Craig's free newsletter designed to give you the edge you need before your exams. The entire registration process is free and takes less than 1 minute.

Visit
**www.actmastery.com/math**

# How to Use This Workbook

This workbook consists of 25 lessons.  Each lesson takes about 15 minutes.  The workbook is designed for you to do one lesson per day.

By the end of the book, you will have mastered 20 math concepts that can each appear as one or more questions on the ACT.

Read through a question, answer it to the best of your ability, then check to see if you got the answer right.  The answer and explanation of each question are directly behind the question being asked.  That makes it easy to cheat, but don't!  You'll only be cheating yourself.

Read through the explanation of how to arrive at the best answer (whether you got it right or wrong).  Then go to the next question.  It's okay to get answers wrong.  That's how you'll learn and get better!

A question may be marked as REVIEW.  If you get that question wrong when you try, the explanation of the answer might direct you to work through some problems again in a previous lesson.  The whole point is to help you get to the point where you remember all of these questions and can use your newfound knowledge to ace the ACT.

If a particular lesson is giving you difficulties, get a teacher or tutor to help you.  It's possible that you may have missed that segment in school and so don't have any idea what the lesson is talking about.  There's nothing wrong with getting help!

And with that, let's begin.

# Lesson 1
# Division

The key to solving division word problems is to first identify what you know from the information provided, and what you are trying to figure out.

For example, in the following word problem:

*If 5 vases cost $5, what is the cost of 1 vase?*

you know the cost of five vases. What you need to figure out is how much one by itself would cost. Whenever you know the total value of a group of things, you can use *division* to figure out the value of ONE thing.

In this case, you would divide $5 by 5, since there are five vases.

5 / 5 = 1

Your answer is $1.00.

Using division to figure out what the value of ONE thing is is often a building block to questions on the ACT. You can use this skill to make the word problems you answer simpler to figure out.

One trick to remember when to use division is to remember the phrase DIVVY UP. If you DIVVY UP something, you split it up evenly among all the people involved. For example, if you have 5 friends helping you run a lemonade stand, you would divvy up the money afterwards, giving each person one dollar until no dollars remained. This is what division does. Use division to figure out what each person would get if the total was split evenly between everyone.

# Lesson 1 - Division

# 1.

If 10 vases cost $10, what is the cost of 1 vase?

- a. $2.00
- b. $1.50
- c. $10.00
- d. $1.00

# 2.

If 15 vases cost $30, what is the cost of 1 vase?

- a. $2.00
- b. $4.50
- c. $7.50
- d. $1.00

# 3.

If 4 tickets cost $6.00, what is the cost of 1 ticket?

- a. $1.50
- b. $2.50
- c. $2.00
- d. $6.00

Math Mastery - Level 1

# 1.

If 10 vases cost $10, what is the cost of 1 vase?

a. $2.00
b. $1.50
c. $10.00
**d. $1.00**

**The correct answer is D.**
$10 divided by 10 vases = $1.00 per vase.
10 / 10 = 1

# 2.

If 15 vases cost $30, what is the cost of 1 vase?

**a. $2.00**
b. $4.50
c. $7.50
d. $1.00

**The correct answer is A.**
$30 divided by 15 vases = $2.00 per vase.
30 / 15 = 2

# 3.

If 4 tickets cost $6.00, what is the cost of 1 ticket?

**a. $1.50**
b. $2.50
c. $2.00
d. $6.00

**The correct answer is A.**
$6 divided by 4 tickets = $1.50 per ticket.  6 / 4 = 1.5
Note: You may have accidentally divided 4 tickets by $6. The problem here is that you now have 0.67 tickets per dollar. This is not the answer you are looking for. You have to make sure the first number is value, and the second number is the number of times you're splitting the value up.

# 4.

If 6 adults can fit in a van, how many vans do you need to transport 24 adults at one time?

    a. 5
    b. 6
    c. 24
    d. 4

# 5.

If 6 adults can fit in a van, how many vans do you need to transport 25 adults at one time?

    a. 5
    b. 4
    c. 6
    d. 25

# 6.

If a back yard has 100 square feet that need grass planted, how many 2 square foot grass squares do you need to plant the whole area?

    a. 40
    b. 100
    c. 50
    d. 30

# 4.

If 6 adults can fit in a van, how many vans do you need to transport 24 adults at one time?

a. 5
b. 6
c. 24
**d. 4**

**The correct answer is D.**
24 adults divided into vans with 6 adults in each van = 4 vans
24 / 6 = 4

# 5.

If 6 adults can fit in a van, how many vans do you need to transport 25 adults at one time?

**a. 5**
b. 4
c. 6
d. 25

**The correct answer is A.**
25 adults divided into vans with 6 adults in each van = 4.17 vans. 25 / 6 = 4.17
Since you can't have a fraction of a van, you have to round up to 5 to fit all of the adults. Be careful of this. On many ACT questions, a whole number is required as the answer.

# 6.

If a back yard has 100 square feet that need grass planted, how many 2 square foot grass squares do you need to plant the whole area?

a. 40
b. 100
**c. 50**
d. 30

**The correct answer is C.**
100 square feet divided by 2 square feet per square = 50 grass squares.
100 / 2 = 50

# Lesson 1 - Division

## 7.

If a back yard has 250 square feet that need grass planted, how many 5 square foot grass squares do you need to plant the whole area?

    a. 40
    b. 50
    c. 250
    d. 1250

## 8.

If a school needs to raise $1000.00 at a fundraiser, and each fundraiser ticket sold earns the school $2.00, how many tickets does the school need to sell?

    a. 500
    b. 2000
    c. 50
    d. 1000

## 9.

If a school needs to raise $2500.00 at a fundraiser, and each fundraiser ticket sold earns the school $3.00, what is the minimum number of tickets that the school needs to sell to reach its goal?

    a. 2500
    b. 834
    c. 835
    d. 9

# 7.

If a back yard has 250 square feet that need grass planted, how many 5 square foot grass squares do you need to plant the whole area?

a. 40
**b. 50**
c. 250
d. 1250

**The correct answer is B.**
250 square feet divided by 5 square feet per square = 50 grass squares.
250 / 5 = 50

# 8.

If a school needs to raise $1000.00 at a fundraiser, and each fundraiser ticket sold earns the school $2.00, how many tickets does the school need to sell?

**a. 500**
b. 2000
c. 50
d. 1000

**The correct answer is A.**
$1000 divided by $2.00 per ticket = 500 tickets
1000 / 2 = 500

# 9.

If a school needs to raise $2500.00 at a fundraiser, and each fundraiser ticket sold earns the school $3.00, what is the minimum number of tickets that the school needs to sell to reach its goal?

a. 2500
**b. 834**
c. 835
d. 9

**The correct answer is B.**
$2500 divided by $3.00 per ticket = 833.33 tickets.  2500 / 3 = 833.33
Since you can't sell a part of a ticket, you have to round up to the nearest whole number to meet the goal.

Lesson 1 - Division

# 10.

A school needs to raise $2500.00 as a fundraiser for its new library. A parent has already donated $250, but the rest will need to be earned through ticket sales. If each fundraiser ticket earns the school $3.00, what is the minimum number of tickets that the school needs to sell to reach its goal?

a. 750
b. 75
c. 834
d. 83

# 11.

Dianna is starting a lemonade stand. Her brother offers to work for her for $10.00. If she earns $1.00 for every drink sold, how many drinks will she need to sell before she has earned enough to pay her brother?

a. 1
b. 100
c. 150
d. 10

# 12.

Dianna is starting a lemonade stand. Her brother offers to work for her for $20.00. If she earns $1.20 for every drink sold, how many drinks will she need to sell before she has earned enough to pay her brother?

a. 17
b. 20
c. 16
d. 5

# 10.

A school needs to raise $2500.00 as a fundraiser for its new library. A parent has already donated $250, but the rest will need to be earned through ticket sales. If each fundraiser ticket earns the school $3.00, what is the minimum number of tickets that the school needs to sell to reach its goal?

a. 750
b. 75
c. 834
d. 83

**The correct answer is A.**
$2500 minus $250 already raised = $2250. $2250 divided by $3.00 per ticket = 750 tickets.
2500 - 250 = 2250.  2250 / 3 = 750.

# 11.

Dianna is starting a lemonade stand. Her brother offers to work for her for $10.00. If she earns $1.00 for every drink sold, how many drinks will she need to sell before she has earned enough to pay her brother?

a. 1
b. 100
c. 150
**d. 10**

**The correct answer is D.**
$10 divided by $1.00 per drink = 10 drinks.
10 / 1 = 10

# 12.

Dianna is starting a lemonade stand. Her brother offers to work for her for $20.00. If she earns $1.20 for every drink sold, how many drinks will she need to sell before she has earned enough to pay her brother?

a. 17
b. 20
c. 16
d. 5

**The correct answer is A.**
$20 divided by $1.20 per drink = 16.67 drinks.  20 / 1.20 = 16.67
Since you can't sell part of a drink, you have to round up to the nearest whole number.

Math Mastery - Level 1

# Lesson 1 - Division

## 13.

If ten shirts cost $120, how much do 2 shirts cost?

    a. $12
    b. $24
    c. $240
    d. $48

## 14.

If twelve shirts cost $150, how much do 3 shirts cost?

    a. $37.50
    b. $50.00
    c. $450
    d. $22.50

## 15.

If five shirts cost $75, how much does 1 shirt cost?

    a. $15
    b. $10
    c. $75
    d. $37.50

# 13.

If ten shirts cost $120, how much do 2 shirts cost?

a. $12
**b. $24**
c. $240
d. $48

**The correct answer is B.**
$120 divided by 10 shirts = $12 per shirt. $12 per shirt times 2 shirts = $24.
120 / 10 = 12. 12 x 2 = 24. You have to figure out the value of one shirt, then you can figure out how much more than one shirt costs.

# 14.

If twelve shirts cost $150, how much do 3 shirts cost?

**a. $37.50**
b. $50.00
c. $450
d. $22.50

**The correct answer is A.**
$150 divided by 12 shirts = $12.50. $12.50 per shirt times 3 shirts = $37.50.
150 / 12 = 12.50. 12.50 x 3 = 37.50. You have to figure out the value of one shirt, then you can figure out how much more than one shirt costs.

# 15.

If five shirts cost $75, how much does 1 shirt cost?

**a. $15**
b. $10
c. $75
d. $37.50

**The correct answer is A.**
$75 divided by five shirts = $15. 75 / 5 = 15.
This problem was easier than the ones before it. Remember that the ACT does not give you questions in order of difficulty. You can have a tough question and right after that an easy one.

# Lesson 2
# Averages

Word problems that ask for averages are a special form of division problem. When you average something, you:

1. ADD UP ALL OF THE VALUES

2. DIVIDE THEM BY THE NUMBER OF THINGS YOU'RE AVERAGING

A good check for whether you got the average right is that the average is almost always in the middle compared to the values you were averaging. For example, in this problem:

Four students scored a 100 on a test, while one student scored a 50. What is the average score of the five students together?

To find the average, you add up all of the values. In this case, the values are:

100

100

100

100

50

100 + 100 + 100 + 100 + 50 = 450.

Then we divide that total by the number of things we are averaging. In this case, we are averaging five things, so we divide 450 by 5.

450 / 5 = 90.

The average score of the five students is 90.

Now we check it.  Is 90 between 100 and 50?  It is.  Notice that because there were a lot of 100s, and only one 50, our average is closer to 100, and not to 50.

What do you think our average would be closer to if there had been four 50s and only one 100?  That's right, it would be closer to 50!

Whenever a question asks you to find the AVERAGE, use this method.  Another word for average is MEAN.  If an ACT question asks you to find the MEAN of a set of numbers, that means the test wants you to find the AVERAGE of the numbers.

## 1.

Four students scored 90 on a test, while one student scored 100. What is the average score of the five students together?

      a. 92
      b. 90
      c. 94
      d. 95

## 2.

Eight students scored the following scores on a science test: 70, 82, 89, 91, 92, 94, 95, 99. What was the average score for this test?

      a. 70
      b. 85
      c. 89
      d. 92

## 3.

John went to the store and purchased five shirts at the following prices: $8.00, $15.00, $30.00, $32.00, and $35.00. What was the average price of the five shirts?

      a. $24
      b. $27
      c. $19
      d. $32

# 1.

Four students scored 90 on a test, while one student scored 100. What is the average score of the five students together?

a. 92
b. 90
c. 94
d. 95

**The correct answer is A.**
The total score of all five students is 90 + 90 + 90 + 90 + 100 = 460. There are five students, so we divide 460 by 5 students to get the average score. 460 / 5 = 92.

# 2.

Eight students scored the following scores on a science test: 70, 82, 89, 91, 92, 94, 95, 99. What was the average score for this test?

a. 70
b. 85
**c. 89**
d. 92

**The correct answer is C.**
The total score of all eight students is 70 + 82 + 89 + 91 + 92 + 94 + 95 + 99 = 712. There are eight students, so we divide 712 by 8 students to get the average score. 712 / 8 = 89.

# 3.

John went to the store and purchased five shirts at the following prices: $8.00, $15.00, $30.00, $32.00, and $35.00. What was the average price of the five shirts?

**a. $24**
b. $27
c. $19
d. $32

**The correct answer is A.**
The total price of the five shirts is $8.00 + $15.00 + $30.00 + $32.00 + $35.00 = $120.00. There are five shirts, so we divide $120.00 by 5 shirts to get the average price. 120 / 5 = 24.

# Lesson 2 - Averages

## 4.

John went to the store and purchased nine shirts at the following prices: $9.00, $4.00, $12.00, $18.00, $27.00, $39.00, $41.00, $43.00, and $50.00.  What was the average price of the nine shirts?

    a. $24.55
    b. $30.00
    c. $27.00
    d. None of the above

## 5.

Ella took a summer job at a store.  They have a small t-shirt section, and her manager has asked her to figure out the average price of all the shirts in the store.  Below is the chart of how many shirts they have at each price level.  What is the average price of the shirts they have in stock, rounded to the nearest cent?

| Price of Shirts | Number in Inventory |
|---|---|
| $6.99 | 3 |
| $7.99 | 2 |
| $8.99 | 2 |
| $9.99 | 1 |

    a. $8.11
    b. $8.12
    c. $8.00
    d. $7.99

## 6.

Ella took a summer job at a store.  They have a small t-shirt section, and her manager asked her to figure out the average price of all the shirts in the store.  Below is the chart of how many shirts they have at each price level.  What is the average price of the shirts they have in stock, rounded to the nearest cent?

| Price of Shirts | Number in Inventory |
|---|---|
| $6.99 | 3 |
| $7.99 | 4 |
| $8.99 | 3 |
| $9.99 | 1 |
| $14.99 | 4 |
| $24.99 | 5 |

    a. $13.75
    b. $13.74
    c. $9.99
    d. $12.32

# 4.

John went to the store and purchased nine shirts at the following prices: $9.00, $4.00, $12.00, $18.00, $27.00, $39.00, $41.00, $43.00, and $50.00. What was the average price of the nine shirts?

a. $24.55
b. $30.00
**c. $27.00**
d. None of the above

**The correct answer is C.**
The total price of the nine shirts is $9 + $4 + $12 + $18 + $27 + $39 + $41 + $43 + $50 = $243. The average price of each shirt is $243 divided by 9 shirts = $27. 243 / 9 = 27

# 5.

Ella took a summer job at a store. They have a small t-shirt section, and her manager has asked her to figure out the average price of all the shirts in the store. Below is the chart of how many shirts they have at each price level. What is the average price of the shirts they have in stock, rounded to the nearest cent?

a. $8.11  **b. $8.12**  c. $8.00  d. $7.99

| Price of Shirts | Number in Inventory |
|---|---|
| $6.99 | 3 |
| $7.99 | 2 |
| $8.99 | 2 |
| $9.99 | 1 |

**The correct answer is B.**
The total price of the shirts is ($6.99 x 3) + ($7.99 x 2) + ($8.99 x 2) + ($9.99 x 1) = $64.92. The average price of the shirts is $64.92 divided by 8 shirts = $8.115. Rounding to the nearest cent, we get $8.12. Note that if you round incorrectly, you'll get A, a wrong answer. Having an answer that's similar to another answer is a good sign you're on the right track - usually!

# 6.

Ella took a summer job at a store. They have a small t-shirt section, and her manager asked her to figure out the average price of all the shirts in the store. Below is the chart of how many shirts they have at each price level. What is the average price of the shirts they have in stock, rounded to the nearest cent?

a. $13.75  **b. $13.74**  c. $9.99  d. $12.32

| Price of Shirts | Number in Inventory |
|---|---|
| $6.99 | 3 |
| $7.99 | 4 |
| $8.99 | 3 |
| $9.99 | 1 |
| $14.99 | 4 |
| $24.99 | 5 |

**The correct answer is B.**
The total price of the shirts is ($6.99 x 3) + ($7.99 x 4) + ($8.99 x 3) + ($9.99 x 1) + ($14.99 x 4) + ($24.99 x 5) = $274.80. The average price of the shirts is $274.80 divided by 20 shirts = $13.74. Note that you don't need to round to the nearest cent, even though the question instructs you to. Don't let this throw you off of a correct answer.

# 7.

Ella took a summer job at a store. They have a small t-shirt section, and her manager asked her to figure out the average price of all the shirts in the store. Below is the chart of how many shirts they have at each price level. What is the average price of the shirts they have in stock, rounded to the nearest cent?

| Price of Shirts | Number in Inventory |
|---|---|
| $6.99 | 4 |
| $7.99 | 5 |
| $8.99 | 2 |
| $9.99 | 3 |
| $14.99 | 1 |
| $24.99 | 2 |

a. $10.64
b. $10.63
c. $9.49
d. $10.99

# 8.

Damien did an internship in the accounting department of a large corporation. He was asked to do a little math for them. The company earned a yearly profit of $7.0 million dollars for three years. For the next two years, the company earned $7.5 million each year. What was the average profit earned by the company in this five-year period?

a. $7.25 million
b. $7.0 million
c. $7.2 million
d. $7.3 million

# 9.

Damien did an internship in the accounting department of a large corporation. He was asked to do a little math for them. The company earned a yearly profit of $9.0 million dollars for three years. For the next two years, the company earned $3.2 million each year. What was the average profit earned by the company in this five-year period?

a. $6.1 million
b. $6.67 million
c. $6.68 million
d. $5 million

# 7.

Ella took a summer job at a store. They have a small t-shirt section, and her manager asked her to figure out the average price of all the shirts in the store. Below is the chart of how many shirts they have at each price level. What is the average price of the shirts they have in stock, rounded to the nearest cent?

| Price of Shirts | Number in Inventory |
|---|---|
| $6.99 | 4 |
| $7.99 | 5 |
| $8.99 | 2 |
| $9.99 | 3 |
| $14.99 | 1 |
| $24.99 | 2 |

a. **$10.64**   b. $10.63   c. $9.49   d. $10.99

**The correct answer is A.**
The total price of the shirts is ($6.99 x 4) + ($7.99 x 5) + ($8.99 x 2) + ($9.99 x 3) + ($14.99 x 1) + ($24.99 x 2) = $180.83. The average price of the shirts is $180.83 divided by 17 shirts = $10.63705. Rounding to the nearest cent, we get $10.64. Note that if you round incorrectly, you'll get B, a wrong answer.

# 8.

Damien did an internship in the accounting department of a large corporation. He was asked to do a little math for them. The company earned a yearly profit of $7.0 million dollars for three years. For the next two years, the company earned $7.5 million each year. What was the average profit earned by the company in this five-year period?

a. $7.25 million   b. $7.0 million   **c. $7.2 million**   d. $7.3 million

**The correct answer is C.**
$7.0 million per year x 3 years = $21 million. $7.5 million per year x 2 years = $15 million. The total amount of profit in five years is $21 million + $15 million = $36 million. The average profit per year is $36 million divided into 5 years = $7.2 million.

# 9.

Damien did an internship in the accounting department of a large corporation. He was asked to do a little math for them. The company earned a yearly profit of $9.0 million dollars for three years. For the next two years, the company earned $3.2 million each year. What was the average profit earned by the company in this five-year period?

a. $6.1 million   b. $6.67 million   **c. $6.68 million**   d. $5 million

**The correct answer is C.**
$9.0 million per year x 3 years = $27 million. $3.2 million x 2 = $6.4 million. The total profit earned in five years is $27 milion + $6.4 million = $33.4 million. The average profit per years is $33.4 million per year divided into 5 years = $6.68 million.

# 10.

Tabitha made the following scores in her math class:

| Test | 1 | 2 | 3 | 4 | 5 |
|---|---|---|---|---|---|
| Score | 80 | 100 | 99 | 96 | ? |

In her school an overall average score of 94 or more is given a A.  What is the minimum score she needs to get on her fifth test in order to score an A in the class?

      a. 94
      b. 95
      c. 96
      d. 100

# 11.

Tabitha made the following scores in her math class:

| Test | 1 | 2 | 3 | 4 | 5 |
|---|---|---|---|---|---|
| Score | 94 | 97 | 85 | 98 | ? |

In her school an overall average score of 94 or more is given a A.  What is the minimum score she needs to get on her fifth test in order to score an A in the class?

      a. 94
      b. 95
      c. 96
      d. 97

# 12.

Tabitha made the following scores in her math class:

| Test | 1 | 2 | 3 | 4 | 5 |
|---|---|---|---|---|---|
| Score | 97 | 88 | 98 | 99 | ? |

In her school an overall average score of 94 or more is given a A.  What is the minimum score she needs to get on her fifth test in order to score an A in the class?

      a. 75
      b. 95
      c. 90
      d. 88

# 10.

Tabitha made the following scores in her math class. In her school an overall average score of 94 or more is given a A. What is the minimum score she needs to get on her fifth test in order to score an A in the class?

a. 94   **b. 95**   c. 96   d. 100

| Test  | 1  | 2   | 3  | 4  | 5 |
|-------|----|-----|----|----|---|
| Score | 80 | 100 | 99 | 96 | ? |

**The correct answer is B.**

To answer this problem, we have to work backwards with what we know about averages. We need to find out what TOTAL score is needed to have an average of 94. In other words, what number divided by 5 = 94?

x / 5 = 94

Multiply both sides by 5 and you get x = 94 • 5

x = 470. So the TOTAL score needs to be 470. Currently we have a total score of 80 + 100+ 99 + 96 = 375. So we need a minimum score of 470 - 375 = 95.

# 11.

Tabitha made the following scores in her math class. In her school an overall average score of 94 or more is given a A. What is the minimum score she needs to get on her fifth test in order to score an A in the class?

a. 94   b. 95   **c. 96**   d. 97

| Test  | 1  | 2  | 3  | 4  | 5 |
|-------|----|----|----|----|---|
| Score | 94 | 97 | 85 | 98 | ? |

**The correct answer is C.**

To answer this problem, we have to work backwards with what we know about averages. We need to find out what TOTAL score is needed to have an average of 94. In other words, what number divided by 5 = 94?

x / 5 = 94

Multiply both sides by 5 and you get x = 94 • 5

x = 470. So the TOTAL score needs to be 470. Currently we have a total score of 94 + 97 + 85 + 98 = 374. So we need a minimum score of 470 - 374 = 96.

# 12.

Tabitha made the following scores in her math class. In her school an overall average score of 94 or more is given a A. What is the minimum score she needs to get on her fifth test in order to score an A in the class?

a. 75   b. 95   c. 90   **d. 88**

| Test  | 1  | 2  | 3  | 4  | 5 |
|-------|----|----|----|----|---|
| Score | 97 | 88 | 98 | 99 | ? |

**The correct answer is D.**

To answer this problem, we have to work backwards with what we know about averages. We need to find out what TOTAL score is needed to have an average of 94. In other words, what number divided by 5 = 94?

x / 5 = 94

Multiply both sides by 5 and you get x = 94 • 5

x = 470. So the TOTAL score needs to be 470. Currently we have a total score of 97 + 88 + 98 + 99 = 382. So we need a minimum score of 470 - 382 = 88.

# 13.

Jim is trying to save up for a car over the summer. The car costs $2000.00. He has started a job where he earns $7.00 per hour. If the summer lasts ten weeks, what is the minimum average number of hours per week that he needs to work in order to earn enough for the car, rounded to the nearest hour?

a. 29
b. 30
c. 31
d. 286

# 14.

Jim is trying to save up for a car over the summer. The car costs $2500.00. He has started a job where he earns $7.50 per hour. If the summer lasts ten weeks, what is the minimum average number of hours per week that he needs to work in order to earn enough for the car, rounded to the nearest hour?

a. 31
b. 32
c. 34
d. 33

# 15.

Jim is trying to save up for a car over the summer. The car costs $2500.00. He has decided to start a summer job but can only work 20 hours per week. If the summer lasts ten weeks, what is the minimum average amount he needs to earn per hour to save up for the car by the end of the summer, rounded to the nearest cent?

a. $12.50
b. $13.00
c. $11.50
d. $250.00

# 13.

Jim is trying to save up for a car over the summer. The car costs $2000.00. He has started a job where he earns $7.00 per hour. If the summer lasts ten weeks, what is the minimum average number of hours per week that he needs to work in order to earn enough for the car, rounded to the nearest hour?

**a. 29**  b. 30  c. 31  d. 286

**The correct answer is A.**
Jim needs to work $2000 divided by $7.00 per hour = 285.71 hours. The average number of hours per week he needs to work is 285.71 hours divided into 10 weeks = 28.57 hours. We round this to the nearest hour for our answer, 29.

# 14.

Jim is trying to save up for a car over the summer. The car costs $2500.00. He has started a job where he earns $7.50 per hour. If the summer lasts ten weeks, what is the minimum average number of hours per week that he needs to work in order to earn enough for the car, rounded to the nearest hour?

a. 31  b. 32  c. 34  **d. 33**

**The correct answer is D.**
Jim needs to earn $2500 divided by $7.50 per hour = 333.33 hours. The average number of hours per week he needs to work is 333.33 hours divided into 10 weeks = 33.33 hours. We round this down to the nearest hour for our answer, 33.

# 15.

Jim is trying to save up for a car over the summer. The car costs $2500.00. He has decided to start a summer job but can only work 20 hours per week. If the summer lasts ten weeks, what is the minimum average amount he needs to earn per hour to save up for the car by the end of the summer, rounded to the nearest cent?

**a. $12.50**  b. $13.00  c. $11.50  d. $250.00

**The correct answer is A.**
Jim is able to work 20 hours per week x 10 weeks = 200 total hours this summer. Jim needs to earn an average of $2500 divided into 200 hours = $12.50. 2500 / 200 = 12.50

## Lesson 3
# Probability

Probability problems ask you for how likely or how unlikely something is to happen. A probability tells you that if a certain task is attempted a certain number of times, chances are that a certain number of desired results will happen.

For example, if I have one orange marble and three red marbles in a bag, and I draw them from the bag four times, chances are that I will draw the orange marble one time and the red marbles three times.

Probability is figured out this way: Total number of desired outcomes divided by total number of possible outcomes. So in this example, there is a 1 divided by 4 chance of drawing an orange marble. That's because there is one orange marble (desired outcome) and four total marbles (possible outcomes).

What are our chances of drawing a red marble? Well there are three red marbles (desired outcome) and four total marbles (possible outcomes), so there is a 3 divided by 4 chance of drawing an orange marble.

Probability gets a little trickier than this because there are a few ways that you can answer a probability problem. The test may ask you for a fraction.

If they ask you for a fraction, instead of saying 3 divided by 4 you would say ¾. This is the same thing.

They may ask you to answer as a percentage. The way to arrive at a percentage is to divide the numbers. 3 divided by 4 is .75. Then you multiply by 100. In this example, you would end up with 75%.

Or they may ask you for a ratio. A ratio is expressed this way…

Total Desired Outcomes : Total Undesired Outcomes

In this case, the ratio would be 3:1. The way you read this is "3 to 1".

All of these are saying the same thing.  The probability of drawing a red marble is:

3 divided by 4

¾

75%

3:1

.75

Let's begin so you can see this in practice...

# 1.

If a marble is drawn randomly from a bag that contains exactly 5 marbles, 2 of which are red and 3 of which are orange, what is the probability of drawing a red marble?

- a. 3/5
- b. 2/5
- c. 3/2
- d. 2/3

# 2.

If a marble is drawn randomly from a bag that contains exactly 7 marbles, 3 of which are white and four of which are blue, what is the probability of drawing a blue marble?

- a. 7/4
- b. 4/3
- c. 3/4
- d. 4/7

# 3.

If a marble is drawn randomly from a bag that contains exactly 9 marbles, 4 of which are red, two of which are blue, and three of which are white, what is the probability of drawing a blue marble?

- a. 6/9
- b. 2/9
- c. 3/9
- d. 4/9

# 1.

If a marble is drawn randomly from a bag that contains exactly 5 marbles, 2 of which are red and 3 of which are orange, what is the probability of drawing a red marble?

a. 3/5   **b. 2/5**   c. 3/2   d. 2/3

**The correct answer is B.**
The probability of drawing a red marble is 2 desired outcomes divided by 5 total possible outcomes.  2/5

# 2.

If a marble is drawn randomly from a bag that contains exactly 7 marbles, 3 of which are white and four of which are blue, what is the probability of drawing a blue marble?

a. 7/4   b. 4/3   c. 3/4   **d. 4/7**

**The correct answer is D.**
The probability of drawing a blue marble is 4 desired outcomes divided by 7 total possible outcomes.  4/7

# 3.

If a marble is drawn randomly from a bag that contains exactly 9 marbles, 4 of which are red, two of which are blue, and three of which are white, what is the probability of drawing a blue marble?

a. 6/9   **b. 2/9**   c. 3/9   d. 4/9

**The correct answer is B.**
The probability of drawing a blue marble is 2 desired outcomes divided by 9 total possible outcomes.  2/9

# 4.

If a marble is drawn randomly from a bag that contains exactly 9 marbles, 4 of which are red, two of which are blue, and three of which are white, what is the probability of NOT drawing a red marble?

   a. 2/9
   b. 5/9
   c. 4/9
   d. 1/3

# 5.

If a marble is taken randomly from a bag that contains exactly 13 marbles, 5 of which are red, 5 of which are white, and 3 of which are blue, what is the probability of NOT drawing a blue marble?

   a. 10/13
   b. 5/13
   c. 8/13
   d. 3/13

# 6.

Joann and nine other students are being randomly assigned to one of four classes: PE, Math, Science, and Social Studies.  3 students are being assigned to PE.  2 students are being assigned to Math.  2 students are being assigned to Science, and 3 students are being assigned to Social Studies.  Joann loves Social Studies.  What is the probability that she will be assigned to Social Studies?

   a. 30%
   b. 20%
   c. 50%
   d. 80%

Math Mastery - Level 1

# 4.

If a marble is drawn randomly from a bag that contains exactly 9 marbles, 4 of which are red, two of which are blue, and three of which are white, what is the probability of NOT drawing a red marble?

a. 2/9   **b. 5/9**   c. 4/9   d. 1/3

**The correct answer is B.**
There are 2 + 3 = 5 possible outcomes that are NOT drawing a red marble. The probability of NOT drawing a red marble is 5 desired outcomes divided by 9 total possible outcomes. 5/9
Note that if you missed seeing the word NOT, you would have answered C and been incorrect.

# 5.

If a marble is taken randomly from a bag that contains exactly 13 marbles, 5 of which are red, 5 of which are white, and 3 of which are blue, what is the probability of NOT drawing a blue marble?

**a. 10/13**   b. 5/13   c. 8/13   d. 3/13

**The correct answer is A.**
There are 5 + 5 = 10 desired outcomes. The probability of NOT drawing a blue marble is 10 desired outcomes divided by 13 total possible outcomes. 10/13

# 6.

Joann and nine other students are being randomly assigned to one of four classes: PE, Math, Science, and Social Studies. 3 students are being assigned to PE. 2 students are being assigned to Math. 2 students are being assigned to Science, and 3 students are being assigned to Social Studies. Joann loves Social Studies. What is the probability that she will be assigned to Social Studies?

**a. 30%**   b. 20%   c. 50%   d. 80%

**The correct answer is A.**
The probability of being assigned to Social Studies is 3 desired outcomes divided by 10 possible outcomes. 3 divided by 10 = 0.3 = 30%

# Lesson 3 - Probability

# 7.

Joe and nine other students are being randomly assigned to one of four classes: PE, Math, Science, and Social Studies. 3 students are being assigned to PE. 2 students are being assigned to Math. 2 students are being assigned to Science, and 3 students are being assigned to Social Studies. Joe doesn't like Math. What is the probability that he will NOT be assigned to Math?

- a. 9/10
- b. 1/5
- c. 3/10
- d. 4/5

# 8.

Frank and nine other students are being randomly assigned to one of four classes: PE, Math, Science, and Social Studies. 3 students are being assigned to PE. 2 students are being assigned to Math. 2 students are being assigned to Science, and 3 students are being assigned to Social Studies. Frank likes PE and Science. What is the probability that he will be assigned to PE or Science?

- a. 4/5
- b. 9/10
- c. 1/2
- d. 1/5

# 9.

Danny and Jim are playing a guessing game. Danny rolls an 8-sided die, with each side numbered 1 through 8, and Jim tries to guess what number it will be. This time Jim guesses 7. What is the probability that Jim's guess is correct?

- a. 87.5%
- b. 12.5%
- c. 20%
- d. 50%

## 7.

Joe and nine other students are being randomly assigned to one of four classes: PE, Math, Science, and Social Studies. 3 students are being assigned to PE. 2 students are being assigned to Math. 2 students are being assigned to Science, and 3 students are being assigned to Social Studies. Joe doesn't like Math. What is the probability that he will NOT be assigned to Math?

a. 9/10   b. 1/5   c. 3/10   **d. 4/5**

**The correct answer is D.**
There are 3 + 2 + 3 = 8 desired outcomes. The probability of NOT being assigned to Math is 8 desired outcomes divided by 10 total possible outcomes. 8/10 = 4/5. Note that you have to simplify all fractions when doing probability, which is why 8/10 is not an available choice.

## 8.

Frank and nine other students are being randomly assigned to one of four classes: PE, Math, Science, and Social Studies. 3 students are being assigned to PE. 2 students are being assigned to Math. 2 students are being assigned to Science, and 3 students are being assigned to Social Studies. Frank likes PE and Science. What is the probability that he will be assigned to PE or Science?

a. 4/5   b. 9/10   **c. 1/2**   d. 1/5

**The correct answer is C.**
There are 3 + 2 = 5 desired outcomes. The probability of being assigned to PE or Science is 5 divided by 10 total possible outcomes. 5/10 = 1/2. Note that you have to simplify all fractions when doing probability, so 5/10 would not be the best choice and is not an option on this question.

## 9.

Danny and Jim are playing a guessing game. Danny rolls an 8-sided die, with each side numbered 1 through 8, and Jim tries to guess what number it will be. This time Jim guesses 7. What is the probability that Jim's guess is correct?

a. 87.5%   **b. 12.5%**   c. 20%   d. 50%

**The correct answer is B.**
The probability of 7 being the correct guess is 1 desired outcome divided by 8 possible outcomes. 1/8 = .125 = 12.5%. Note that you may have gotten tripped up by the desired outcome being a number, so watch out for this on the test.

# 10.

Danny and Jim are playing a guessing game. Danny rolls an 8-sided die, with each side numbered 1 through 8, and Jim guesses three numbers that it could be. This time Jim guesses 2, 4, and 6. What is the probability that one of Jim's guesses is correct?

a. 12.5%
b. 62.5%
c. 37.5%
d. 50%

# 11.

Danny and Jim are playing a guessing game. Danny rolls an 8-sided die, with each side numbered 1 through 8, and Jim guesses five numbers that it could be. This time Jim guesses 2, 4, and 6, 7 and 8. What is the probability that one of Jim's guesses is correct?

a. 62.5%
b. 12.5%
c. 37.5%
d. 25%

# 12.

Ellen is trying to pick out a dress, but she can't decide. Her friends finally tell her that they are going to play a game. They have numbered the dresses one through five. She has to pick a number, and that's the dress they'll buy her. The dresses are each a color – red, green, blue, pink, and orange. What are the odds that she will pick the blue dress?

a. 4:1
b. 3:2
c. 1:4
d. 1:1

# 10.

Danny and Jim are playing a guessing game. Danny rolls an 8-sided die, with each side numbered 1 through 8, and Jim guesses three numbers that it could be. This time Jim guesses 2, 4, and 6. What is the probability that one of Jim's guesses is correct?

a. 12.5%   b. 62.5%   **c. 37.5%**   d. 50%

**The correct answer is C.**
The probability of 2, 4 or 6 being the correct guess is 3 desired outcomes divided by 8 possible outcomes. 3/8 = .375= 37.5%.

# 11.

Danny and Jim are playing a guessing game. Danny rolls an 8-sided die, with each side numbered 1 through 8, and Jim guesses five numbers that it could be. This time Jim guesses 2, 4, and 6, 7 and 8. What is the probability that one of Jim's guesses is correct?

**a. 62.5%**   b. 12.5%   c. 37.5%   d. 25%

**The correct answer is A.**
The probability of 2, 4, 6, 7 or 8 being the correct guess is 5 desired outcomes divided by 8 possible outcomes. 5/8 = .625= 62.5%.

# 12.

Ellen is trying to pick out a dress, but she can't decide. Her friends finally tell her that they are going to play a game. They have numbered the dresses one through five. She has to pick a number, and that's the dress they'll buy her. The dresses are each a color – red, green, blue, pink, and orange. What are the odds that she will pick the blue dress?

a. 4:1   b. 3:2   **c. 1:4**   d. 1:1

**The correct answer is C.**
The odds that she will pick the blue dress is 1 desired outcome vs. 4 undesired outcomes = 1:4.

# 13.

Ellen is trying to pick out a dress, but she can't decide. Her friends finally tell her that they are going to play a game. They have numbered the dresses one through five. She has to pick a number, and that's the dress they'll buy her. Two dresses are red, one is green, one is blue, and one is pink. What are the odds that she will pick a red dress?

- a. 2:3
- b. 1:4
- c. 3:2
- d. 5:3

# 14.

Ellen is trying to pick out a dress, but she can't decide. Her friends finally tell her that they are going to play a game. They have numbered the dresses one through five. She has to pick a number, and that's the dress they'll buy her. Two dresses are red, one is green, one is blue, and one is pink. What are the odds that she will pick something else besides a red dress?

- a. 2:3
- b. 3:2
- c. 4:1
- d. 1:4

# 15.

Ellen is trying to pick out a dress, but she can't decide. Her friends finally tell her that they are going to play a game. They have numbered the dresses one through five. She has to pick a number, and that's the dress they'll buy her. Three of the dresses cost less than $20, while two of the dresses cost more than $20. What are the odds that she will pick something that costs more than $20?

- a. 2:3
- b. 3:2
- c. 4:1
- d. 1:4

## 13.

Ellen is trying to pick out a dress, but she can't decide. Her friends finally tell her that they are going to play a game. They have numbered the dresses one through five. She has to pick a number, and that's the dress they'll buy her. Two dresses are red, one is green, one is blue, and one is pink. What are the odds that she will pick a red dress?

**a. 2:3**   b. 1:4   c. 3:2   d. 5:3

**The correct answer is A.**
The odds that she will pick the blue dress is 2 desired outcomes vs. 3 undesired outcomes = 2:3.

## 14.

Ellen is trying to pick out a dress, but she can't decide. Her friends finally tell her that they are going to play a game. They have numbered the dresses one through five. She has to pick a number, and that's the dress they'll buy her. Two dresses are red, one is green, one is blue, and one is pink. What are the odds that she will pick something else besides a red dress?

a. 2:3   **b. 3:2**   c. 4:1   d. 1:4

**The correct answer is B.**
The odds that she will pick something besides the red dress is is 3 desired outcomes vs. 2 undesired outcomes = 3:2.

## 15.

Ellen is trying to pick out a dress, but she can't decide. Her friends finally tell her that they are going to play a game. They have numbered the dresses one through five. She has to pick a number, and that's the dress they'll buy her. Three of the dresses cost less than $20, while two of the dresses cost more than $20. What are the odds that she will pick something that costs more than $20?

**a. 2:3**   b. 3:2   c. 4:1   d. 1:4

**The correct answer is A.**
The odds that she will pick a dress that costs more than $20 is 2 desired outcomes vs. 3 undesired outcomes = 2:3.

## Lesson 4
# Combinations

Some questions on the ACT are going to ask you about how many different combinations of something are possible. The way to figure out how many combinations are possible is to multiply the number of possibilities.

For example, if there are 4 different sets of jeans, and each set of jeans has three different colors, then there are a total of 3 times 4 = 12 possible jeans combinations.

This works for simple problems like the ones you'll see in the following lesson.

The clue to knowing that the ACT wants you to figure out a combination is that the question that is asked will contain words like "how many are possible" or "how many different."

# Lesson 4 - Combinations

# 1.

Joey is trying to select a t-shirt from a catalog. There are three different collar types available and four different colors. How many different shirt designs are available for Joey to choose from?

      a. 12
      b. 15
      c. 3
      d. 4

# 2.

Joey is selecting a t-shirt from a catalog. There are four different collar types available and two different colors. How many different shirt designs are available for Joey to choose from?

      a. 4
      b. 2
      c. 1
      d. 8

# 3.

Joey is selecting a t-shirt from a catalog. There are four different collar types available and five different colors. There is also an option to add an extra button to the neckline. How many different shirt designs are available for Joey to choose from?

      a. 10
      b. 20
      c. 40
      d. 21

# 1.

Joey is trying to select a t-shirt from a catalog. There are three different collar types available and four different colors. How many different shirt designs are available for Joey to choose from?

    **a. 12**
    b. 15
    c. 3
    d. 4

**The correct answer is A.**
There are 3 collar types x 4 different colors = 12 shirt designs.
3 x 4 = 12

# 2.

Joey is selecting a t-shirt from a catalog. There are four different collar types available and two different colors. How many different shirt designs are available for Joey to choose from?

    a. 4
    b. 2
    c. 1
    **d. 8**

**The correct answer is D.**
There are 4 collar types x 2 colors = 8 shirt designs.
4 x 2 = 8

# 3.

Joey is selecting a t-shirt from a catalog. There are four different collar types available and five different colors. There is also an option to add an extra button to the neckline. How many different shirt designs are available for Joey to choose from?

    a. 10   b. 20   **c. 40**   d. 21

**The correct answer is C.**
There are 4 collar types x 5 colors x 2 button options = 40 shirt designs.
Whenever you have a yes/no option, that means there are two different choices (yes and no).
Note: If you counted the button as only 1 option, your incorrectly calculated the combination as
4 x 5 x 1 = 20, which gives you a wrong answer.

# Lesson 4 - Combinations

## 4.

Joey is selecting a t-shirt from a catalog. There are three different collar types available and eight different colors. There is an option to add an extra button to the neckline, as well as the choice between smooth and rough fabric. How many different t-shirt designs are available for Joey to choose from?

a. 24
b. 15
c. 192
d. 96

## 5.

Brianna is choosing school supplies. There are five different types of pens she can get, four different types of binders, and three different kinds of notebooks. She has to choose one of each. How many different combinations of school supplies are possible?

a. 60
b. 30
c. 12
d. 120

## 6.

Brianna is choosing school supplies. There are eight different types of pens she can get, five different types of binders, and five different kinds of notebooks. She has to choose one of each. How many different combinations of school supplies are possible?

a. 400
b. 40
c. 18
d. 200

## 4.

Joey is selecting a t-shirt from a catalog. There are three different collar types available and eight different colors. There is an option to add an extra button to the neckline, as well as the choice between smooth and rough fabric. How many different t-shirt designs are available for Joey to choose from?

a. 24   b. 15   c. 192   **d. 96**

The correct answer is D.
There are 3 collars x 8 colors x 2 button options x 2 fabric options = 96 shirt designs.
3 x 8 x 2 x 2 = 96.

## 5.

Brianna is choosing school supplies. There are five different types of pens she can get, four different types of binders, and three different kinds of notebooks. She has to choose one of each. How many different combinations of school supplies are possible?

**a. 60**   b. 30   c. 12   d. 120

The correct answer is A.
There are 5 pens x 4 binders x 3 notebooks = 60 school supply combinations.
5 x 4 x 3 = 60

## 6.

Brianna is choosing school supplies. There are eight different types of pens she can get, five different types of binders, and five different kinds of notebooks. She has to choose one of each. How many different combinations of school supplies are possible?

a. 400   b. 40   c. 18   **d. 200**

**The correct answer is D.**
There are 8 pens x 5 binders x 5 notebooks = 200 school supply combinations.
8 x 5 x 5 = 200

# 7.

Brianna is selecting school supplies. There are seven different types of pens she can get, six different types of binders, and seven different types of notebooks. She has to choose one of each. Additionally, she can choose to add a pack of mechanical pencils, if she wants. How many different combinations of school supplies are possible?

a. 20
b. 294
c. 42
d. 588

# 8.

Brianna is selecting school supplies. There are five different types of pens she can get, nine different types of binders, and six different types of notebooks. She has to choose one of each. Additionally, she can choose to add a pack of mechanical pencils, if she wants. How many different combinations of school supplies are possible?

a. 540
b. 1080
c. 270
d. 135

# 9.

Dominique and Jared own a sandwich shop. They offer 5 kinds of bread, 6 kinds of meat, and 4 kinds of cheese. Each type of sandwich on their menu has a combination of 1 bread, 1 meat, and 1 cheese. How many types of sandwiches are possible?

a. 120
b. 60
c. 240
d. 15

# 7.

Brianna is selecting school supplies. There are seven different types of pens she can get, six different types of binders, and seven different types of notebooks. She has to choose one of each. Additionally, she can choose to add a pack of mechanical pencils, if she wants. How many different combinations of school supplies are possible?

a. 20   b. 294   c. 42   **d. 588**

**The correct answer is D.**
There are 7 pens x 6 binders x 7 notebooks x 2 pencil options = 588 school supply combinations. The mechanical pencil option is counted as two because she can either say YES or NO to it, so there are two possibilities there.

# 8.

Brianna is selecting school supplies. There are five different types of pens she can get, nine different types of binders, and six different types of notebooks. She has to choose one of each. Additionally, she can choose to add a pack of mechanical pencils, if she wants. How many different combinations of school supplies are possible?

**a. 540**   b. 1080   c. 270   d. 135

**The correct answer is A.**
There are 5 pens x 9 binders x 6 notebooks x 2 pencil options = 540 school supply combinations. The mechanical pencil option is counted as two because she can either say YES or NO to it, so there are two possibilities there.

# 9.

Dominique and Jared own a sandwich shop. They offer 5 kinds of bread, 6 kinds of meat, and 4 kinds of cheese. Each type of sandwich on their menu has a combination of 1 bread, 1 meat, and 1 cheese. How many types of sandwiches are possible?

**a. 120**   b. 60   c. 240   d. 15

**The correct answer is A.**
There are 5 breads x 6 meats x 4 cheeses = 120 sandwiches possible.
5 x 6 x 4 = 120

Lesson 4 - Combinations

# 10.

Dominique and Jared own a sandwich shop. They offer 7 kinds of bread, 4 kinds of meat, and 5 kinds of cheese. Each type of sandwich on their menu has a combination of 1 bread, 1 meat, and 1 cheese. How many types of sandwiches are possible?

a. 280
b. 140
c. 70
d. 16

# 11.

Dominique and Jared own a sandwich shop. They offer 2 kinds of bread, 10 kinds of meat, and 3 kinds of cheese. Each type of sandwich on their menu has a combination of 1 bread, 1 meat, and 1 cheese. How many types of sandwiches are possible?

a. 15
b. 36
c. 120
d. 60

# 12.

Dominique and Jared own a sandwich shop. They offer 3 kinds of bread, 7 kinds of meat, and 5 kinds of cheese. Each type of sandwich on their menu has a combination of 1 bread, 1 meat, and 1 cheese. How many types of sandwiches are possible?

a. 210
b. 15
c. 105
d. 315

# 10.

Dominique and Jared own a sandwich shop. They offer 7 kinds of bread, 4 kinds of meat, and 5 kinds of cheese. Each type of sandwich on their menu has a combination of 1 bread, 1 meat, and 1 cheese. How many types of sandwiches are possible?

a. 280   **b. 140**   c. 70   d. 16

**The correct answer is B.**
7 breads x 4 meats x 5 cheeses = 140 sandwich combinations.
7 x 4 x 5 = 140

# 11.

Dominique and Jared own a sandwich shop. They offer 2 kinds of bread, 10 kinds of meat, and 3 kinds of cheese. Each type of sandwich on their menu has a combination of 1 bread, 1 meat, and 1 cheese. How many types of sandwiches are possible?

a. 15   b. 36   c. 120   **d. 60**

**The correct answer is D.**
2 breads x 10 meats x 3 cheeses = 60 sandwich combinations.
2 x 10 x 3 = 60

# 12.

Dominique and Jared own a sandwich shop. They offer 3 kinds of bread, 7 kinds of meat, and 5 kinds of cheese. Each type of sandwich on their menu has a combination of 1 bread, 1 meat, and 1 cheese. How many types of sandwiches are possible?

a. 210   b. 15   **c. 105**   d. 315

**The correct answer is C.**
3 breads x 7 meats x 5 cheeses = 105 sandwich combinations.
3 x 7 x 5 = 105

# 13.

Dominique and Jared own a sandwich shop. They offer 3 kinds of bread, 7 kinds of meat, and 5 kinds of cheese. Each type of sandwich on their menu has a combination of 1 bread, 1 meat, and 1 cheese. A "Value Deal" consists of one sandwich and one drink. There are 5 drink options. How many different "Value Deal" combinations are possible?

a. 525
b. 105
c. 110
d. 1050

# 14.

Dominique and Jared own a sandwich shop. They offer 4 kinds of bread, 2 kinds of meat, and 11 kinds of cheese. Each type of sandwich on their menu has a combination of 1 bread, 1 meat, and 1 cheese. A "Value Deal" consists of one sandwich and one drink. There are 7 drink options. How many different "Value Deal" combinations are possible?

a. 24
b. 616
c. 88
d. 462

# 15.

Dominique and Jared own a sandwich shop. They offer 12 kinds of bread, 13 kinds of meat, and 8 kinds of cheese. Each type of sandwich on their menu has a combination of 1 bread, 1 meat, and 1 cheese. A "Value Deal" consists of one sandwich and one drink. There are 12 drink options. How many different "Value Deal" combinations are possible?

a. 12892
b. 23922
c. 14976
d. 15491

# 13.

Dominique and Jared own a sandwich shop. They offer 3 kinds of bread, 7 kinds of meat, and 5 kinds of cheese. Each type of sandwich on their menu has a combination of 1 bread, 1 meat, and 1 cheese. A "Value Deal" consists of one sandwich and one drink. There are 5 drink options. How many different "Value Deal" combinations are possible?

**a. 525**  b. 105  c. 110  d. 1050

**The correct answer is A.**
There are 3 breads x 7 meats x 5 cheeses x 5 drinks = 525 "Value Deal" combinations. The question seems to separate the drinks from the sandwich options. To arrive at the correct answer, you have to know to multiply it all together.

# 14.

Dominique and Jared own a sandwich shop. They offer 4 kinds of bread, 2 kinds of meat, and 11 kinds of cheese. Each type of sandwich on their menu has a combination of 1 bread, 1 meat, and 1 cheese. A "Value Deal" consists of one sandwich and one drink. There are 7 drink options. How many different "Value Deal" combinations are possible?

a. 24  **b. 616**  c. 88  d. 462

**The correct answer is B.**
There are 4 breads x 2 meats x 11 cheeses x 7 drinks = 616 combinations.
4 x 2 x 11 x 7 = 616

# 15.

Dominique and Jared own a sandwich shop. They offer 12 kinds of bread, 13 kinds of meat, and 8 kinds of cheese. Each type of sandwich on their menu has a combination of 1 bread, 1 meat, and 1 cheese. A "Value Deal" consists of one sandwich and one drink. There are 12 drink options. How many different "Value Deal" combinations are possible?

a. 12892  b. 23922  **c. 14976**  d. 15491

**The correct answer is C.**
There are 12 breads x 13 meats x 8 cheeses x 12 drinks = 14976 combinations.
12 x 13 x 8 x 12 = 14976. Don't let yourself be thrown off by the big numbers. You solve the problem the same way as with the earlier questions. Use your calculator for problems like this!

# Lesson 5
# Review

In the past four lessons, you practiced solving problems using division, solving problems involving averages, solving problems involving probability, and solving problems involving combinations.

In this lesson you will review what you have learned. You will also answer problems that require you to combine these skills.

On the answer side of the pages, you will sometimes see a note that says: "If you answered incorrectly, see pages ____ ."

If you miss a problem, go back to the indicated page and review the concept again. Go through the motions of answering them - even though you already answered them! This is going to refresh you on what you've already learned.

Don't cheat on this. The review is what will help you remember these concepts all the way to the test.

Some of you at this point will have had no problem answering any of these problems. That's okay. This work is still helping you. Why? Because the ACT is a timed test. Your level of CERTAINTY and SPEED play a huge role in whether you score highly or not. So there is a big difference between answering a question you know in 30 seconds and answering it in 15 seconds. That extra 15 seconds can help you answer a question you might not have gotten to.

That's why you need to go back to review anything that you miss. That's what these review sections are for. Do this, and your certainty and speed will increase, and your ACT score will go up, too!

# Lesson 5 - Review

## 1.

If eight shirts cost $240, how much do 3 shirts cost?

a. $90
b. $180
c. $30
d. $80

## 2.

Dominique and Jared own a sandwich shop. They offer 4 kinds of bread, 7 kinds of meat, and 3 kinds of cheese. Each type of sandwich on their menu has a combination of 1 bread, 1 meat, and 1 cheese. A "Value Deal" consists of one sandwich and one drink. There are 8 drink options. How many different "Value Deal" combinations are possible?

a. 84   b. 891   c. 672   d. 432

## 3.

Dominique and Jared own a sandwich shop. They offer 3 kinds of bread, 2 kinds of meat, and 8 kinds of cheese. Each type of sandwich on their menu has a combination of 1 bread, 1 meat, and 1 cheese. A "Value Deal" consists of one sandwich and one drink. There are 6 drink options. How many different "Value Deal" combinations are possible?

a. 24   b. 288   c. 88   d. 350

# 1.

If eight shirts cost $240, how much do 3 shirts cost?

**a. $90**
b. $180
c. $30
d. $80

**The correct answer is A.**
$240 divided by 8 shirts = $30 per shirt. $30 per shirt times 3 shirts = $90.
240 / 8 = 30. 30 x 3 = 90. You have to figure out the value of one shirt, then you can figure out how much more than one shirt costs. Missed this? Review Lesson 1.

# 2.

Dominique and Jared own a sandwich shop. They offer 4 kinds of bread, 7 kinds of meat, and 3 kinds of cheese. Each type of sandwich on their menu has a combination of 1 bread, 1 meat, and 1 cheese. A "Value Deal" consists of one sandwich and one drink. There are 8 drink options. How many different "Value Deal" combinations are possible?

a. 84   b. 891   **c. 672**   d. 432

**The correct answer is C.**
There are 4 breads x 7 meats x 3 cheeses x 8 drinks = 672 combinations.
4 * 7 * 3 * 8 = 672. Use your calculator. Missed this? Review Lesson 4.

# 3.

Dominique and Jared own a sandwich shop. They offer 3 kinds of bread, 2 kinds of meat, and 8 kinds of cheese. Each type of sandwich on their menu has a combination of 1 bread, 1 meat, and 1 cheese. A "Value Deal" consists of one sandwich and one drink. There are 6 drink options. How many different "Value Deal" combinations are possible?

a. 24   **b. 288**   c. 88   d. 350

**The correct answer is B.**
There are 3 breads * 2 meats * 8 cheeses * 6 drinks = 288 combinations.
3 * 2 * 8 * 6 = 288. Use your calculator. Missed this? Review Lesson 4.

## 4.

Ellen is trying to pick out a dress, but she can't decide. Her friends finally tell her that they are going to play a game. They have numbered the dresses one through five. She has to pick a number, and that's the dress they'll buy her. Three dresses are red, one is green, one is blue, one is orange, and one is pink. What are the odds that she will pick something else besides a red dress?

a. 2:3   b. 4:3   c. 4:1   d. 1:4

## 5.

Jim is trying to save up for a car over the summer. The car costs $2800.00. He has started a job where he earns $8.50 per hour. If the summer lasts ten weeks, what is the minimum average number of hours per week that he needs to work in order to earn enough for the car, rounded to the nearest hour?

a. 31   b. 32   c. 34   d. 33

## 6.

If fifteen shirts cost $150, how much do 3 shirts cost?

a. $30.00
b. $60.00
c. $10.00
d. $15.00

# 4.

Ellen is trying to pick out a dress, but she can't decide. Her friends finally tell her that they are going to play a game. They have numbered the dresses one through five. She has to pick a number, and that's the dress they'll buy her. Three dresses are red, one is green, one is blue, one is orange, and one is pink. What are the odds that she will pick something else besides a red dress?

a. 2:3  **b. 4:3**  c. 4:1  d. 1:4

**The correct answer is B.**
The odds that she will pick something besides the red dress is 4 desired outcomes vs. 3 undesired outcomes = 4:3. Missed this question? Review Lesson 3.

# 5.

Jim is trying to save up for a car over the summer. The car costs $2800.00. He has started a job where he earns $8.50 per hour. If the summer lasts ten weeks, what is the minimum average number of hours per week that he needs to work in order to earn enough for the car, rounded to the nearest hour?

a. 31  b. 32  c. 34  **d. 33**

**The correct answer is D.**
Jim needs to earn $2800 divided by $8.50 per hour = 329.41 hours. The average number of hours per week he needs to work is 329.41 hours divided into 10 weeks = 32.94 hours. We round this up to the nearest hour for our answer, 33. Missed this question? Review Lesson 2.

# 6.

If fifteen shirts cost $150, how much do 3 shirts cost?

**a. $30.00**
b. $60.00
c. $10.00
d. $15.00

**The correct answer is A.**
$150 divided by 15 shirts = $10.00. $10.00 per shirt times 3 shirts = $30.00.
150 / 15 = 10.00. 10.00 x 3 = 30.00. You have to figure out the value of one shirt, then you can figure out how much more than one shirt costs. Missed this question? Review Lesson 1.

# Lesson 5 - Review

# 7.

Jim is trying to save up for a car over the summer. The car costs $2000.00. He has decided to start a summer job but can only work 25 hours per week. If the summer lasts ten weeks, what is the minimum average amount he needs to earn per hour to save up for the car by the end of the summer, rounded to the nearest cent?

a. $8.00   b. $10.00   c. $11.50   d. $200.00

# 8.

Ellen is trying to pick out a dress, but she can't decide. Her friends finally tell her that they are going to play a game. They have numbered the dresses one through five. She has to pick a number, and that's the dress they'll buy her. Two of the dresses cost less than $20, while three of the dresses cost more than $20. What is the probability that she will pick something that costs more than $20?

a. 3/5   b. 2/5   c. 3/2   d. 2/3

# 9.

If seven shirts cost $175, how much do nine shirts cost?

a. $225
b. $250
c. $200
d. $25

# 7.

Jim is trying to save up for a car over the summer. The car costs $2000.00. He has decided to start a summer job but can only work 25 hours per week. If the summer lasts ten weeks, what is the minimum average amount he needs to earn per hour to save up for the car by the end of the summer, rounded to the nearest cent?

a. **$8.00**   b. $10.00   c. $11.50   d. $200.00

**The correct answer is A.**
Jim is able to work 25 hours per week x 10 weeks = 250 total hours this summer. Jim needs to earn an average of $2000 divided into 250 hours = $8.00. 2000 / 250 = 8.00
Missed this question? Review Lesson 2.

# 8.

Ellen is trying to pick out a dress, but she can't decide. Her friends finally tell her that they are going to play a game. They have numbered the dresses one through five. She has to pick a number, and that's the dress they'll buy her. Two of the dresses cost less than $20, while three of the dresses cost more than $20. What is the probability that she will pick something that costs more than $20?

a. **3/5**   b. 2/5   c. 3/2   d. 2/3

**The correct answer is A.**
The probability that she will pick a dress that costs more than $20 is 3 desired outcomes vs. 5 total possible outcomes = 3/5. Missed this question? Review Lesson 3.

# 9.

If seven shirts cost $175, how much do nine shirts cost?

a. **$225**
b. $250
c. $200
d. $25

**The correct answer is A.**
$175 divided by 7 shirts = $25 per shirt. $25 per shirt times 9 shirts = $225.
175 / 7 = 25. 25 x 9 = 225. You have to figure out the value of one shirt, then you can figure out how much more than one shirt costs. Missed this? Review Lesson 1.

Lesson 5 - Review

# 10.

If four shirts cost $240, how much do seven shirts cost?

a. $90
b. $60
c. $420
d. $210

# 11.

Dominique and Jared own a sandwich shop. They offer 8 kinds of bread, 2 kinds of meat, and 3 kinds of cheese. Each type of sandwich on their menu has a combination of 1 bread, 1 meat, and 1 cheese. A "Value Deal" consists of one sandwich and one drink. There are 10 drink options. How many different "Value Deal" combinations are possible?

a. 84   b. 891   c. 480   d. 432

# 12.

Dominique and Jared own a sandwich shop. They offer 6 kinds of bread, 5 kinds of meat, and 5 kinds of cheese. Each type of sandwich on their menu has a combination of 1 bread, 1 meat, and 1 cheese. A "Value Deal" consists of one sandwich and one drink. There are 5 drink options. How many different "Value Deal" combinations are possible?

a. 500   b. 750   c. 850   d. 450

Math Mastery - Level 1

# 10.

If four shirts cost $240, how much do seven shirts cost?

a. $90
b. $60
**c. $420**
d. $210

**The correct answer is C.**
$240 divided by 4 shirts = $60 per shirt. $60 per shirt times 7 shirts = $420.
240 / 4 = 60. 60 x 7 = 420. You have to figure out the value of one shirt, then you can figure out how much more than one shirt costs. Missed this? Review Lesson 1.

# 11.

Dominique and Jared own a sandwich shop. They offer 8 kinds of bread, 2 kinds of meat, and 3 kinds of cheese. Each type of sandwich on their menu has a combination of 1 bread, 1 meat, and 1 cheese. A "Value Deal" consists of one sandwich and one drink. There are 10 drink options. How many different "Value Deal" combinations are possible?

a. 84   b. 891   **c. 480**   d. 432

**The correct answer is C.**
There are 8 breads * 2 meats * 3 cheeses * 10 drinks = 480 combinations.
8 * 2 * 3 * 10 = 480. Use your calculator. Missed this? Review Lesson 4.

# 12.

Dominique and Jared own a sandwich shop. They offer 6 kinds of bread, 5 kinds of meat, and 5 kinds of cheese. Each type of sandwich on their menu has a combination of 1 bread, 1 meat, and 1 cheese. A "Value Deal" consists of one sandwich and one drink. There are 5 drink options. How many different "Value Deal" combinations are possible?

a. 500   **b. 750**   c. 850   d. 450

**The correct answer is B.**
There are 6 breads * 5 meats * 5 cheeses * 5 drinks = 750 combinations.
6 * 5 * 5 * 5 = 750. Use your calculator. Missed this? Review Lesson 4.

# Lesson 5 - Review

## 13.

Ellen is trying to pick out a dress, but she can't decide. Her friends finally tell her that they are going to play a game. They have numbered the dresses one through five. She has to pick a number, and that's the dress they'll buy her. Eight dresses are red, one is green, one is blue, and one is pink. What are the odds that she will pick something else besides a red dress?

a. 2:3   b. 3:8   c. 4:1   d. 1:4

## 14.

Jim is trying to save up for a car over the summer. The car costs $3000.00. He has started a job where he earns $12.50 per hour. If the summer lasts ten weeks, what is the minimum average number of hours per week that he needs to work in order to earn enough for the car, rounded to the nearest hour?

a. 27   b. 20   c. 30   d. 24

## 15.

If twelve shirts cost $24, how much do 3 shirts cost?

a. $6.00
b. $12.00
c. $72.00
d. $36.00

# 13.

Ellen is trying to pick out a dress, but she can't decide. Her friends finally tell her that they are going to play a game. They have numbered the dresses one through five. She has to pick a number, and that's the dress they'll buy her. Eight dresses are red, one is green, one is blue, and one is pink. What are the odds that she will pick something else besides a red dress?

a. 2:3  **b. 3:8**  c. 4:1  d. 1:4

**The correct answer is B.**
The odds that she will pick something besides a red dress are 3 desired outcomes vs. 8 undesired outcomes = 3:8. Missed this question? Review Lesson 3.

# 14.

Jim is trying to save up for a car over the summer. The car costs $3000.00. He has started a job where he earns $12.50 per hour. If the summer lasts ten weeks, what is the minimum average number of hours per week that he needs to work in order to earn enough for the car, rounded to the nearest hour?

a. 27  b. 20  c. 30  **d. 24**

**The correct answer is D.**
Jim needs to earn $3000 divided by $12.50 per hour = 240 hours. The average number of hours per week he needs to work is 240 hours divided into 10 weeks = 24 hours. Missed this question? Review Lesson 2.

# 15.

If twelve shirts cost $24, how much do 3 shirts cost?

**a. $6.00**
b. $12.00
c. $72.00
d. $36.00

**The correct answer is A.**
$24 divided by 12 shirts = $2.00. $2.00 per shirt times 3 shirts = $6.00.
24 / 12 = 2.00. 2.00 x 3 = 6.00. You have to figure out the value of one shirt, then you can figure out how much more than one shirt costs. Missed this question? Review Lesson 1.

# Lesson 6
# Combinations with Removal

The next set of questions focuses on a special version of our combination rule. Note that the rule doesn't change – you still multiply the different options – but what does change is making sure that you correctly calculate the number of options available.

Here is a sample problem:

George has 4 different classes to choose from to fill his schedule. His schedule has a first period, a second period, a third period, and a fourth period. George cannot schedule any one class more than once. How many different schedules is it possible for George to make?

In this case, you first have to figure out how many options he has for each choice. Obviously when choosing his first class, he has 4 options. But when he gets to choosing the second class, he only has 3 options left. When he gets to his third period, he only has 2 options left. And on his fourth period, he only has 1 option left. So the correct answer would be

4 x 3 x 2 x 1 = 24

We'll explore this more fully in the questions that follow in this lesson.

# 1.

George has 10 different classes to choose from to fill his schedule. His schedule has a first period, a second period, a third period, and a fourth period. George cannot schedule any one class more than once. How many different schedules is it possible for George to make?

a. 720
b. 5040
c. 10000
d. 40

# 2.

George has 12 different classes to choose from to fill his schedule. His schedule has a first period, a second period, a third period, a fourth period, and a fifth period. George cannot schedule any one class more than once. How many different schedules is it possible for George to make?

a. 50
b. 248832
c. 95040
d. 100000

# 3.

George has 15 different classes to choose from to fill his schedule. His schedule has a first period, a second period, a third period, and a fourth period. George cannot schedule any one class more than once. How many different schedules is it possible for George to make?

a. 32760
b. 50625
c. 60
d. 54

## 1.

George has 10 different classes to choose from to fill his schedule. His schedule has a first period, a second period, a third period, and a fourth period. George cannot schedule any one class more than once. How many different schedules is it possible for George to make?

a. 720  **b. 5040**  c. 10000  d. 40

**The correct answer is B.**
There are 10 x 9 x 8 x 7 = 5040 possible class schedules. The answer is NOT 10 x 10 x 10 x 10 = 10000 because each time George selects a class, he cannot select that class again. So for the second period, there are only 9 possibilities, for the third period, there are only 8 possibilities, and for the fourth period, there are only 7 possibilities.

## 2.

George has 12 different classes to choose from to fill his schedule. His schedule has a first period, a second period, a third period, a fourth period, and a fifth period. George cannot schedule any one class more than once. How many different schedules is it possible for George to make?

a. 50  b. 248832  **c. 95040**  d. 100000

**The correct answer is C.**
There are 12 x 11 x 10 x 9 x 8 = 95040 possible class schedules. The answer is NOT 12 x 12 x 12 x 12 x 12 = 248832 because each time George selects a class, he cannot select that class again. So for the second period, there are only 11 possibilities, for the third period, there are only 10 possibilities, and so on.

## 3.

George has 15 different classes to choose from to fill his schedule. His schedule has a first period, a second period, a third period, and a fourth period. George cannot schedule any one class more than once. How many different schedules is it possible for George to make?

**a. 32760**  b. 50625  c. 60  d. 54

**The correct answer is A.**
There are 15 x 14 x 13 x 12 = 32760 possible class schedules. The answer is NOT 15 x 15 x 15 x 15 = 50625 because each time George selects a class, he cannot select that class again. So for the second period, there are only 14 possibilities, for the third period, there are only 13 possibilities, and so on.

# Lesson 6 - Combinations with Removal

## 4.

George has 9 different classes to choose from to fill his schedule. His schedule has a first period, a second period, a third period, a fourth period, a fifth period, and a sixth period. George cannot schedule any one class more than once. How many different schedules is it possible for George to make?

a. 39
b. 54
c. 531441
d. 60480

## 5.

Monique is making a game schedule for a little league soccer tournament. Her sister's team, the Hornets, and seven other teams are in the tournament. The tournament has three rounds. Teams can only play each other once. How many different schedules could the Hornets have in this tournament?

a. 210
b. 343
c. 21
d. 72

## 6.

Monique is making a game schedule for a little league soccer tournament. Her sister's team, the Hornets, and nine other teams are in the tournament. The tournament has three rounds. Teams can only play each other once. How many different schedules could the Hornets have in this tournament?

a. 504
b. 729
c. 24
d. 27

# 4.

George has 9 different classes to choose from to fill his schedule. His schedule has a first period, a second period, a third period, a fourth period, a fifth period, and a sixth period. George cannot schedule any one class more than once. How many different schedules is it possible for George to make?

a. 39   b. 54   c. 531441   **d. 60480**

**The correct answer is D.**

There are 9 x 8 x 7 x 6 x 5 x 4 = 60480 possible class schedules. The answer is NOT 9 x 9 x 9 x 9 x 9 x 9 = 531441 because each time George selects a class, he cannot select that class again. So for the second period, there are only 8 possibilities, and so on.

# 5.

Monique is making a game schedule for a little league soccer tournament. Her sister's team, the Hornets, and seven other teams are in the tournament. The tournament has three rounds. Teams can only play each other once. How many different schedules could the Hornets have in this tournament?

**a. 210**   b. 343   c. 21   d. 72

**The correct answer is A.**

There are 7 x 6 x 5 = 210 different schedules the Hornets can play. The first round, there are 7 teams they can play against. The second round, there are 6 teams, since they can't play the same team again. The third round, there are 5 teams they can possibly play. 7 x 6 x 5 = 210

# 6.

Monique is making a game schedule for a little league soccer tournament. Her sister's team, the Hornets, and nine other teams are in the tournament. The tournament has three rounds. Teams can only play each other once. How many different schedules could the Hornets have in this tournament?

**a. 504**   b. 729   c. 24   d. 27

**The correct answer is A.**

There are 9 x 8 x 7 = 504 different schedules the Hornets can play. The first round, there are 9 teams they can play against. The second round, there are 8 teams, since they can't play the same team again. The third round, there are 7 teams they can possibly play. 9 x 8 x 7 = 504

## 7.

Monique is making a game schedule for a little league soccer tournament. Her sister's team, the Hornets, and seven other teams are in the tournament. The tournament has five rounds. Teams can only play each other once. How many different schedules could the Hornets have in this tournament?

a. 16807
b. 2520
c. 35
d. 25

## 8.

Monique is making a game schedule for a little league soccer tournament. Her sister's team, the Hornets, and seven other teams are in the tournament. The tournament has seven rounds. Teams can only play each other once. How many different schedules could the Hornets have in this tournament?

a. 2520
b. 5040
c. 49
d. 28

## 9.

James is picking runners for a race. There are fifteen runners and six slots at the starting line numbered one through six for them to stand at. How many different combinations of runners are possible at the starting line?

a. 90
b. 729
c. 3603600
d. 11390625

# 7.

Monique is making a game schedule for a little league soccer tournament. Her sister's team, the Hornets, and seven other teams are in the tournament. The tournament has five rounds. Teams can only play each other once. How many different schedules could the Hornets have in this tournament?

a. 16807   **b. 2520**   c. 35   d. 25

### The correct answer is B.
There are 7 x 6 x 5 x 4 x 3 = 2520 different schedules the Hornets can play. The first round, there are 7 teams they can play against. The second round, there are 6 teams, since they can't play the same team again, and so on. 7 x 6 x 5 x 4 x 3 = 2520

# 8.

Monique is making a game schedule for a little league soccer tournament. Her sister's team, the Hornets, and seven other teams are in the tournament. The tournament has seven rounds. Teams can only play each other once. How many different schedules could the Hornets have in this tournament?

a. 2520   **b. 5040**   c. 49   d. 28

### The correct answer is B.
There are 7 x 6 x 5 x 4 x 3 x 2 x 1 = 5040 different schedules the Hornets can play. The first round, there are 7 teams they can play against. The second round, there are 6 teams, since they can't play the same team again, and so on. 7 x 6 x 5 x 4 x 3 x 2 x 1 = 5040

# 9.

James is picking runners a the race. There are fifteen runners and six slots at the starting line numbered one through six for them to stand at. How many different combinations of runners are possible at the starting line?

a. 90   b. 729   **c. 3603600**   d. 11390625

### The correct answer is C.
There are 15 x 14 x 13 x 12 x 11 x 10 = 3603600 different combinations of runners. Don't let the big numbers throw you off. The way you solve this problem is the same. In the first lane, there are 15 different runners you can select. In the second lane, there are 14 (since you can't assign a runner to two lanes). And so on... 15 x 14 x 13 x 12 x 11 x 10 = 3603600

# 10.

James is picking runners for a race. There are twenty-one runners and six slots at the starting line numbered one through six for them to stand at. How many different combinations of runners are possible at the starting line?

a. 105
b. 126
c. 72014002
d. 39070080

# 11.

James is picking runners for a race. There are ten runners and nine slots at the starting line numbered one through nine for them to stand at. How many different combinations of runners are possible at the starting line?

a. 90
b. 7354400
c. 3628800
d. 45

# 12.

James is picking runners a the race. There are seventeen runners and seven slots at the starting line numbered one through seven for them to stand at. How many different combinations of runners are possible at the starting line?

a. 119
b. 72900212
c. 98017920
d. 1960172320

# 10.

James is picking runners for a race. There are twenty-one runners and six slots at the starting line numbered one through six for them to stand at. How many different combinations of runners are possible at the starting line?

a. 105   b. 126   c. 72014002   **d. 39070080**

**The correct answer is D.**
There are 21 x 20 x 19 x 18 x 17 x 16 = 39070080 different combinations of runners. Don't let the big numbers throw you off. USE A CALCULATOR. The way you solve this problem is the same. In the first lane, there are 21 different runners you can select. In the second lane, there are 20 (since you can't assign a runner to two lanes). And so on... 21 x 20 x 19 x 18 x 17 x 16 = 39070080

# 11.

James is picking runners for a race. There are ten runners and nine slots at the starting line numbered one through nine for them to stand at. How many different combinations of runners are possible at the starting line?

a. 90   b. 7354400   **c. 3628800**   d. 45

**The correct answer is C.**
There are 10 x 9 x 8 x 7 x 6 x 5 x 4 x 3 x 2= 3628800 different combinations of runners. Don't let the big numbers throw you off. USE A CALCULATOR. In the first lane, there are 10 different runners you can select. In the second lane, there are 9 (since you can't assign a runner to two lanes). And so on... 10 x 9 x 8 x 7 x 6 x 5 x 4 x 3 x 2= 3628800

# 12.

James is picking runners for a race. There are seventeen runners and seven slots at the starting line numbered one through seven for them to stand at. How many different combinations of runners are possible at the starting line?

a. 119   b. 72900212   **c. 98017920**   d. 1960172320

**The correct answer is C.**
There are 17 x 16 x 15 x 14 x 13 x 12 x 11= 98017920 different combinations of runners. Don't let the big numbers throw you off. USE A CALCULATOR. In the first lane, there are 17 different runners you can select. In the second lane, there are 16 (since you can't assign a runner to two lanes). And so on... 17 x 16 x 15 x 14 x 13 x 12 x 11= 98017920

Lesson 6 - Combinations with Removal

## 13.

There are 10 pieces of paper in a hat, numbered one through 10. Jeff pulls 1 piece of paper at a time out of the hat and writes down the number he drew. If each time he draws the piece of paper he leaves it outside of the hat, how many different combinations of numbers can he write if he draws a total of three times?

a. 720
b. 30
c. 27
d. 1440

## 14.

There are 12 pieces of paper in a hat, numbered one through 12. Jeff pulls 1 piece of paper at a time out of the hat and writes down the number he drew. If each time he draws the piece of paper he leaves it outside of the hat, how many different combinations of numbers can he write if he draws a total of four times?

a. 48
b. 42
c. 5400
d. 11880

## 15.

There are 8 pieces of paper in a hat, numbered one through 8. Jeff pulls 1 piece of paper at a time out of the hat and writes down the number he drew. If each time he draws the piece of paper he leaves it outside of the hat, how many different combinations of numbers can he write if he draws a total of 6 times?

a. 20
b. 48
c. 10080
d. 20160

# 13.

There are 10 pieces of paper in a hat, numbered one through 10. Jeff pulls 1 piece of paper at a time out of the hat and writes down the number he drew. If each time he draws the piece of paper he leaves it outside of the hat, how many different combinations of numbers can he write if he draws a total of three times?

**a. 720**  b. 30  c. 27  d. 1440

**The correct answer is A.**

Jeff can write 10 x 9 x 8 = 720 different combinations of numbers. The first draw, there are 10 different possibilities. The second draw, there are only 9 possibilities (one piece of paper is left out). The third draw, there are only 8 possibilities. 10 x 9 x 8 = 720

# 14.

There are 12 pieces of paper in a hat, numbered one through 12. Jeff pulls 1 piece of paper at a time out of the hat and writes down the number he drew. If each time he draws the piece of paper he leaves it outside of the hat, how many different combinations of numbers can he write if he draws a total of four times?

a. 48  b. 42  c. 5400  **d. 11880**

**The correct answer is D.**

Jeff can write 12 x 11 x 10 x 9 = 11880 different combinations of numbers. The first draw, there are 12 different possibilities. The second draw, there are only 11 possibilities (one piece of paper is left out). The third draw, there are only 10 possibilities, and so on. 12 x 11 x 10 x 9 = 11880

# 15.

There are 8 pieces of paper in a hat, numbered one through 8. Jeff pulls 1 piece of paper at a time out of the hat and writes down the number he drew. If each time he draws the piece of paper he leaves it outside of the hat, how many different combinations of numbers can he write if he draws a total of 6 times?

a. 20  b. 48  c. 10080  **d. 20160**

**The correct answer is D.**

Jeff can write 8 x 7 x 6 x 5 x 4 x 3 = 20160 different combinations of numbers. The first draw, there are 8 different possibilities. The second draw, there are only 7 possibilities (one piece of paper is left out). The third draw, there are only 6 possibilities, and so on. 8 x 7 x 6 x 5 x 4 x 3 = 20160

# *Lesson 7*
# Multiplication

Some word problems on the ACT will be looking for you to do a simple multiplication. Word problems like this typically tell you that there are so many pounds or miles or inches for every step or minute or dollar. The key words to look for are PER or EACH, or anything that gives you a clue that you need to figure out how many of something there is based on a proportion like MILES PER HOURS or POUNDS PER GALLON etc.

The trick here is to not overthink it. You have to recognize when the test simply wants you to multiply.

For example, in the following question:

A milk truck can hold 1,000 gallons of milk. Each gallon of milk weighs approximately 8 pounds. About how many pounds of milk can a milk truck hold?

To arrive at our answer, we multiply 1,000 gallons of milk per truck times 8 pounds per gallon. 1000 x 8 = 8000 pounds of milk.

# 1.

A milk truck can hold 2,000 gallons of milk.  Each gallon of milk weighs approximately 8 pounds.  About how many pounds of milk can a milk truck hold?

a. 8000
b. 16000
c. 500
d. 1000

# 2.

A milk truck can hold 2,500 gallons of milk.  Each gallon of milk weighs approximately 8 pounds.  About how many pounds of milk can a milk truck hold?

a. 20000
b. 40000
c. 16000
d. 650

# 3.

A gasoline truck can hold 1,200 gallons of gasoline.  Each gallon of gasoline weighs approximately 7 pounds.  About how many pounds of gasoline can a gasoline truck hold?

a. 16800
b. 8400
c. 4200
d. 175

# 1.

A milk truck can hold 2,000 gallons of milk. Each gallon of milk weighs approximately 8 pounds. About how many pounds of milk can a milk truck hold?

a. 8000
**b. 16000**
c. 500
d. 1000

**The correct answer is B.**
2000 gallons x 8 pounds per gallon = 16000 pounds. 2000 x 8 = 16000

# 2.

A milk truck can hold 2,500 gallons of milk. Each gallon of milk weighs approximately 8 pounds. About how many pounds of milk can a milk truck hold?

**a. 20000**
b. 40000
c. 16000
d. 650

**The correct answer is A.**
2500 gallons x 8 pounds per gallon = 20000 pounds. 2500 x 8 = 20000

# 3.

A gasoline truck can hold 1,200 gallons of gasoline. Each gallon of gasoline weighs approximately 7 pounds. About how many pounds of gasoline can a gasoline truck hold?

a. 16800
**b. 8400**
c. 4200
d. 175

**The correct answer is B.**
1200 gallons x 7 pounds per gallon = 8400 pounds. 1200 x 7 = 8400

# 4.

A milk truck can hold 1,150 gallons of milk. Each gallon of milk weighs approximately 8 pounds. About how many pounds of milk can a milk truck hold?

    a. 10000
    b. 9200
    c. 8000
    d. 115

# 5.

Each time Tim takes one step left, he takes three steps forward. How many steps has Tim taken forward after he has taken 100 steps left?

    a. 33
    b. 100
    c. 300
    d. 500

# 6.

How many miles has a car driving 70 miles per hour gone after three hours?

    a. 70
    b. 20
    c. 140
    d. 210

# 4.

A milk truck can hold 1,150 gallons of milk. Each gallon of milk weighs approximately 8 pounds. About how many pounds of milk can a milk truck hold?

a. 10000
**b. 9200**
c. 8000
d. 115

**The correct answer is B.**
1150 gallons x 8 pounds per gallon = 9200 pounds. 1150 x 8 = 9200

# 5.

Each time Tim takes one step left, he takes three steps forward. How many steps has Tim taken forward after he has taken 100 steps left?

a. 33
b. 100
**c. 300**
d. 500

**The correct answer is C.**
Tim takes three steps forward for every step left. So 100 steps left x 3 = 300. 100 x 3 = 300

# 6.

How many miles has a car driving 70 miles per hour traveled after three hours?

a. 70
b. 20
c. 140
**d. 210**

**The correct answer is D.**
70 miles per hour x 3 hours = 210 miles. 70 x 3 = 210

# 7.

How far has a car driving 50 miles per hour traveled after two and a half hours?

      a. 100
      b. 125
      c. 150
      d. 52.5

# 8.

How many miles has a car driving 40 miles per hour traveled after 75 minutes?

      a. 50
      b. 60
      c. 40
      d. 120

# 9.

How many miles has a car driving 50 miles per hour traveled after 15 minutes?

      a. 25
      b. 12.5
      c. 50
      d. 6.25

# 7.

How far has a car driving 50 miles per hour traveled after two and a half hours?

    a. 100
**b. 125**
    c. 150
    d. 52.5

**The correct answer is B.**
50 miles per hour x 2.5 hours = 125 miles.  50 x 2.5 = 125

# 8.

How many miles has a car driving 40 miles per hour traveled after 75 minutes?

**a. 50**  b. 60  c. 40  d. 120

**The correct answer is A.**
To solve this problem, first you have to convert 75 minutes into hours.  75 minutes / 60 minutes per hour = 1.25 hours.  40 miles per hour x 1.25 hours = 50 miles.  Before you multiply in these types of problems, you have to make sure the units of measure match up.  You can't multiply hours and minutes together.

# 9.

How many miles has a car driving 50 miles per hour traveled after 15 minutes?

a. 25  **b. 12.5**  c. 50  d. 6.25

**The correct answer is B.**
To solve this problem, first you have to convert 15 minutes into hours.  15 minutes / 60 minutes per hour = .25 hours.  50 miles per hour x .25 hours = 12.5 miles.  Before you multiply in these types of problems, you have to make sure the units of measure match up.  You can't multiply hours and minutes together.

## 10.

Jim can travel 30 miles on one gallon of gas. How many miles can he travel on ten gallons of gas?

        a. 100
        b. 200
        c. 300
        d. 600

## 11.

Jim can travel 27 miles on one gallon of gas. How many miles can he travel on 30 gallons of gas?

        a. 57
        b. 540
        c. 270
        d. 810

## 12.

Jim can travel 18 miles on one gallon of gas. How many miles can he travel on 23 gallons of gas?

        a. 414
        b. 207
        c. 41
        d. 42

# 10.

Jim can travel 30 miles on one gallon of gas. How many miles can he travel on ten gallons of gas?

      a. 100
      b. 200
      **c. 300**
      d. 600

**The correct answer is C.**
Jim can travel 30 miles per gallon x 10 gallons = 300 miles. 30 x 10 = 300.

# 11.

Jim can travel 27 miles on one gallon of gas. How many miles can he travel on 30 gallons of gas?

      a. 57
      b. 540
      c. 270
      **d. 810**

**The correct answer is D.**
Jim can travel 27 miles per gallon x 30 gallons = 810 miles. 27 x 30 = 810.

# 12.

Jim can travel 18 miles on one gallon of gas. How many miles can he travel on 23 gallons of gas?

      **a. 414**
      b. 207
      c. 41
      d. 42

**The correct answer is A.**
Jim can travel 18 miles per gallon x 23 gallons = 414 miles. 18 x 23 = 414.

# 13.

Jim can travel 20 miles on one gallon of gas. How many miles can he travel on half of a gallon of gas?

a. 5
b. 40
c. 20
d. 10

# 14.

Jim can travel 23 miles on one gallon of gas. How many miles can he travel on 50 gallons of gas?

a. 2300
b. 73
c. 1150
d. 23

# 15.

Jim can travel 25 miles on one gallon of gas. His gas tank holds 16 gallons of gas. What is the furthest distance (in miles) he can travel without needing to refuel?

a. 400 mi
b. 200 mi
c. 41 mi
d. 800 mi

# 13.

Jim can travel 20 miles on one gallon of gas. How many miles can he travel on half of a gallon of gas?

a. 5
b. 40
c. 20
**d. 10**

**The correct answer is D.**
Half a gallon of gas = .5 gallons. Jim can travel 20 miles per gallon x .5 gallons = 10 miles.
20 x .5 = 10

# 14.

Jim can travel 23 miles on one gallon of gas. How many miles can he travel on 50 gallons of gas?

a. 2300
b. 73
**c. 1150**
d. 23

**The correct answer is C.**
Jim can travel 23 miles per gallon x 50 gallons = 1150 miles.
23 x 50 = 1150

# 15.

Jim can travel 25 miles on one gallon of gas. His gas tank holds 16 gallons of gas. What is the furthest distance (in miles) he can travel without needing to refuel?

**a. 400 mi**
b. 200 mi
c. 41 mi
d. 800 mi

**The correct answer is A.**
Jim can travel 25 miles per gallon x 16 gallons = 400 mi.
25 x 16 = 400

# Lesson 8
# Algebra

The next set of questions consists of algebra problems.

ALGEBRA is the math subject that involves figuring out unknown quantities. Usually a variable, such as $x$, is used in the math problem.

It's called a VARIABLE because it is unknown. What $x$ is from problem to problem can VARY (meaning change), although it's always the same in any one problem. You just don't know what it is. That's what you have to find out.

Typically simple algebra problems are presented as EQUATIONS.

An EQUATION has two sides. It says that something EQUALS something else.

For example, x + 2 = 4 is an equation. One side of the equals sign is the same as the other side.

The secret of algebra problems is to simplify things so that the variable, in this case $x$, is all by itself on one side of the equation.

You can add, subtract, multiply and divide both sides of the equation, as long as you do it to both sides equally.

For example, to solve x + 2 = 4, you subtract 2 from both sides.

x + 2 - 2 = 4 - 2

x = 2

Sometimes you have to subtract or add variables to the problem. For example,

2x + 3 = x - 2

First subtract x from both sides.

(2x + 3) - x = (x - 2) - x

x + 3 = -2

Then you subtract 3 from both sides.

(x + 3) - 3 = (-2) - 3

x = -5

You'll get a chance to practice this more in the questions that follow.

Lesson 8 - Algebra

# 1.

If 4x + 5 = 9x − 2, then x = ?

a. 5/7   b. 7/5   c. 2   d. 5

# 2.

If 5x + 2 = 12x − 5, then x = ?

a. -1   b. 4   c. 2   d. 1

# 3.

If 2x + 7 = 4x + 3, then x = ?

a. 3   b. 2   c. 1/2   d. -2

# 1.

If 4x + 5 = 9x − 2, then x = ?

a. 5/7   **b. 7/5**   c. 2   d. 5

**The correct answer is B.**
Subtract 4x from both sides.
5 = 5x - 2
Add 2 to both sides.
7 = 5x
Divide both sides by 5.
x = 7/5

# 2.

If 5x + 2 = 12x − 5, then x = ?

a. -1   b. 4   c. 2   **d. 1**

**The correct answer is D.**
Subtract 5x from both sides.
2 = 7x - 5
Add 5 to both sides.
7 = 7x
Divide both sides by 7.
x = 1

# 3.

If 2x + 7 = 4x + 3, then x = ?

a. 3   **b. 2**   c. 1/2   d. -2

**The correct answer is B.**
Subtract 2x from both sides.
7 = 2x + 3
Subtract 3 from both sides.
4 = 2x
Divide both sides by 2.
x = 2

# 4.

If 3x +2 = 4x + 3, then x = ?

a. -1    b. 4    c. -2    d. -4

# 5.

If 9x -20 = 5x + 4, then x = ?

a. 1    b. 6    c. 4    d. -3

# 6.

If 15x + 5 = 5x + 35, then x = ?

a. -3    b. 35    c. 5    d. 3

Lesson 8 - Algebra

# 4.

If 3x +2 = 4x + 3, then x = ?

**a. -1**   b. 4   c. -2   d. -4

The correct answer is A.
Subtract 3x from both sides.
2 = x + 3
Subtract 3 from both sides.
x = -1

# 5.

If 9x -20 = 5x + 4, then x = ?

a. 1   **b. 6**   c. 4   d. -3

**The correct answer is B.**
Subtract 5x from both sides.
4x - 20 = 4
Add 20 to both sides.
4x = 24
Divide both sides by 4.
x = 6

# 6.

If 15x + 5 = 5x + 35, then x = ?

a. -3   b. 35   c. 5   **d. 3**

**The correct answer is D.**
Subtract 5x from both sides.
10x + 5 = 35
Subtract 5 from both sides.
10x = 30
Divide both sides by 10.
x = 3

# 7.

If 2x + 5 = 7x + 20, then x = ?

a. 3   b. -3   c. 7   d. 10

# 8.

If 3x + 3 = 4x + 9, then x = ?

a. -4   b. 3   c. -6   d. 6

# 9.

If 7x + 22 = 17x − 28, then x = ?

a. 5   b. 10   c. -5   d. -1

# 7.

If 2x + 5 = 7x + 20, then x = ?

a. 3   **b. -3**   c. 7   d. 10

**The correct answer is B.**
Subtract 2x from both sides.
5 = 5x + 20
Subtract 20 from both sides.
-15 = 5x
Divide both sides by 5.
x = -3

# 8.

If 3x + 3 = 4x + 9, then x = ?

a. -4   b. 3   **c. -6**   d. 6

The correct answer is C.
Subtract 3x from both sides.
3 = x + 9
Subtract 9 from both sides.
x = -6

# 9.

If 7x + 22 = 17x − 28, then x = ?

**a. 5**   b. 10   c. -5   d. -1

**The correct answer is A.**
Subtract 7x from both sides.
22 = 10x - 28
Add 28 to both sides.
50 = 10x
Divide both sides by 10
x = 5

# 10.

If 41x - 1 = x − 121, then x = ?

a. 3   b. -3   c. 5   d. -5

# 11.

If x +2 = 2x +12, then x = ?

a. -1/10   b. 1/10   c. 10   d. -10

# 12.

If 19x + 10 = 12x + 45, then x = ?

a. 3   b. 4   c. -5   d. 5

# 10.

If 41x - 1 = x − 121, then x = ?

a. 3  **b. -3**  c. 5  d. -5

**The correct answer is B.**
Subtract x from both sides.
40x - 1 = -121
Add 1 to both sides.
40x = -120
Divide both sides by 40.
x = -3

# 11.

If x +2 = 2x +12, then x = ?

a. -1/10  b. 1/10  c. 10  **d. -10**

**The correct answer is D.**
Subtract x from both sides.
2 = x + 12
Subtract 12 from both sides
x = -10

# 12.

If 19x + 10 = 12x + 45, then x = ?

a. 3  b. 4  c. -5  **d. 5**

The correct answer is D.
Subtract 12x from both sides.
7x + 10 = 45
Subtract 10 from both sides.
7x = 35
Divide both sides by 7
x = 5

Lesson 8 - Algebra

# 13.

If 12x + 8 = 4x − 24, then x = ?

a. 3   b. -4   c. 4   d. -3

# 14.

If -4x + 2 = 7x − 20, then x = ?

a. -2   b. 2   c. 1/2   d. -1/2

# 15.

If -6x + 8 = 2x + 6, then x = ?

a. -4   b. 4   c. 1/4   d. -1/4

# 13.

If 12x + 8 = 4x − 24, then x = ?

a. 3    **b. -4**    c. 4    d. -3

**The correct answer is B.**
Subtract 4x from both sides.
8x + 8 = -24
Subtract 8 from both sides.
8x = -32
Divide both sides by 8.
x = -4

# 14.

If -4x + 2 = 7x − 20, then x = ?

a. -2    **b. 2**    c. 1/2    d. -1/2

The correct answer is B.
Add 4x to both sides.
2 = 11x - 20
Add 20 to both sides.
22 = 11x
Divide both sides by 11.
x = 2

# 15.

If -6x + 8 = 2x + 6, then x = ?

a. -4    b. 4    **c. 1/4**    d. -1/4

**The correct answer is C.**
Add 6x to both sides.
8 = 8x + 6
Subtract 6 from both sides
2 = 8x
Divide both sides by 8
x = 2/8 = 1/4

# Lesson 9
# Multiplication using FOIL

The next set of questions deals with using the FOIL method to solve algebra problems.

FOIL stands for First, Outer, Inner, Last, and tells you what to do when you have to multiply an equation that looks like this:

$(x + 2)(x + 3) = ?$

To arrive at the correct answer, you multiply the first terms inside each set of parenthases. Then you multiply the outer terms, then the inner terms, then the last terms. Then you add all of these up.

FIRST: $x * x = x^2$

OUTER: $x * 3 = 3x$

INNER: $2 * x = 2x$

LAST: $2 * 3 = 6$

So the solution is $x^2 + 3x + 2x + 6 =$ **$x^2 + 5x + 6$**

There are a couple variations of this that you might encounter on the ACT. For example, you might be asked to simplify this statement:

$(x - 3)^2$

To solve this problem using the FOIL method, you need to first turn $(x - 3)^2$ into:

$(x - 3)(x - 3)$

From there apply the normal FOIL method, as described above.

You might also have to work backwards from the FOIL method. For example, you may be given the problem:

$4x^2 + 6x + 2 = 0, x = ?$

This is called FACTORING. You are finding the factors that when multiplied together create the expanded equation. To solve this problem, you need to reverse the FOIL method. Start with empty parentheses:

(        ) (        )

You know that your FIRST = $4x^2$, you know that your OUTER + INNER = 6x, and you know that your LAST = 2. Use a little trial and error to find the correct answer.

$(4x + 1)(x + 2)$ doesn't work. It FOILs out to $4x^2 + 9x + 2$.

$(2x + 1)(2x + 2) = 0$ works! Multiply it out using the FOIL method and you'll arrive back at the original problem, $4x^2 + 6x + 2$.

Now to solve the problem, $2x + 1 = 0$ OR $2x + 2 = 0$. So x = -1/2 OR -1.

You almost always have two answers for X when solving a problem like this.

Now we get to practice. Refer to these instructions again once you get to question 11 to refresh.

# Lesson 9 - Multiplication using FOIL

# 1.

$(x + 2)(x + 3) = ?$

a. $x^2 + 5x + 6$
b. $x^2 + 5x - 6$
c. $2x^2 - 3x + 2$
d. $2x^2 - 2$

# 2.

$(4x + 5)(-2x + 3) = ?$

a. $-4x^2 + 2x + 15$
b. $8x^2 - 2x - 15$
c. $-8x^2 + 2x + 15$
d. $x^2 - 2x - 8$

# 3.

$(9x - 3)(-3x - 4) = ?$

a. $27x^2 + 27x + 12$
b. $-27x^2 - 27x + 12$
c. $9x^2 + 6x - 12$
d. $-9x^2 - 6x - 6$

# 1.

$(x + 2)(x + 3) = ?$

a. $x^2 + 5x + 6$
b. $x^2 + 5x - 6$
c. $2x^2 - 3x + 2$
d. $2x^2 - 2$

**The correct answer is A.**
FIRST: $x * x = x^2$. OUTER: $x * 3 = 3x$. INNER: $2 * x = 2x$. LAST: $2 * 3 = 6$.
$x^2 + 3x + 2x + 6 = x^2 + 5x + 6$.

# 2.

$(4x + 5)(-2x + 3) = ?$

a. $-4x^2 + 2x + 15$
b. $8x^2 - 2x - 15$
c. $-8x^2 + 2x + 15$
d. $x^2 - 2x - 8$

**The correct answer is C.**
FIRST: $4x * -2x = -8x^2$. OUTER: $4x * 3 = 12x$. INNER: $5 * -2x = -10x$. LAST: $5 * 3 = 15$.
$-8x^2 + 12x - 10x + 15 = -8x^2 + 2x + 15$.

# 3.

$(9x - 3)(-3x - 4) = ?$

a. $27x^2 + 27x + 12$
b. $-27x^2 - 27x + 12$
c. $9x^2 + 6x - 12$
d. $-9x^2 - 6x - 6$

**The correct answer is B.**
FIRST: $9x * -3x = -27x2$. OUTER: $9x * -4 = -36x$. INNER: $-3 * -3x = 9x$. LAST: $-3 x -4 = 12$.
$-27x^2 - 36x + 9x + 12 = -27x^2 - 27x + 12$.

# Lesson 9 - Multiplication using FOIL

## 4.

$(3x + 2)(3x + 3) = ?$

a. $x^2 - 15x - 6$
b. $-x^2 + 15x - 6$
c. $-9x^2 - 15x + 6$
d. $9x^2 + 15x + 6$

## 5.

$(2x - 5)^2 = ?$

a. $-2x^2 - 20x + 25$
b. $2x^2 - 20x + 25$
c. $-4x^2 - 20x + 25$
d. $4x^2 - 20x + 25$

## 6.

$(3x - 5)^2 = ?$

a. $9x^2 - 30x - 25$
b. $-9x^2 + 30x - 25$
c. $9x^2 - 30x + 25$
d. $-9x^2 - 30x + 25$

# 4.

$(3x + 2)(3x + 3) = ?$

a. $x^2 - 15x - 6$
b. $-x^2 + 15x - 6$
c. $-9x^2 - 15x + 6$
**d. $9x^2 + 15x + 6$**

**The correct answer is D.**
FIRST: $3x * 3x = 9x^2$. OUTER: $3x * 3 = 9x$. INNER: $2 * 3x = 6x$. LAST: $2 * 3 = 6$.
$9x^2 + 9x + 6x + 6 = 9x^2 + 15x + 6$.

# 5.

$(2x - 5)^2 = ?$

a. $-2x^2 - 20x + 25$
b. $2x^2 - 20x + 25$
c. $-4x^2 - 20x + 25$
**d. $4x^2 - 20x + 25$**

**The correct answer is D.**
$(2x - 5)^2 = (2x - 5)(2x - 5)$
FIRST: $2x * 2x = 4x^2$. OUTER: $2x * -5 = -10x$. INNER: $2x * -5 = -10x$. LAST: $-5 * -5 = 25$.
$4x^2 - 10x - 10x + 25 = 4x^2 - 20x + 25$

# 6.

$(3x - 5)^2 = ?$

a. $9x^2 - 30x - 25$
b. $-9x^2 + 30x - 25$
**c. $9x^2 - 30x + 25$**
d. $-9x^2 - 30x + 25$

**The correct answer is C.**
$(3x - 5)^2 = (3x - 5)(3x - 5)$
FIRST: $3x * 3x = 9x^2$. OUTER: $3x * -5 = -15x$. INNER: $3x * -5 = -15x$. OUTER: $-5 * -5 = 25$.
$9x2 - 15x - 15x + 25 = 9x^2 - 30x + 25$

# 7.

$(4x - 2)^2 = ?$

a. $16x^2 - 16x + 4$
b. $-16x^2 - 16x + 4$
c. $4x^2 - 16x + 2$
d. $4x^2 + 16x + 2$

# 8.

$(5x + 5)^2 = ?$

a. $25x^2 + 50x + 25$
b. $-25x^2 - 50x + 25$
c. $10x^2 + 10x + 10$
d. $-10x^2 + 25x + 25$

# 9.

$(9x + 4)^2 = ?$

a. $-81x^2 - 72x + 16$
b. $81x^2 + 72x + 16$
c. $9x^2 + 18x + 4$
d. $-9x^2 + 18x - 4$

# 7.

$(4x - 2)^2 = ?$

   **a. $16x^2 - 16x + 4$**
   b. $-16x^2 - 16x + 4$
   c. $4x^2 - 16x + 2$
   d. $4x^2 + 16x + 2$

**The correct answer is A.**
$(4x - 2)^2 = (4x - 2)(4x - 2)$
FIRST: $4x * 4x = 16x^2$. OUTER: $4x * -2 = -8x$. INNER: $4x * -2 = -8x$. LAST: $-2 * -2 = 4$.
$16x^2 - 8x - 8x + 4 = 16x^2 - 16x + 4$

# 8.

$(5x + 5)^2 = ?$

   **a. $25x^2 + 50x + 25$**
   b. $-25x^2 - 50x + 25$
   c. $10x^2 + 10x + 10$
   d. $-10x^2 + 25x + 25$

**The correct answer is A.**
$(5x + 5)^2 = (5x + 5)(5x + 5)$
FIRST: $5x * 5x = 25x^2$. OUTER: $5x * 5 = 25x$. INNER: $5x * 5 = 25x$. LAST: $5 * 5 = 25$.
$25x^2 + 25x + 25x + 25 = 25x^2 + 50x + 25$

# 9.

$(9x + 4)^2 = ?$

   a. $-81x^2 - 72x + 16$
   **b. $81x^2 + 72x + 16$**
   c. $9x^2 + 18x + 4$
   d. $-9x^2 + 18x - 4$

**The correct answer is B.**
$(9x + 4)^2 = (9x + 4)(9x + 4)$
FIRST: $9x * 9x = 81x^2$. OUTER: $9x * 4 = 36x$. INNER: $9x * 4 = 36x$. LAST: $4 * 4 = 16$.
$81x^2 + 36x + 36x + 16 = 81x^2 + 72x + 16$.

# Lesson 9 - Multiplication using FOIL

## 10.

$(7x - 7)^2 = ?$

a. $7x^2 + 14x + 7$
b. $7x^2 - 49x + 7$
c. $49x^2 - 98x + 49$
d. $-49x^2 + 98x - 49$

## 11.

Note: Please refer back to the instructions at the beginning of this lesson before continuing.

$x^2 - 5x + 6 = 0$, $x = ?$

a. -2 or -3
b. 2 or 3
c. 0
d. 1 or 4

## 12.

$2x^2 + 3x - 9 = 0$, $x = ?$

a. -1 or 4
b. -3/2 or 3
c. 1 or 4
d. 3/2 or -3

# 10.

$(7x - 7)^2 = ?$

    a. $7x^2 + 14x + 7$
    b. $7x^2 - 49x + 7$
    **c. $49x^2 - 98x + 49$**
    d. $-49x^2 + 98x - 49$

**The correct answer is C.**
$(7x - 7)^2 = (7x - 7)(7x - 7)$
FIRST: $7x * 7x = 49x^2$. OUTER: $7x * -7 = -49x$. INNER: $7x * -7 = -49x$. LAST: $-7 * -7 = 49$.
$49x^2 - 49x - 49x + 49 = 49x^2 - 98x + 49$

# 11.

$x^2 - 5x + 6 = 0, \ x = ?$

    a. -2 or -3
    **b. 2 or 3**
    c. 0
    d. 1 or 4

**The correct answer is B.**
We know that FIRST = $x^2$, OUTER + INNER = $-5x$, and LAST = 6.
Throuh trial and error, we find that $x^2 - 5x + 6 = (x - 3)(x - 2)$
x = 2 or 3

# 12.

$2x^2 + 3x - 9 = 0, \ x = ?$

    a. -1 or 4
    b. -3/2 or 3
    c. 1 or 4
    **d. 3/2 or -3**

**The correct answer is D.**
We know that FIRST = $2x^2$, OUTER + INNER = $3x$, and LAST = -9. Through trial and error, we find that $2x^2 + 3x - 9 = (2x - 3)(x + 3)$
x = 3/2 or -3

# 13.

$8x^2 - 2x - 1 = 0$, $x = ?$

    a. -1/8 or 1/4
    b. 1/8 or -1/4
    c. 1/4 or -1/2
    d. -1/4 or 1/2

# 14.

$3x^2 + 14x + 8 = 0$, $x = ?$

    a. -2/3 or -4
    b. 2/3 or 4
    c. 1 or 5/3
    d. -1 or -5/3

# 15.

$6x^2 + 5x + 9 = 10$, $x = ?$

    a. 1/6 or -1
    b. -1/6 or 1
    c. 1/6 or 1
    d. -1/6 or -1

# 13.

$8x^2 - 2x - 1 = 0$, $x = ?$

a. -1/8 or 1/4
b. 1/8 or -1/4
c. 1/4 or -1/2
**d. -1/4 or 1/2**

The correct answer is D.
We know that FIRST = $8x^2$, OUTER + INNER = -2x, and LAST = -1. Through trial and error, we find that $(4x + 1)(2x - 1) = 0$.
$x = -1/4$ or $1/2$

# 14.

$3x^2 + 14x + 8 = 0$, $x = ?$

**a. -2/3 or -4**
b. 2/3 or 4
c. 1 or 5/3
d. -1 or -5/3

The correct answer is A.
We know that FIRST = $3x^2$, OUTER + INNER = 14x, and LAST = 8. Through trial and error, we find that $3x^2 + 14x + 8 = (3x + 2)(x + 4) = 0$.
$x = -2/3$ or $-4$

# 15.

$6x^2 + 5x + 9 = 10$, $x = ?$

**a. 1/6 or -1**
b. -1/6 or 1
c. 1/6 or 1
d. -1/6 or -1

The correct answer is A.
First we have to simplify the problem by subtracting 10 from both sides. Now we have: $6x^2 + 5x - 1 = 0$. We know that FIRST = $6x^2$, OUTER + INNER = 5x, and LAST = -1. Through trial and error, we find that $6x^2 + 5x + 9 = 10 = (6x - 1)(x + 1) = 0$. $x = 1/6$ or $-1$.

## Lesson 10
# Review

In this lesson, we'll review everything that's been covered from lessons one through nine. Any concept (or any combination of concepts) from lessons one through nine are fair game.

You may experience knowing how to use the method we've gone over, but not being sure WHAT method to use. As you practice more, this will become second nature to you.

Another good check for whether or not you are using the correct method is that chances are, if you use the wrong method, then you won't find your answer among the multiple choices. Instead of trying over and over again using the same method, take a step back and figure out what approach you need to take.

For example, if you don't realize that you're solving a COMBINATION WITH REMOVAL, and solve it instead as a simple COMBINATION, you're going to come up with the wrong answer.

Identifying HOW to solve the problem is the major part of the battle. Once you've figured out how to solve the problem, actually solving it is just a matter of doing simple math and double-checking your answer.

Ask yourself on each question on the ACT: how am I going to solve this problem? What are they really asking for on this question? What do I need to figure out in order to turn this problem into simple math?

# Lesson 10 - Review

## 1.

$4x^2 + 4x - 8 = 0$, x = ?

- a. -2 or 1
- b. 2 or -1
- c. 1/2 or -1/2
- d. -1 or 1

## 2.

Dominique and Jared own a sandwich shop. They offer 4 kinds of bread, 2 kinds of meat, and 11 kinds of cheese. Each type of sandwich on their menu has a combination of 1 bread, 1 meat, and 1 cheese. A "Value Deal" consists of one sandwich and one drink. There are 7 drink options. How many different "Value Deal" combinations are possible?

a. 24   b. 616   c. 88   d. 462

## 3.

Dominique and Jared own a sandwich shop. They offer 10 kinds of bread, 11 kinds of meat, and 12 kinds of cheese. Each type of sandwich on their menu has a combination of 1 bread, 1 meat, and 1 cheese. A "Value Deal" consists of one sandwich and one drink. There are 12 drink options. How many different "Value Deal" combinations are possible?

a. 16250   b. 13525   c. 15840   d. 15491

# 1.

$4x^2 + 4x - 8 = 0, x = ?$

**a. -2 or 1**
b. 2 or -1
c. 1/2 or -1/2
d. -1 or 1

**The correct answer is A.**
We know that FIRST = $4x^2$, OUTER + INNER = $4x$, and LAST = -8. Through trial and error, we find that $4x^2 + 4x - 8 = (4x + 8)(x - 1) = 0$.
x = -2 or 1. Missed this question? Review Lesson 9.

# 2.

Dominique and Jared own a sandwich shop. They offer 4 kinds of bread, 2 kinds of meat, and 11 kinds of cheese. Each type of sandwich on their menu has a combination of 1 bread, 1 meat, and 1 cheese. A "Value Deal" consists of one sandwich and one drink. There are 7 drink options. How many different "Value Deal" combinations are possible?

a. 24  **b. 616**  c. 88  d. 462

**The correct answer is B.**
There are 4 breads x 2 meats x 11 cheeses x 7 drinks = 616 combinations.
4 x 2 x 11 x 7 = 616
Missed this question? Review Lesson 4.

# 3.

Dominique and Jared own a sandwich shop. They offer 10 kinds of bread, 11 kinds of meat, and 12 kinds of cheese. Each type of sandwich on their menu has a combination of 1 bread, 1 meat, and 1 cheese. A "Value Deal" consists of one sandwich and one drink. There are 12 drink options. How many different "Value Deal" combinations are possible?

a. 16250   b. 13525   **c. 15840**   d. 15491

**The correct answer is C.**
There are 10 breads x 11 meats x 12 cheeses x 12 drinks = 15840 combinations.
10 x 11 x 12 x 12 = 15840. Use your calculator for problems like this!
Missed this question? Review Lesson 4.

## 4.

If ten shirts cost $120, how much do 8 shirts cost?

a. $48
b. $96
c. $60
d. $32

## 5.

Jim is trying to save up for a car over the summer. The car costs $3500.00. He has started a job where he earns $17.50 per hour. If the summer lasts nine weeks, what is the minimum average number of hours per week that he needs to work in order to earn enough for the car, rounded to the nearest hour?

a. 35   b. 20   c. 24   d. 22

## 6.

Ellen is trying to pick out a dress, but she can't decide. Her friends finally tell her that they are going to play a game. They have numbered the dresses one through five. She has to pick a number, and that's the dress they'll buy her. Two dresses are red, one is green, one is blue, and one is pink. What are the odds that she will pick a red dress?

a. 3:2   b. 2:3   c. 4:1   d. 1:4

# 4.

If ten shirts cost $120, how much do 8 shirts cost?

a. $48
**b. $96**
c. $60
d. $32

**The correct answer is B.**
$120 divided by 10 shirts = $12 per shirt. $12 per shirt times 8 shirts = $96. 120 / 10 = 12. 12 x 8 = 96. You have to figure out the value of one shirt, then you can figure out how much more than one shirt costs. Missed this question? Review Lesson 1.

# 5.

Jim is trying to save up for a car over the summer. The car costs $3500.00. He has started a job where he earns $17.50 per hour. If the summer lasts nine weeks, what is the minimum average number of hours per week that he needs to work in order to earn enough for the car, rounded to the nearest hour?

a. 35   b. 20   c. 24   **d. 22**

**The correct answer is D.**
Jim needs to work $3500 divided by $17.50 per hour = 200 hours. The average number of hours per week he needs to work is 200 hours divided into 9 weeks = 22.22 hours. We round this down to the nearest hour for our answer, 22. Missed this question? Review Lesson 2.

# 6.

Ellen is trying to pick out a dress, but she can't decide. Her friends finally tell her that they are going to play a game. They have numbered the dresses one through five. She has to pick a number, and that's the dress they'll buy her. Two dresses are red, one is green, one is blue, and one is pink. What are the odds that she will pick a red dress?

a. 3:2   **b. 2:3**   c. 4:1   d. 1:4

**The correct answer is B.**
The odds that she will pick the red dress is 2 desired outcomes vs. 3 undesired outcomes = 2:3. Missed this question? Review Lesson 4.

# 7.

Jim can travel 30 miles on one gallon of gas. His gas tank holds 15 gallons of gas. What is the furthest distance (in miles) he can travel without needing to refuel?

a. 450 mi
b. 400 mi
c. 45 mi
d. 800 mi

# 8.

There are 10 pieces of paper in a hat, numbered 1 through 10. Jeff pulls 1 piece of paper at a time out of the hat and writes down the number he drew. If each time he draws the piece of paper he leaves it outside of the hat, how many different combinations of numbers can he write if he draws a total of 5 times?

a. 100000   b. 40   c. 26280   d. 30240

# 9.

If -4x + 18 = 2x + 6, then x = ?

a. -1/2   b. 1/2   c. 2   d. -2

## 7.

Jim can travel 30 miles on one gallon of gas. His gas tank holds 15 gallons of gas. What is the furthest distance (in miles) he can travel without needing to refuel?

**a. 450 mi**
b. 400 mi
c. 45 mi
d. 800 mi

**The correct answer is A.**
Jim can travel 30 miles per gallon x 15 gallons = 450 mi.
30 x 15 = 450. Missed this question? Review Lesson 7.

## 8.

There are 10 pieces of paper in a hat, numbered 1 through 10. Jeff pulls 1 piece of paper at a time out of the hat and writes down the number he drew. If each time he draws the piece of paper he leaves it outside of the hat, how many different combinations of numbers can he write if he draws a total of 5 times?

a. 100000   b. 40   c. 26280   **d. 30240**

**The correct answer is D.**
Jeff can write 10 * 9 * 8 * 7 * 6 = 30240 different combinations of numbers. The first draw, there are 10 different possibilities. The second draw, there are only 9 possibilities (one piece of paper is left out). The third draw, there are only 8 possibilities, and so on. 10 * 9 * 8 * 7 * 6 = 30240. Use your calculator. Missed this question? Review Lesson 6.

## 9.

If -4x + 18 = 2x + 6, then x = ?

a. -1/2   b. 1/2   **c. 2**   d. -2

**The correct answer is C.**
Add 4x to both sides.
18 = 6x + 6
Subtract 6 from both sides
12 = 6x
Divide both sides by 6
x = 2. Missed this question? Review Lesson 8.

# 10.

Jim can travel 23 miles on one gallon of gas.  How many miles can he travel on 40 gallons of gas?

a. 1050
b. 900
c. 920
d. 63

# 11.

Tabitha made the following scores in her math class.  In her school an overall average score of 88 or more is given a B.  What is the minimum score she needs to get on her fifth test in order to score a B in the class?

a. 75   b. 65   c. 55   d. 95

| Test | 1 | 2 | 3 | 4 | 5 |
|---|---|---|---|---|---|
| Score | 80 | 100 | 99 | 96 | ? |

# 12.

$3x^2 + 2x + 9 = 10$.  X = ?

a. 1/3 or -1
b. -1/3 or 1
c. 1/3 or 1
d. -1/3 or -1

# 10.

Jim can travel 23 miles on one gallon of gas. How many miles can he travel on 40 gallons of gas?

a. 1050
b. 900
**c. 920**
d. 63

**The correct answer is C.**
Jim can travel 23 miles per gallon x 40 gallons = 920 miles.
23 x 40 = 920
Missed this question? Review Lesson 7.

# 11.

Tabitha made the following scores in her math class. In her school an overall average score of 88 or more is given a B. What is the minimum score she needs to get on her fifth test in order to score a B in the class?

a. 75  **b. 65**  c. 55  d. 95

| Test | 1 | 2 | 3 | 4 | 5 |
|---|---|---|---|---|---|
| Score | 80 | 100 | 99 | 96 | ? |

**The correct answer is B.**
To answer this problem, we have to work backwards with what we know about averages. We need to find out what TOTAL score is needed to have an average of 88. In other words, what number divided by 5 = 88?
$x / 5 = 88$
Multiply both sides by 5 and you get x = 88 • 5
x = 440. So the TOTAL score needs to be 440. Currently we have a total score of 80 + 100+ 99 + 96 = 375. So we need a minimum score of 440 - 375 = 65. Missed this question? Review Lesson 2.

# 12.

$3x^2 + 2x + 9 = 10$. X = ?

**a. 1/3 or -1**
b. -1/3 or 1
c. 1/3 or 1
d. -1/3 or -1

The correct answer is A.
First we have to simplify the problem by subtracting 10 from both sides. Now we have:
$3x^2 + 2x - 1 = 0$. We know that FIRST = $3x^2$, OUTER + INNER = 2x, and LAST = -1. Through trial and error, we find that (3x - 1)(x + 1). x = 1/3 or -1. Missed this question? Review Lesson 9.

122

# 13.

$4x^2 - 18x + 8 = 0$, x = ?

    a. 1/2 or 4
    b. -1/2 or 4
    c. 1 or 4
    d. -1 or -4

# 14.

If 9x + 8 = 4x + 33, then x = ?

a. -5   b. 5   c. 1/5   d. -1/5

# 15.

(2x + 2)(5x - 3) = ?

    a. $x^2 - 16x - 6$
    b. $-x^2 + 16x - 6$
    c. $-10x^2 - 4x + 6$
    d. $10x^2 + 4x - 6$

# 13.

$4x^2 - 18x + 8 = 0$, x = ?

    **a. 1/2 or 4**
    b. -1/2 or 4
    c. 1 or 4
    d. -1 or -4

**The correct answer is A.**
We know that FIRST = $4x^2$, OUTER + INNER = -18x, and LAST = 8. Through trial and error, we find that $4x^2 - 18x + 8 = (4x - 2)(x - 4) = 0$.
x = 1/2 or 4. Missed this question? Review Lesson 9.

# 14.

If 9x + 8 = 4x + 33, then x = ?

a. -5    **b. 5**    c. 1/5    d. -1/5

**The correct answer is B.**
Subtract 4x from both sides.
5x + 8 = 33
Subtract 8 from both sides.
5x = 25
Divide both sides by 5.
x = 5. Missed this question? Review Lesson 8.

# 15.

$(2x + 2)(5x - 3)$ = ?

    a. $x^2 - 16x - 6$
    b. $-x^2 + 16x - 6$
    c. $-10x^2 - 4x + 6$
    **d. $10x^2 + 4x - 6$**

**The correct answer is D.**
FIRST: 2x * 5x = $10x^2$. OUTER: 2x * -3 = -6x. INNER: 2 * 5x = 10x. LAST: 2 * -3 = -6.
$10x^2 - 6x + 10x - 6 = 10x^2 + 4x - 6$.
Missed this question? Review Lesson 9.

# Lesson 11
# Working Backwards

In some math problems on the ACT, you'll need to work backwards from one number to figure out what you started with.

For example, you will be told how much money Susan had in the third year, and you'll be asked how much money she started with.

For example, in this problem:

A class had 5 more students the second year than the first, and the class size for the third year was double the size of the class on the second year. If the class size in the third year was 50 students, what was the size of the class in the first year?

You start with a class size of 50 in the third year. If this is double the size of the class in the second year, we divide by two to figure out how many students were in the class the second year.

50 / 2 = 25 students in the class the second year.

Since the class had 5 more students in it the second year compared to the first year, we can subtract 5 to figure out how many students were in the class the first year.

25 - 5 = 20.

Our answer is 20 students in the first year.

# Lesson 11 - Working Backwards

# 1.

Sales for a business were 4 million dollars more the second year than the first, and sales for the third year were double the sales for the second year.  If sales for the third year were 40 million dollars, what were the sales, in millions of dollars, of the first year?

    a.  30 million   b.  20 million   c.  16 million   d.  10 million

# 2.

Sales for a business were 4 million dollars more the second year than the first, and sales for the third year were double the sales for the second year.  If sales for the third year were 40 million dollars, what were the sales, in millions of dollars, of the second year?

    a.  30 million   b.  20 million   c.  16 million   d.  10 million

# 3.

Sales for a business were 8 million dollars more the second year than the first, and sales for the third year were triple the sales for the second year.  If sales for the third year were 72 million dollars, what were the sales, in millions of dollars, of the first year?

    a.  30 million   b.  20 million   c.  16 million   d.  10 million

# 1.

Sales for a business were 4 million dollars more the second year than the first, and sales for the third year were double the sales for the second year. If sales for the third year were 40 million dollars, what were the sales, in millions of dollars, of the first year?

a. 30 million   b. 20 million   **c. 16 million**   d. 10 million

**The correct answer is C.**
Working backwards from year 3: 40 million / 2 = 20 million in year 2.  20 million - 4 million = 16 million in year 1.

# 2.

Sales for a business were 4 million dollars more the second year than the first, and sales for the third year were double the sales for the second year. If sales for the third year were 40 million dollars, what were the sales, in millions of dollars, of the second year?

a. 30 million   **b. 20 million**   c. 16 million   d. 10 million

**The correct answer is B.**
This is a bit of trick question.  They are asking for the SECOND year, so working back from year 3: 40 million / 2 = 20 million in year 2.  That's your answer.

# 3.

Sales for a business were 8 million dollars more the second year than the first, and sales for the third year were triple the sales for the second year. If sales for the third year were 72 million dollars, what were the sales, in millions of dollars, of the first year?

a. 30 million   b. 20 million   **c. 16 million**   d. 10 million

**The correct answer is C.**
Working backwards from year 3: 72 million divided by 3 = 24 million in year 2.  24 million - 8 million = 16 million in year 1.

# 4.

Sales for a business were 10 million dollars more the second year than the first, and sales for the third year were quadruple the sales for the second year. If sales for the third year were 96 million dollars, what were the sales, in millions of dollars, of the first year?

a. 14 million   b. 17 million   c. 20 million   d. 472 million

# 5.

Sales for a business were 7 million dollars more the second year than the first, and sales for the third year were quintuple the sales for the second year. If sales for the third year were 100 million dollars, what were the sales, in millions of dollars, of the first year?

a. 13 million   b. 10 million   c. 16 million   d. 20 million

# 6.

Bill has arrived at the bank at 5:29 p.m. Thirty minutes before that, he was leaving his job, and exactly eight hours before that, he arrived at his job. What time did Bill arrive at his job?

a. 8:59 p.m.   b. -4:59   c. 8:59 a.m.   d. 9:29 a.m.

# 4.

Sales for a business were 10 million dollars more the second year than the first, and sales for the third year were quadruple the sales for the second year. If sales for the third year were 96 million dollars, what were the sales, in millions of dollars, of the first year?

**a. 14 million**   b. 17 million   c. 20 million   d. 472 million

**The correct answer is A.**
Working backwards from year 3: 96 million divided by 4 = 24 million in year 2. 24 million - 10 million = 14 million in year 1.

# 5.

Sales for a business were 7 million dollars more the second year than the first, and sales for the third year were quintuple the sales for the second year. If sales for the third year were 100 million dollars, what were the sales, in millions of dollars, of the first year?

**a. 13 million**   b. 10 million   c. 16 million   d. 20 million

**The correct answer is A.**
Working backwards from year 3: 100 million divided by 5 = 20 million in year 2. 20 million - 7 million = 13 million in year 1.

# 6.

Bill has arrived at the bank at 5:29 p.m. Thirty minutes before that, he was leaving his job, and exactly eight hours before that, he arrived at his job. What time did Bill arrive at his job?

a. 8:59 p.m.   b. -4:59   **c. 8:59 a.m.**   d. 9:29 a.m.

**The correct answer is C.**
Working backwards from Bill arriving at the bank: 5:29 p.m. - 30 minutes = 4:59 p.m. 4:59 p.m. - 8 hours = 8:59 a.m. Bill arrived at work at 8:59 a.m. Be sure to remember that one hour before 1:59 p.m. is 12:59 p.m., and then 11:59 a.m.

## 7.

Bill has arrived at the bank at 3:29 p.m. Twenty-three minutes before that, he was leaving his job, and exactly four hours before that, he arrived at his job. What time did Bill arrive at his job?

a. 3:29 a.m.   b. 9:39 p.m.   c. 11:06 p.m.   d. 11:06 a.m.

## 8.

Bill has arrived at the bank at 5:29 p.m. One hour and twenty minutes before that, he was leaving his job, and exactly four hours before that, he arrived at his job. What time did Bill arrive at his job?

a. 11:09 a.m.   b. 12:09 p.m.   c. 1:09 p.m.   d. 12:29 p.m.

## 9.

A math teacher wrote a number on the board, and then each day at the beginning of class he doubled it. On the fourth day, after he doubled it, the number was 32. What was the number on the first day?

a. 4   b. 8   c. 2   d. 256

# 7.

Bill has arrived at the bank at 3:29 p.m.  Twenty-three minutes before that, he was leaving his job, and exactly four hours before that, he arrived at his job.  What time did Bill arrive at his job?

a. 3:29 a.m.   b. 9:39 p.m.   c. 11:06 p.m.   **d. 11:06 a.m.**

**The correct answer is D.**
Working backwards from Bill arriving at the bank: 3:29 p.m. - 23 minutes = 3:06 p.m.  3:06 p.m. - 4 hours = 11:06 a.m.  Bill arrived at work at 11:06 a.m.   Be sure to remember that one hour before 1:06 p.m. is 12:06 p.m., and then one hour before that is 11:06 a.m.

# 8.

Bill has arrived at the bank at 5:29 p.m.  One hour and twenty minutes before that, he was leaving his job, and exactly four hours before that, he arrived at his job.  What time did Bill arrive at his job?

a. 11:09 a.m.   **b. 12:09 p.m.**   c. 1:09 p.m.   d. 12:29 p.m.

**The correct answer is B.**
Working backwards from Bill arriving at the bank: 5:29 p.m. - 1 hour and 20 minutes = 4:09 p.m.  4:09 p.m. - 4 hours = 12:09 p.m.  Bill arrived at his job at 12:09 p.m.   Be sure to remember that one hour before 1:09 p.m. is 12:09 p.m., not 0:09 p.m.

# 9.

A math teacher wrote a number on the board, and then each day at the beginning of class he doubled it.  On the fourth day, after he doubled it, the number was 32.  What was the number on the first day?

**a. 4**   b. 8   c. 2   d. 256

**The correct answer is A.**
Working backwards from the number 32 on the 4th day: 32 / 2 = 16 on the 3rd day.  16 / 2 = 8 on the 2nd day.  8 / 2 = 4 on the 1st day.
32 / 2 = 16.  16 / 2 = 8.  8 / 2 = 4.

Lesson 11 - Working Backwards

# 10.

A math teacher wrote a number on the board, and then each day at the beginning of class he added one and then doubled it. On the third day, after he added one and then doubled it, the number was 38. What was the number on the first day?

a. 7   b. 8.75   c. 8   d. 9

# 11.

A math teacher wrote a number on the board, and then each day at the beginning of class he tripled it. On the fourth day, after he tripled it, the number was 405. What was the number on the first day?

a. 45   b. 90   c. 3645   d. 15

# 12.

A math teacher wrote a number on the board, and then each day at the beginning of class he doubled it and then subtracted 5. On the fourth day, after he doubled it and then subtracted five, the number was 21. What was the number on the first day?

a. 9   b. 7   c. 21   d. 8

133

## 10.

A math teacher wrote a number on the board, and then each day at the beginning of class he added one and then doubled it. On the third day, after he added one and then doubled it, the number was 38. What was the number on the first day?

a. 7   b. 8.75   **c. 8**   d. 9

**The correct answer is C.**
Working backwards from the number 38 on the 3rd day: 38 / 2 = 19 - 1 = 18 on the 2nd day. 18 / 2 = 9 - 1 = 8 on the 1st day. To solve this correctly, you have to work backwards, meaning the last action is the first action you undo. If you subtract one, then divide for each day, you won't arrive at the correct answer.

## 11.

A math teacher wrote a number on the board, and then each day at the beginning of class he tripled it. On the fourth day, after he tripled it, the number was 405. What was the number on the first day?

a. 45   b. 90   c. 3645   **d. 15**

**The correct answer is D.**
Working backwards from the number 405 on the 4th day: 405 / 3 = 135 on the 3rd day. 135 / 3 = 45 on the 2nd day. 45 / 3 = 15 on the 1st day. Note that to undo multiplication, you divide. If you multiply by 3 instead of dividing by 3, you won't arrive at the correct answer.

## 12.

A math teacher wrote a number on the board, and then each day at the beginning of class he doubled it and then subtracted 5. On the fourth day, after he doubled it and then subtracted five, the number was 21. What was the number on the first day?

a. 9   **b. 7**   c. 21   d. 8

**The correct answer is B.**
Working backwards from the number 21 on the 4th day: 21 + 5 = 26 / 2 = 13 on the 3rd day. 13 + 5 = 18 / 2 = 9 on the 2nd day. 9 + 5 = 14 / 2 = 7 on the first day.

## 13.

A math teacher wrote a number on the board, and then each day at the beginning of class he doubled it and then subtracted 5. On the tenth day, after he doubled it and then subtracted five, the number was 5. What was the number on the first day?

a. 7   b. 9765625   c. 6   d. 5

## 14.

Joe started the day with a full tank of gas. Each hour, he burned two gallons of gas. After driving for five hours, Joe had six gallons of gas left. How many gallons of gas did he start with?

a. 14   b. 18   c. 1   d. 16

## 15.

Joe started the day with a tank of gas ¾ full. Each hour, he burned three gallons of gas. After driving for 4 hours, Joe's tank was empty. How many gallons of gas can his tank hold when it's full?

a. 20   b. 16   c. 12   d. 8

# 13.

A math teacher wrote a number on the board, and then each day at the beginning of class he doubled it and then subtracted 5. On the tenth day, after he doubled it and then subtracted five, the number was 5. What was the number on the first day?

a. 7   b. 9765625   c. 6   **d. 5**

**The correct answer is D.**
Working backwards from the number 5 on the 10th day: 5 + 5 = 10 / 2 = 5 on the 9th day. 5 + 5 = 10 / 2 = 5 on the 8th day. You can either continue to calculate this all the way to the first day, or recognize the pattern that every day remains 5. Either way, the correct answer is 5 on the first day.

# 14.

Joe started the day with a full tank of gas. Each hour, he burned two gallons of gas. After driving for five hours, Joe had six gallons of gas left. How many gallons of gas did he start with?

a. 14   b. 18   c. 1   **d. 16**

**The correct answer is D.**
We know that Joe burned 2 gallons of gas per hour * 5 hours = 10 gallons of gas. He was left with 6 gallons of gas + 10 gallons burned = 16 gallons started with.

# 15.

Joe started the day with a tank of gas ¾ full. Each hour, he burned three gallons of gas. After driving for 4 hours, Joe's tank was empty. How many gallons of gas can his tank hold when it's full?

a. 20   **b. 16**   c. 12   d. 8

**The correct answer is B.**
We know that Joe burned 3 gallons per hour * 4 hours = 12 gallons of gas. 12 gallons of gas = 3/4 of a tank. We can solve this as a proportion or as an algebra problem. 12 = 3/4x. Multiply both sides by 4/3. x = 48/3. x = 16.

# Lesson 12
# Sequences & Patterns

There are always some questions on the ACT that will ask you to identify a pattern or a sequence.

A pattern or sequence is a list of numbers that are changing, from one to the next. There is always a rule that you have to identify that causes the numbers to change.

For example, the pattern:

1, 2, 3, 4, 5...

uses the rule "add one each time."

The pattern:

2, 4, 8, 16, 32...

uses the rule "multiply by 2 each time."

The rule never changes between the numbers in the pattern. Only the numbers change.

Here are a few definitions that will help you:

ARITHMETIC SEQUENCE: a pattern where the rules only use addition and subtraction.

GEOMETRIC SEQUENCE: a pattern where the rules can include multiplication, division, and other operations.

In general, an arithmetic sequence will be easier to figure out than a geometric sequence.

The way to figure out a pattern is to ask yourself:

- What changed between #1 & #2?
- What changed between #2 & #3?
- What changed between #3 & #4?
- What is the rule that covers all of these changes?

# 1.

Which of the following statements is true about the arithmetic sequence 20, 15, 10, 5, … ?

a. The fifth term is 2.
b. The fifth term is 0.
c. The numbers are multiplied by 2 each time in the sequence.
d. The fifth term is 4.

# 2.

Which of the following statements is true about the arithmetic sequence 14, 24, 34, 44, … ?

a. The fifth term is 54.
b. The sixth term is 72.
c. The fifth term is 64.
d. The fifth term is 50.

# 3.

Which of the following statements is true about the arithmetic sequence 1, 4, 7, 10, …?

a. The numbers are being increased by 4 each time.
b. The fifth term is 13.
c. The fifth term is 10.
d. The fourth term is 7.

# 1.

Which of the following statements is true about the arithmetic sequence 20, 15, 10, 5, ... ?

a. The fifth term is 2.
**b. The fifth term is 0.**
c. The numbers are multiplied by 2 each time in the sequence.
d. The fifth term is 4.

**The correct answer is B.**
The term is being subtracted by 5 each time. The change between 20 and 15 is -5. The change between 15 and 10 is -5. This is the pattern. 5 - 5 = 0.

# 2.

Which of the following statements is true about the arithmetic sequence 14, 24, 34, 44, ... ?

**a. The fifth term is 54.**
b. The sixth term is 72.
c. The fifth term is 64.
d. The fifth term is 50.

**The correct answer is A.**
The term is being increased by 10 each time. The difference between 14 and 24 is +10. The difference between 24 and 34 is +10. This is the pattern. 44 + 10 = 54.

# 3.

Which of the following statements is true about the arithmetic sequence 1, 4, 7, 10, ...?

a. The numbers are being increased by 4 each time.
**b. The fifth term is 13.**
c. The fifth term is 10.
d. The fourth term is 7.

**The correct answer is B.**
The term is being increased by 3 each time. The change between 1 and 4 is +3. The change between 4 and 7 is +3. This is the pattern. 10 + 3 = 13.

# Lesson 12 - Sequences & Patterns

## 4.

Which of the following statements is true about the arithmetic sequence 18, 16, 14, 12, ... ?

    a. The fifth term is 2.
    b. The fifth term is 10.
    c. The numbers are multiplied by 3 each time in the sequence.
    d. The fifth term is 5.

## 5.

Which of the following statements is true about the geometric sequence 2, 4, 8, 16, ...?

    a. The fifth term is 32.
    b. The sixth term is 16.
    c. The fifth term is 64.
    d. The fifth term is 24.

## 6.

Which of the following statements is true about the geometric sequence 3, 9, 27, 81, ...?

    a. The fifth term is 54.
    b. The terms are being multiplied by 3 each time.
    c. The fifth term is 162.
    d. The fourth term is 27.

# 4.

Which of the following statements is true about the arithmetic sequence 18, 16, 14, 12, … ?

a. The fifth term is 2.
**b. The fifth term is 10.**
c. The numbers are multiplied by 3 each time in the sequence.
d. The fifth term is 5.

**The correct answer is B.**
The term is having 2 subtracted from it each time. The change between 18 and 16 is -2. The change between 16 and 14 is -2. This is the pattern. 12 - 2 = 10.

# 5.

Which of the following statements is true about the geometric sequence 2, 4, 8, 16, …?

**a. The fifth term is 32.**
b. The sixth term is 16.
c. The fifth term is 64.
d. The fifth term is 24.

**The correct answer is A.**
The term is being multiplied by 2 each time. The 4 is double 2. 8 is double 4. This is the pattern. 16 * 2 = 32.

# 6.

Which of the following statements is true about the geometric sequence 3, 9, 27, 81, …?

a. The fifth term is 54.
**b. The terms are being multiplied by 3 each time.**
c. The fifth term is 162.
d. The fourth term is 27.

**The correct answer is B.**
The term is being multiplied by 3 each time. The change between 3 and 9 being multiplied by 3. The change between 9 and 27 is being multiplied by 3. This is the pattern. 81 * 3 = 243.

## 7.

What is the next number in the pattern? -1, 3, -9, 27, … ?

      a. 81
      b. -27
      c. 27
      d. -81

## 8.

What is the next number in the pattern? -2, 4, -8, 16, … ?

      a. -16
      b. 24
      c. -32
      d. 32

## 9.

What is the next number in the pattern? 5, 25, 125, … ?

      a. 625
      b. 225
      c. 375
      d. 500

# 7.

What is the next number in the pattern? -1, 3, -9, 27, ... ?

    a. 81
    b. -27
    c. 27
    **d. -81**

**The correct answer is D.**
The term is being multiplied by -3 each time. The change between -1 and 3 is +4. The change between 3 and -9 is -12. This tells us that it isn't an arithmetic sequence. Then we ask: what number could we multiply by each time to get this pattern? The answer is -3. Note that a pattern oscillating between positive and negative usually indicates that the terms are being multiplied by a negative number. Now we apply the rule to find the next term in the sequence.
27 * -3 = -81

# 8.

What is the next number in the pattern? -2, 4, -8, 16, ... ?

    a. -16
    b. 24
    **c. -32**
    d. 32

**The correct answer is C.**
The term is being multiplied by -2 each time. The change between -2 and 4 is +6. The change between 4 and -8 is +12. This tells us that it isn't an arithmetic sequence. Then we ask: what number could we multiply by each time to get this pattern? The answer is -2. Note that a pattern oscillating between positive and negative usually indicates that the terms are being multiplied by a negative number. Now we apply the rule to find the next term in the sequence.
16 * -2 = -32

# 9.

What is the next number in the pattern? 5, 25, 125, ... ?

    **a. 625**
    b. 225
    c. 375
    d. 500

**The correct answer is A.**
The term is being multiplied by 5 each time. You have to ask yourself: what do I need to do to this term each time to get the next term? Addition doesn't work, because adding 20 to 5 will give you 25, but then adding the same 20 to 25 will not give you 125. Multiplication does work. Multiply 5 * 5 = 25. 5 * 25 = 125. There's your pattern. Now apply the rule to find the next term. 125 * 5 = 625.

# 10.

What is the next number in the pattern? 1, 1, 2, 3, 5, 8, ... ?

      a. 10
      b. 13
      c. 11
      d. 15

# 11.

What is the next number in the pattern? 4, 6, 9, 13.5, ... ?

      a. 22.5
      b. 20.25
      c. 21
      d. 35

# 12.

What is the next number in the pattern? 1, 3, 7, 15, ... ?

      a. 30
      b. 22
      c. 31
      d. 23

# 10.

What is the next number in the pattern? 1, 1, 2, 3, 5, 8, ... ?

    a. 10
    **b. 13**
    c. 11
    d. 15

**The correct answer is B.**
This is a tricky question that you have to look out for on the ACT. This particular pattern has a name: the Fibonacci Sequence. Half of the tests will include something like it. The next term = the sum of the two terms before it. For example, term three is the sum of term two and term one (1 + 1 = 2). Term five is the sum of terms four and three (2 + 3 = 5). Therefore, term seven = 8 + 5 = 13.

# 11.

What is the next number in the pattern? 4, 6, 9, 13.5, ... ?

    a. 22.5
    **b. 20.25**
    c. 21
    d. 35

**The correct answer is B.**
The term is being multiplied by 1.5 each time. 4 * 1.5 = 6. 6 * 1.5 = 9. 9 * 1.5 = 13.5. We apply this rule to find the next term. 13.5 x 1.5 = 20.25.

# 12.

What is the next number in the pattern? 1, 3, 7, 15, ... ?

    a. 30
    b. 22
    **c. 31**
    d. 23

**The correct answer is C.**
This is a complex pattern. Each term is being doubled, and then having 1 added to it. 1 * 2 + 1 = 3. 3 * 2 + 1 = 7. 7 * 2 +1 = 15. We apply this rule to 15 to arrive at the next term. 15 * 2 + 1 = 31.

# 13.

What is the next number in the pattern? 4, 7, 10, 13, … ?

       a. 16
       b. 14
       c. 15
       d. 17

# 14.

What is the next number in the pattern? 128, 64, 32, 16 … ?

       a. 4
       b. 6
       c. 8
       d. 48

# 15.

What is the next number in the pattern? ½, ¼, 1/8, 1/16, …?

       a. 32
       b. 16
       c. 1/32
       d. 1/24

# 13.

What is the next number in the pattern? 4, 7, 10, 13, … ?

    **a. 16**
    b. 14
    c. 15
    d. 17

**The correct answer is A.**
The change between each term is +3. The rule is to add 3 to each term. We apply this rule to figure out the next number in the pattern. 13 + 3 = 16. Note that this problem is easier than the ones that came before it. On the ACT, the questions are not ordered from easiest to hardest. If you can't figure a question out, skip it and go on to the next. Chances are the next question will be easier!

# 14.

What is the next number in the pattern? 128, 64, 32, 16 … ?

    a. 4
    b. 6
    **c. 8**
    d. 48

**The correct answer is C.**
Each term in the pattern is being divided by 2. 128 / 2 = 64. 64 / 2 = 32. 32 / 2 = 16. To figure out the next number in the pattern, we apply the rule: 16 / 2 = 8.

# 15.

What is the next number in the pattern? ½, ¼, 1/8, 1/16, …?

    a. 32
    b. 16
    **c. 1/32**
    d. 1/24

**The correct answer is C.**
Each term is being multiplied by 1/2. 1/2 * 1/2 = 1/4. 1/4 * 1/2 = 1/8. 1/8 * 1/2 = 1/16. To find the next number in the pattern, we apply the rule to the last term. 1/16 * 1/2 = 1/32.

# Lesson 13
# Perimeter

Questions that ask you to find the perimeter of an object are asking you to find out how long the lines are that make up the sides of a shape.

Usually these are pretty straightforward. Sometimes you have to use a bit of logic or work backwards from what you know. For example, a problem might ask you:

A triangle with 2 sides measuring 4 inches and 5 inches has a perimeter of 12 inches. What is the measure of the triangle's third side?

In this question, you know that a triangle has three sides, and that two of those sides have a total length of 10 inches. So 9 + x = 12 inches. Subtract both sides by 9 and you find that x = 3 inches. Your third side has a length of 3 inches.

It can help to draw out what the problem is talking about. Most perimeter questions on the ACT are just words. By drawing out what is described, you can make your life a lot easier.

Remember that in the math section, you are often juggling around many different parts of a given problem in your mind in order to solve it. The more you can write down in black and white, the closer you are to solving it and moving on to the next question.

Keep in mind that rectangles and parallelograms have two sets of equal sides, and that there is a formula for the perimeter of a circle ($2\pi r$).

# 1.

A rectangle is 8 inches tall by 4 inches wide.  What is its perimeter?

   a. 16 inches
   b. 12 inches
   c. 32 inches
   d. 24 inches

# 2.

A rectangle is 7 inches tall by 5 inches wide.  What is its perimeter?

   a. 12 inches
   b. 35 inches
   c. 24 inches
   d. 36 inches

# 3.

A rectangle is 17 centimeters tall by 33 centimeters wide.  What is its perimeter?

   a. 16 cm
   b. 50 cm
   c. 100 cm
   d. 561 cm

# 1.

A rectangle is 8 inches tall by 4 inches wide. What is its perimeter?

    a. 16 inches
    b. 12 inches
    c. 32 inches
    **d. 24 inches**

**The correct answer is D.**
A rectangle has two sets of equal sides. If the rectangle has 2 sides measuring 8 inches and 4 inches, then it also has 2 other sides measuring 8 inches and 4 inches. 8 + 8 + 4 + 4 = 24 inches.

# 2.

A rectangle is 7 inches tall by 5 inches wide. What is its perimeter?

    a. 12 inches
    b. 35 inches
    **c. 24 inches**
    d. 36 inches

**The correct answer is C.**
A rectangle has two sets of equal sides. If the rectangle has 2 sides measuring 7 inches and 5 inches, then it also has 2 other sides measuring 7 inches and 5 inches. 7 + 7 + 5 + 5 = 24 inches.

# 3.

A rectangle is 17 centimeters tall by 33 centimeters wide. What is its perimeter?

    a. 16 cm
    b. 50 cm
    **c. 100 cm**
    d. 561 cm

**The correct answer is C.**
A rectangle has two sets of equal sides. If the rectangle has 2 sides measuring 17 cm and 33 cm, then it also has 2 other sides measuring 17 cm and 33 cm. 33 + 33 + 17 + 17 = 100 cm.

# Lesson 13 - Perimeter

# 4.

A triangle has 2 sides measuring 4 centimeters and 6 centimeters. Its perimeter its 15 centimeters. What is the length of its third side?

        a. 5 cm
        b. 7 cm
        c. 9 cm
        d. 4 cm

# 5.

A triangle has 2 sides measuring 7 centimeters and 6 centimeters. Its perimeter its 25 centimeters. What is the length of its third side?

        a. 12 cm
        b. 14 cm
        c. 24 cm
        d. 8 cm

# 6.

A triangle has 2 sides measuring 9 centimeters and 4 centimeters. Its perimeter its 19 centimeters. What is the length of its third side?

        a. 32 cm
        b. 4 cm
        c. 8 cm
        d. 6 cm

# 4.

A triangle has 2 sides measuring 4 centimeters and 6 centimeters. Its perimeter its 15 centimeters. What is the length of its third side?

- a. 5 cm
- b. 7 cm
- c. 9 cm
- d. 4 cm

**The correct answer is A.**

This triangle has a total perimeter of 15 inches. Subtract the length of the two sides to find the length of the remaining side. 15 - 4 = 11. 11 - 6 = 5. The third side is 5 inches long.

# 5.

A triangle has 2 sides measuring 7 centimeters and 6 centimeters. Its perimeter its 25 centimeters. What is the length of its third side?

- a. 12 cm
- b. 14 cm
- c. 24 cm
- d. 8 cm

**The correct answer is A.**

This triangle has a total perimeter of 25 centimeters. Subtract the length of the two sides to find the length of the remaining side. 25 - 7 = 18. 18 - 6 = 12. The third side is 12 centimeters long.

# 6.

A triangle has 2 sides measuring 9 centimeters and 4 centimeters. Its perimeter its 19 centimeters. What is the length of its third side?

- a. 32 cm
- b. 4 cm
- c. 8 cm
- d. 6 cm

**The correct answer is D.**

This triangle has a total perimeter of 19 cm. Subtract the length of the two sides to find the length of the remaining side. 19 - 9 = 10. 10 - 4 = 6. The third side is 6 cm long.

# 7.

A circle has a radius of 5 centimeters. What is its perimeter?

   a. $25\pi$ cm
   b. $5\pi$ cm
   c. $10\pi$ cm
   d. $20\pi$ cm

# 8.

A circle has a diameter of 12 centimeters. What is its perimeter, rounded to the nearest tenth of a centimeter?

a. 144 cm   b. 37.7 cm   c. 37.6 cm   d. 36 cm

# 9.

A square has a side of length 5 inches. What is its perimeter?

   a. 10 inches
   b. 20 inches
   c. 25 inches
   d. 30 inches

# 7.

A circle has a radius of 5 centimeters. What is its perimeter?

>    a. 25π cm
>    b. 5π cm
>    **c. 10π cm**
>    d. 20π cm

**The correct answer is C.**
The formula for the perimeter of a circle is 2πr. The radius of this circle is 5 cm, so the perimeter is 2 * π * 5 = 10π cm

# 8.

A circle has a diameter of 12 centimeters. What is its perimeter, rounded to the nearest tenth of a centimeter?

>    a. 144 cm    **b. 37.7 cm**    c. 37.6 cm    d. 36 cm

**The correct answer is B.**
The formula for the perimeter of a circle is 2πr. The diameter of a circle is double the radius, so r = 12 cm / 2 = 6 cm. 2 * π * 6 = 12π. π = approx. 3.14, so for our answer we multiply. 12 * 3.14 = 37.68 cm. Round to the nearest tenth of a cm. 37.7 cm.

# 9.

A square has a side of length 5 inches. What is its perimeter?

>    a. 10 inches
>    **b. 20 inches**
>    c. 25 inches
>    d. 30 inches

**The correct answer is B.**
A square has four equal sides. So if it has one side with length of 5 inches, all four of its sides have length 5 inches. 5 + 5 + 5 + 5 = 20 inches.

# 10.

In the figure below, all line segments are either horizontal or vertical and the dimensions are in inches. What is the perimeter, in inches, of the figure?

4
12
5
6

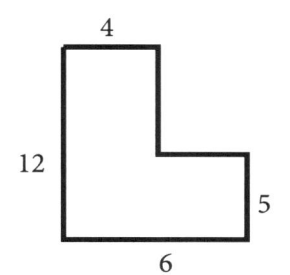

a. 45 in   b. 18 in   c. 27 in   d. 36 in

# 11.

In the figure below, all line segments are either horizontal or vertical and the dimensions are in inches. What is the perimeter, in inches, of the figure?

20
12
25
8

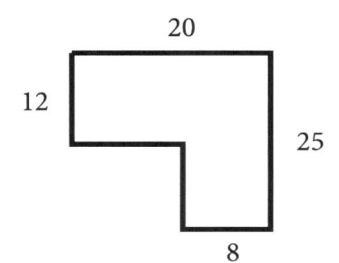

a. 90 in   b. 45 in   c. 65 in   d. 85 in

# 12.

In the figure below, all line segments are either horizontal or vertical and the dimensions are in inches. What is the perimeter, in inches, of the figure?

12
20
9

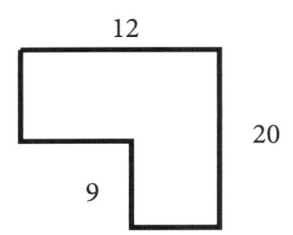

a. 64 in   b. 32 in   c. 24 in   d. 128 in

Math Mastery - Level 1

# 10.

In the figure below, all line segments are either horizontal or vertical and the dimensions are in inches. What is the perimeter, in inches, of the figure?

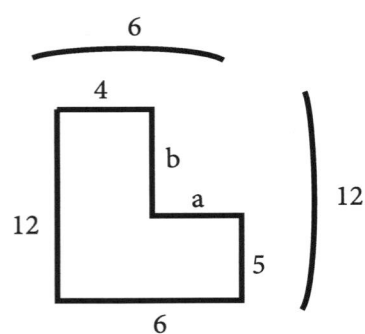

a. 45 in   b. 18 in   c. 27 in   **d. 36 in**

**The correct answer is D.**
With shapes like this, the left side = right side, and the top side = the bottom side. So 4 + a = 6, and 5 + b = 12. Therefore, a = 2 and b = 7. Now we can find the perimeter:
4 + 7 + 2 + 5 + 6 + 12 = 36 in.

# 11.

In the figure below, all line segments are either horizontal or vertical and the dimensions are in inches. What is the perimeter, in inches, of the figure?

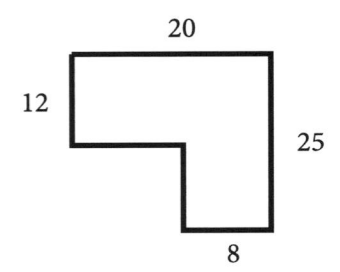

**a. 90 in**   b. 45 in   c. 65 in   d. 85 in

**The correct answer is A.**
First figure out the lengths of the missing sides. Write on the shape as you follow along. The vertical side + 12 = 25, so its length is 13. The horizontal side + 8 = 20, so its length is 12. Now add the sides to find the perimeter:  12 + 20 + 25 + 8 + 13 + 12 = 90 in.

# 12.

In the figure below, all line segments are either horizontal or vertical and the dimensions are in inches. What is the perimeter, in inches, of the figure?

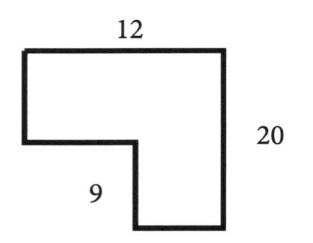

**a. 64 in**   b. 32 in   c. 24 in   d. 128 in

**The correct answer is A.**
First figure out the lengths of the missing sides. Write on the shape as you follow along. The horizontal lines together = 12. We can't figure out how much they are individually, but we know enough to find the perimeter. The vertical line + 9 = 20, so it = 11. Now add the sides to find the perimeter: 12 + 20 + 12 (both of those missing sides together) + 9 + 11 = 64 in.

Lesson 13 - Perimeter

# 13.

In the figure below, all line segments are either horizontal or vertical and the dimensions are in inches. What is the perimeter, in inches, of the figure?

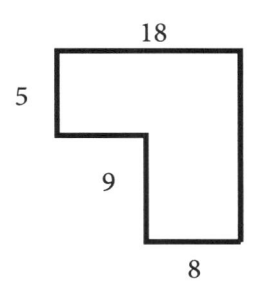

a. 28 in   b. 64 in   c. 40 in   d. 50 in

# 14.

In the figure below, all line segments are either horizontal or vertical and the dimensions are in inches. What is the perimeter, in inches, of the figure?

a. 32 in   b. 64 in   c. 45 in   d. 30 in

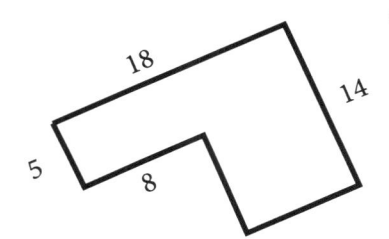

# 15.

In the figure below, all line segments are either horizontal or vertical and the dimensions are in inches. What is the perimeter, in inches, of the figure?

a. 286 in   b. 140 in   c. 70 in   d. 35 in

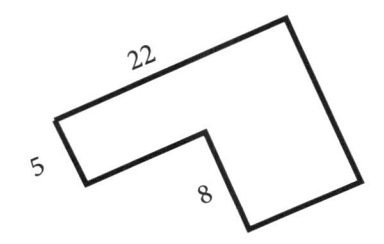

# 13.

In the figure below, all line segments are either horizontal or vertical and the dimensions are in inches. What is the perimeter, in inches, of the figure?

a. 28 in   **b. 64 in**   c. 40 in   d. 50 in

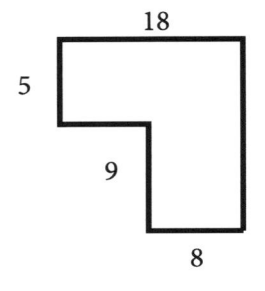

**The correct answer is B.**
The vertical right side of the shape is equal in length to the two vertical sides on the left. 5 + 9 = 14. The horizontal line + 8 = 18, the length of the top horizontal line. So that line segment = 10. Now we add up all the sides to find the perimeter.
18 + 14 + 8 + 9 + 10+ 5 = 64 in.

# 14.

In the figure below, all line segments are either horizontal or vertical and the dimensions are in inches. What is the perimeter, in inches, of the figure?

a. 32 in   **b. 64 in**   c. 45 in   d. 30 in

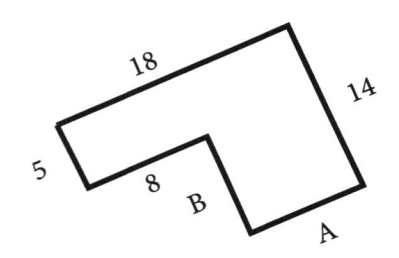

**The correct answer is B.**
First figure out the lengths of the missing sides. Write on the shape as you follow along. The side we labeled A + 8 = 18. So A = 10. The side we labeled B + 5 = 14. So B = 9. Now we can add up all of the sides. 18 + 14 +10 + 9 + 8 + 5 = 64 in.

# 15.

In the figure below, all line segments are either horizontal or vertical and the dimensions are in inches. What is the perimeter, in inches, of the figure?

a. 286 in   b. 140 in   **c. 70 in**   d. 35 in

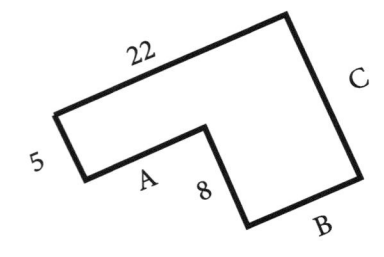

**The correct answer is C.**
First figure out the lengths of the missing sides. Write on the shape as you follow along. The line segments we labeled A & B = 22. The line segment we labeled C = 8 + 5 = 13. Now we can add all of our sides. 22 + 13 + 8 + 5 + 22 = 70 in.

# Lesson 14
# Angles

There will always be a few questions on the ACT Math section that test your knowledge of angles.

There are a few rules you need to know about figuring out angles to be able to get the questions right.

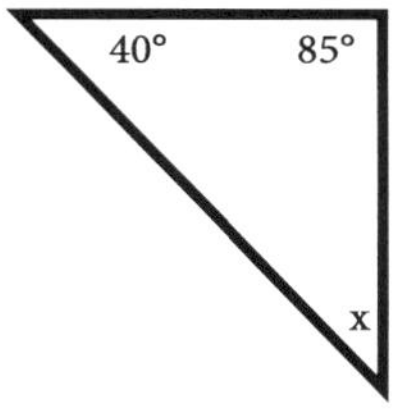

An INTERNAL ANGLE is an angle inside of a shape. An EXTERNAL ANGLE is an angle outside of a shape. In the triangle shown here, both 40° and 85° are internal angles.

A triangle always has 180° of internal angles. A 4-sided shape always has 360°. From there on just add 180° for each additional side to the shape.

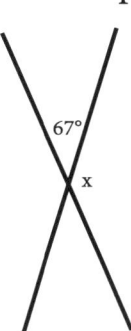

A side of a line always has 180°. So on this graph:

$67 + x = 180$. You could deduce that $x = 113$.

Notice that the other angle opposite x is also 113.

In any intersecting line, the angles opposite one another are always equal.

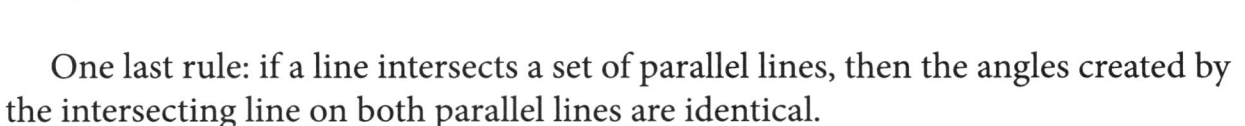

One last rule: if a line intersects a set of parallel lines, then the angles created by the intersecting line on both parallel lines are identical.

Look at the graph on the next page.

161

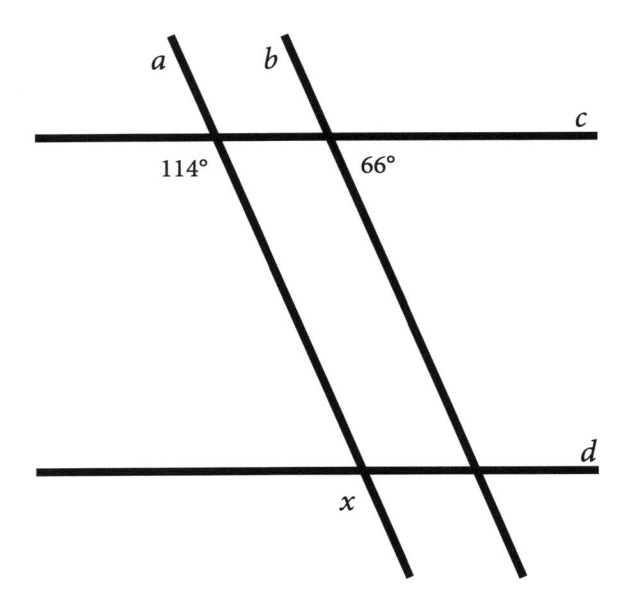

Lines *a* and *b* are parallel. Lines *c* and *d* are parallel. PARALLEL means that two lines run side by side without ever touching.

For that reason, all of the angles created by the intersection of *a* and *c* are the same as the angles created by the intersection of *a* and *d*.

Knowing this, you can say that x = 114, because angle *x* is identical to the angle that has the measure 114°.

Refer back to this introduction whenever you have difficulty remembering one of the rules. But keep practicing until you remember the rules cold!

# Lesson 14 - Angles

## 1.

Angle x = ?

a. 55°   b. 45°   c. 25°   d. 65°

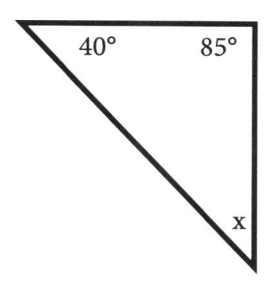

## 2.

Angle x = ?

a. 55°   b. 95°   c. 45°   d. 40°

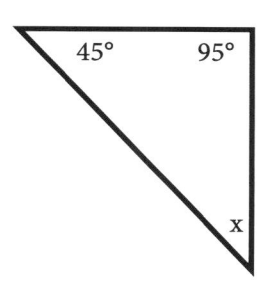

## 3.

Angle x = ?

a. 37°   b. 49°   c. 51°   d. 50°

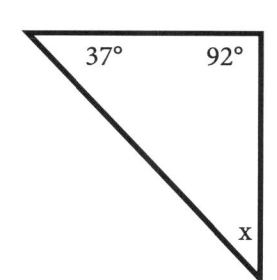

# 1.

Angle x = ?

**a. 55°**  b. 45°  c. 25°  d. 65°

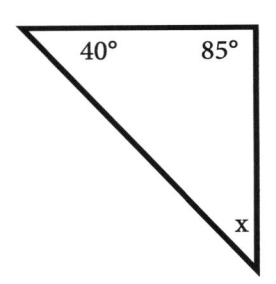

**The correct answer is A.**
A triangle has a total of 180°. Subtract the other two angles to find the third angle.
180 - 40 - 85 = 55°

# 2.

Angle x = ?

a. 55°  b. 95°  c. 45°  **d. 40°**

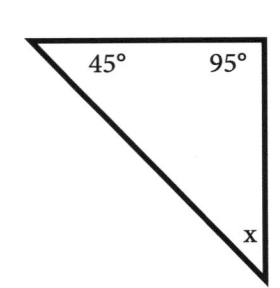

**The correct answer is D.**
A triangle has a total of 180°. Subtract the other two angles to find the third angle.
180 - 45 - 95 = 40°

# 3.

Angle x = ?

a. 37°  b. 49°  **c. 51°**  d. 50°

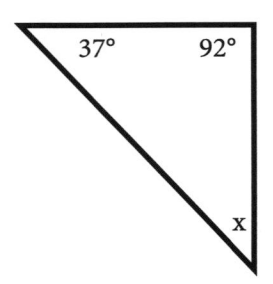

**The correct answer is C.**
A triangle has a total of 180°. Subtract the other two angles to find the third angle.
180 - 37 - 92 = 51°

## 4.

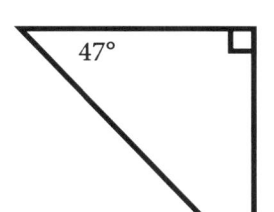

Angle x = ?

a. 133°   b. 43°   c. 25°   d. 47°

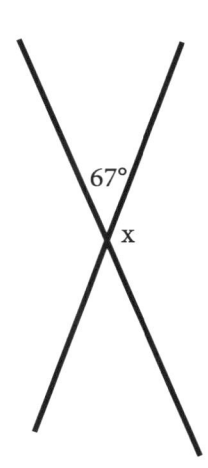

## 5.

Angle x = ?

a. 67°   b. 113°   c. 123°   d. 23°

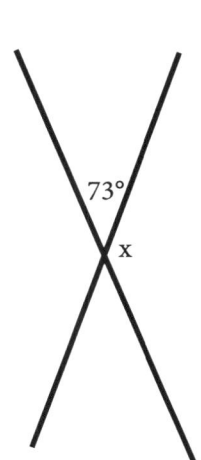

## 6.

Angle x = ?

a. 90°   b. 17°   c. 107°   d. 117°

## 4.

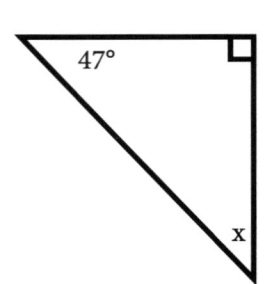

Angle x = ?

a. 133°   **b. 43°**   c. 25°   d. 47°

**The correct answer is B.**
A triangle has a total of 180°. Subtract the other two angles to find the third angle. The box means a 90° angle (also called a RIGHT ANGLE).
180 - 47 - 90 = 43°

## 5.

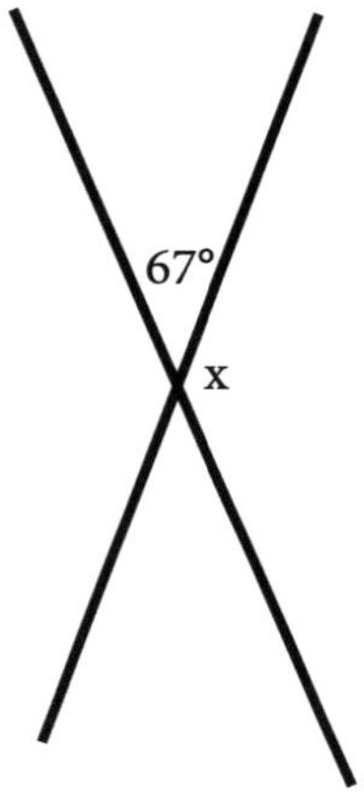

Angle x = ?

a. 67°   **b. 113°**   c. 123°   d. 23°

**The correct answer is B.**
One side of a line has 180°. So x + 67 = 180.
x = 180 - 67
x = 113°

## 6.

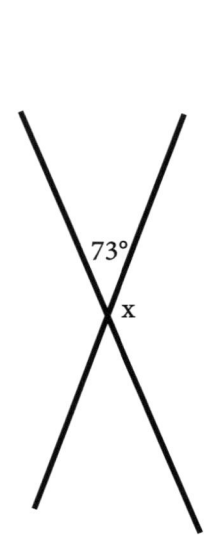

Angle x = ?

a. 90°   b. 17°   **c. 107°**   d. 117°

**The correct answer is C.**
One side of a line has 180°. So x + 73 = 180.
x = 180 - 73
x = 107°

# Lesson 14 - Angles

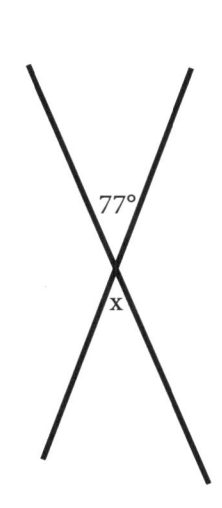

## 7.

Angle x = ?

a. 103°   b. 77°   c. 87°   d. 33°

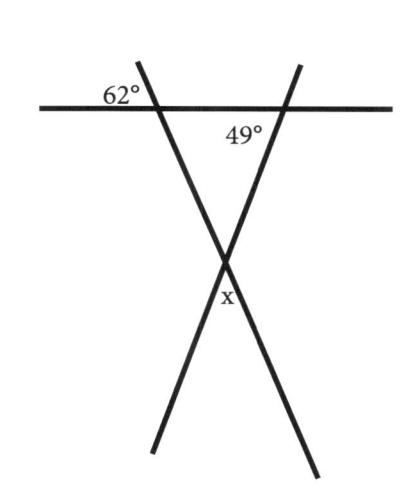

## 8.

Angle x = ?

a. 69°   b. 62°   c. 49°   d. 72°

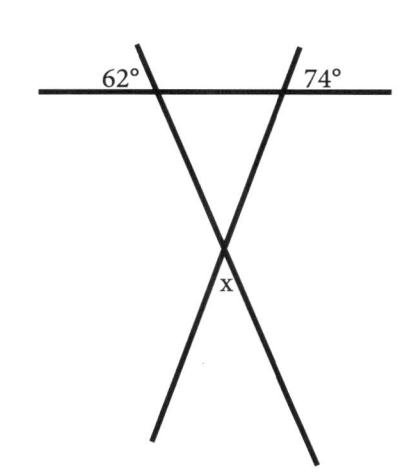

## 9.

Angle x = ?

a. 44°   b. 50°   c. 55°   d. 60°

# 7.

Angle x = ?

a. 103°   **b. 77°**   c. 87°   d. 33°

**The correct answer is B.**
In any intersection of two lines, the angles directly opposite one another are identical. x = 77°. You can also figure it out by saying that any line has 180° on one side, so one of the angles next to the 77° angle is 180 - 77 = 103°.
Then you could say that x = 180 - 103 = 77°.

# 8.

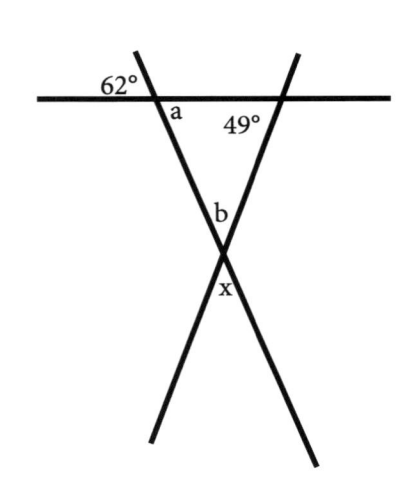

Angle x = ?

**a. 69°**   b. 62°   c. 49°   d. 72°

**The correct answer is A.**
To solve this problem requires a few steps. We know that the angle we've labeled A = 62°. We know that the angle we've labeled B = 180 - 62 - 49 = 69 because there are 180° in a triangle.
Therefore, x = 69°, because it is identical to the angle directly opposite from it.

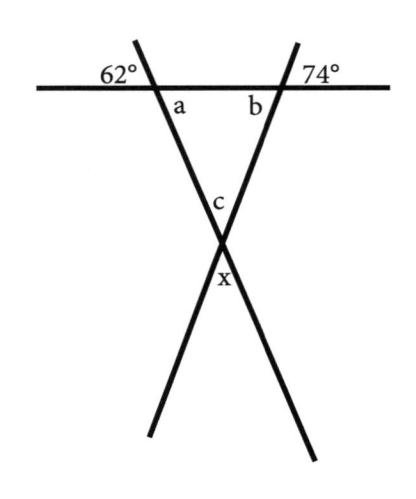

# 9.

Angle x = ?

**a. 44°**   b. 50°   c. 55°   d. 60°

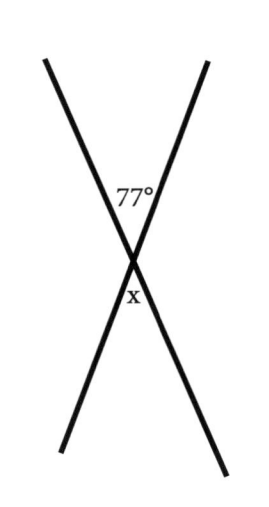

**The correct answer is A.**
Solving this problem requires a few steps. We know that the angle we've labeled A = 62°. We know that the angle we've labeled B = 74°. We know that the angle we've labeled C = 180 - 62 - 74 = 44 because there are 180° in a triangle.
Therefore, x = 44°, because it is identical to the angle directly opposite from it.

# Lesson 14 - Angles

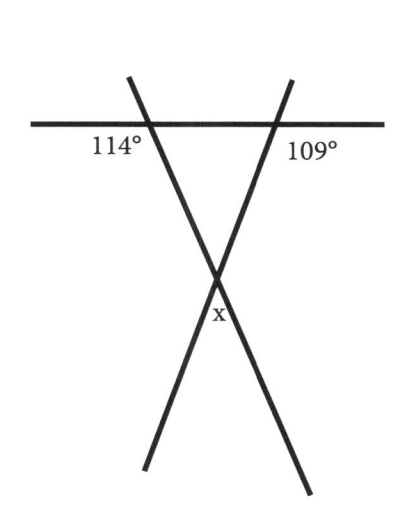

## 10.

Angle x = ?

a. 28°   b. 43°   c. 44°   d. 48°

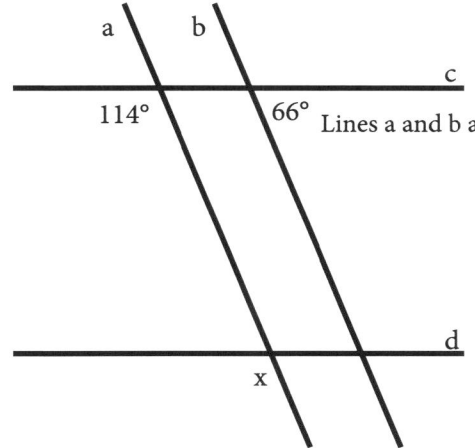

## 11.

Lines a and b are parallel. Lines c and d are parallel. Angle x = ?

a. 24°   b. 66°   c. 114°   d. 110°

## 12.

Lines a and b are parallel. Lines c and d are parallel. Angle x = ?

a. 115°   b. 70°   c. 65°   d. 60°

# 10.

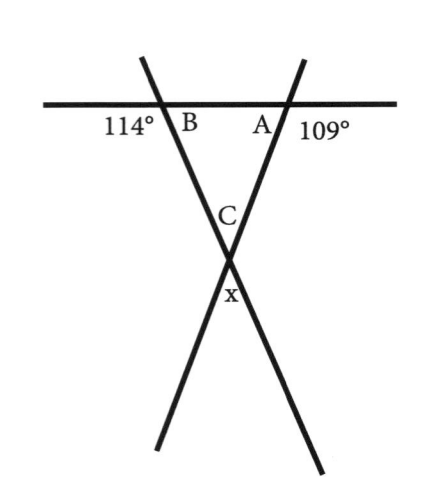

Angle x = ?

a. 28°   **b. 43°**   c. 44°   d. 48°

**The correct answer is B.**
To solve this problem requires a few steps. We know that the angle we've labeled A = 180 - 109 = 71°. We know that the angle we've labeled B = 180 - 114° = 66°. We know that the angle we've labeled C = 180 - 71 - 66 = 43° because there are 180° in a triangle. Therefore, x = 43°, because it is identical to the angle directly opposite from it.

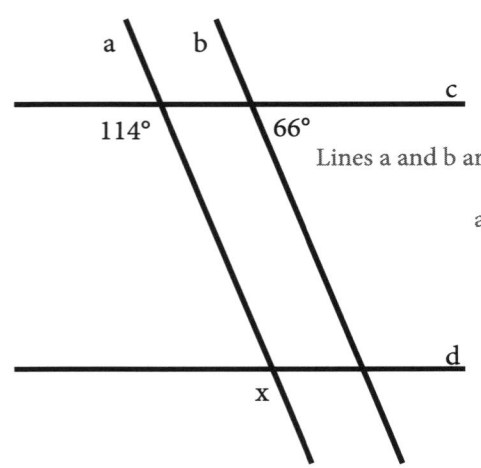

# 11.

Lines a and b are parallel. Lines c and d are parallel. Angle x = ?

a. 24°   b. 66°   **c. 114°**   d. 110°

**The correct answer is C.**
Angle x = 114° because the angles created by the intersection of lines a and c are identical to the angles created by the intersection of lines a and d, because c and d are parallel.

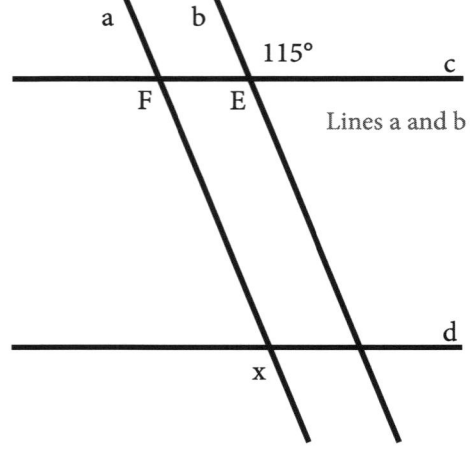

# 12.

Lines a and b are parallel. Lines c and d are parallel. Angle x = ?

**a. 115°**   b. 70°   c. 65°   d. 60°

**The correct answer is A.**
The angle we labeled E = 115° because it is directly opposite the angle given. The angle we labeled F = 115° because lines a and b are parallel, therefore the angles created by their intersection with line c are identical. Angle x = 115° because lines c and d are parallel, therefore the angles created by their intersection with line a are identical.

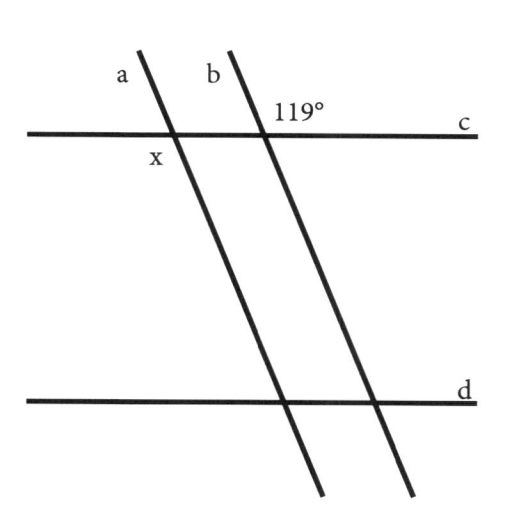

## 13.

Angle x = ?

a. 39°  b. 29°  c. 61°  d. 119°

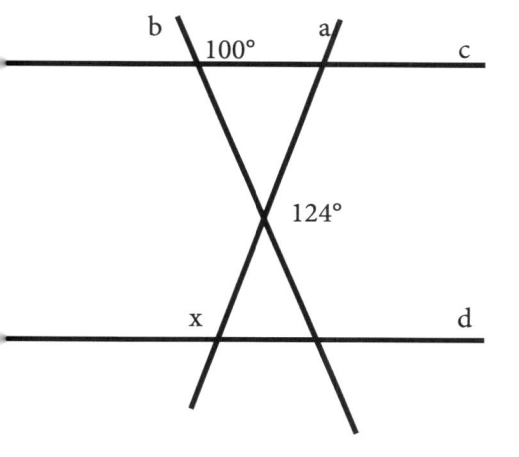

## 14.

Lines c and d are parallel. Angle x = ?

a. 34°  b. 100°  c. 124°  d. 136°

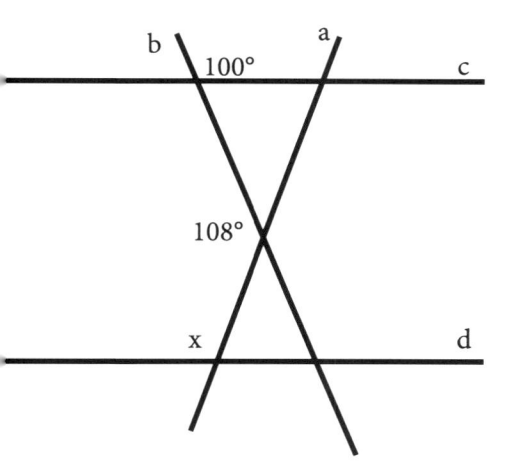

## 15.

Lines c and d are parallel. Angle x = ?

a. 152°  b. 108°  c. 100°  d. 80°

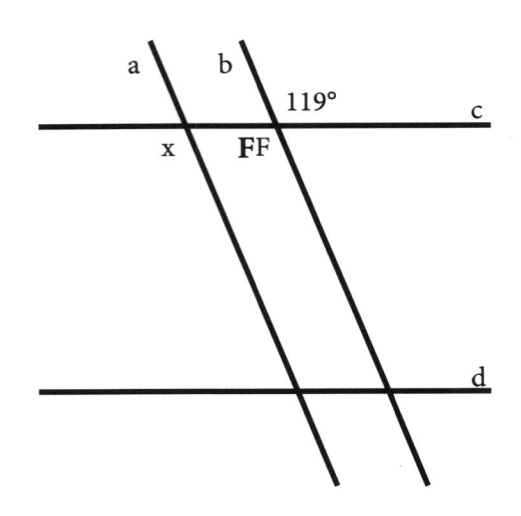

Math Mastery - Level 1

# 13.

Angle x = ?

a. 39°  b. 29°  c. 61°  **d. 119°**

**The correct answer is D.**
The angle we labeled F = 119° because it is identical to the angle directly opposite it. Angle x = 119° because lines a and b are parallel, therefore the angles created by their intersection with line c are identical.

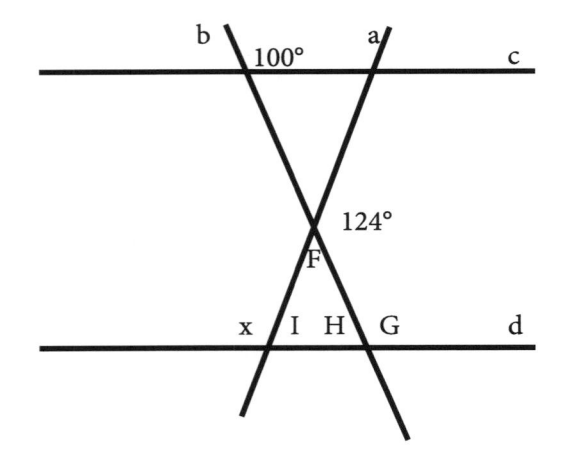

# 14.

Lines c and d are parallel. Angle x = ?

a. 34°  b. 100°  c. 124°  **d. 136°**

**The correct answer is D.**
The angle we've labeled F = 180 - 124 = 56°. The angle we've labeled G = 100° because it is identical to the angle created by the intersection of lines b and c. Angle H = 180 - 100 = 80°. Therefore angle I = 180 - 56 - 80 = 44°. Therefore angle x = 180 - 44 = 136°.

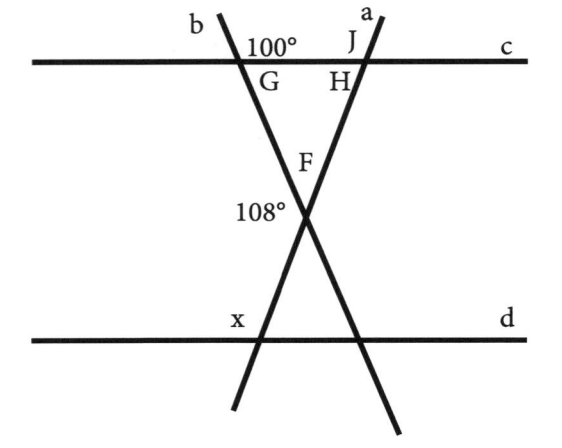

# 15.

Lines c and d are parallel. Angle x = ?

**a. 152°**  b. 108°  c. 100°  d. 80°

**The correct answer is A.**
Angle F = 180 - 108 = 72°. Angle G = 180 - 100 = 80°. Angle H = 180 - 72 - 80 = 28°. Angle J = 180 - 28 = 152°. Therefore, x = 152° because the angles created by the intersection of lines a and c are identical to the angles created by the intersection of lines a and d since c and d are parallel.

## Lesson 15
# Review

In this lesson, everything you've covered in this book from Lesson 1 to Lesson 14 is fair game. You'll be asked to combine what you've learned and to remember things that you haven't covered since the very first lessons.

If you miss a question, follow the instructions and go back and re-do the corresponding lesson.

It doesn't matter that you've already marked the correct answers on the questions in the book. Go through the motions of solving the problems. Your mind needs practice solving the problem correctly.

Think about it this way: If you try to solve the problems five different times, and you get it right on the last time, what does your mind have more experience in? Getting it right or getting it wrong? That's correct, your mind will have more experience in getting it wrong. So you have to practice PAST the point of getting it right once. Practice until you've gotten it right over and over again to the point where there's no way you'll get it wrong. Then you'll be fast in the Math section, fast enough to answer at least one problem per minute...fast enough to ace the Math ACT.

# Lesson 15 - Review

## 1.

In the figure below, all line segments are either horizontal or vertical and the dimensions are in inches. What is the perimeter, in inches, of the figure?

a. 90 in   b. 60 in   c. 84 in   d. 70 in

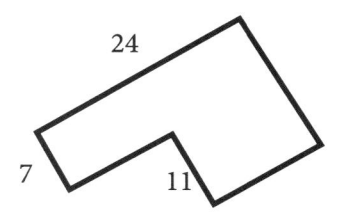

## 2.

Jim is trying to save up for a car over the summer. The car costs $1500.00. He has started a job where he earns $7.50 per hour. If the summer lasts eight weeks, what is the minimum average number of hours per week that he needs to work in order to earn enough for the car, rounded to the nearest hour?

a. 200   b. 20   c. 30   d. 25

## 3.

$4x^2 - 4x + 6 = 5$, $x = ?$

a. 1/2
b. -1/2
c. 1/2 or -1/2
d. 0

## 1.

In the figure below, all line segments are either horizontal or vertical and the dimensions are in inches. What is the perimeter, in inches, of the figure?

a. 90 in   b. 60 in   **c. 84 in**   d. 70 in

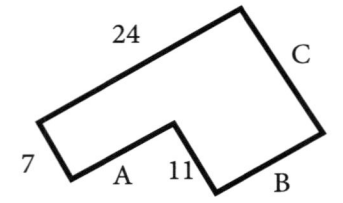

**The correct answer is C.**
First figure out the lengths of the missing sides. Write on the shape as you follow along. The line segments we labeled A & B = 24. The line segment we labeled C = 7 + 11 = 18. Now we can add all of our sides. 24 + 7 + 11 + 18 + 24 = 84 in.
Missed this question? Review Lesson 13.

## 2.

Jim is trying to save up for a car over the summer. The car costs $1500.00. He has started a job where he earns $7.50 per hour. If the summer lasts eight weeks, what is the minimum average number of hours per week that he needs to work in order to earn enough for the car, rounded to the nearest hour?

a. 200   b. 20   c. 30   **d. 25**

**The correct answer is D.**
Jim needs to work $1500 divided by $7.50 per hour = 200 hours. The average number of hours per week he needs to work is 200 hours divided into 8 weeks = 25 hours.
Missed this question? Review Lesson 2.

## 3.

$4x^2 - 4x + 6 = 5, x = ?$

**a. 1/2**
b. -1/2
c. 1/2 or -1/2
d. 0

The correct answer is A.
First we have to simplify the problem by subtracting 5 from both sides. Now we have: $4x^2 - 4x + 1 = 0$. We know that FIRST = $4x^2$, OUTER + INNER = -4x, and LAST = 1. Through trial and error, we find that (2x - 1)(2x - 1) = 0. x = 1/2. Missed this question? Review Lesson 9.

# Lesson 15 - Review

## 4.

$3x^2 - 7x - 6 = 0$, x = ?

a. -2/3 or 3
b. 2/3 or 3
c. 1 or 5/3
d. -1 or -5/3

## 5.

Joe started the day with a tank of gas 1/2 full. Each hour, he burned three gallons of gas. After driving for 2 hours, Joe's tank was empty. How many gallons of gas can his tank hold when it's full?

a. 16   b. 12   c. 8   d. 20

## 6.

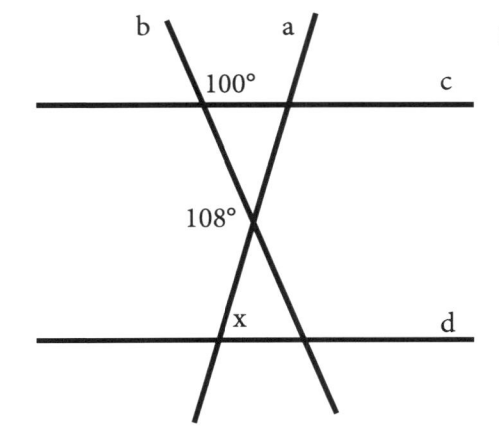

Lines c and d are parallel. Angle x = ?

a. 28°   b. 108°   c. 100°   d. 80°

## 4.

$3x^2 - 7x - 6 = 0$, $x = ?$

**a. -2/3 or 3**
b. 2/3 or 3
c. 1 or 5/3
d. -1 or -5/3

**The correct answer is A.**
We know that FIRST = $3x^2$, OUTER + INNER = -7x, and LAST = -6. Through trial and error, we find that $3x^2 - 7x - 6 = (3x + 2)(x - 3) = 0$.
x = -2/3 or 3. Missed this question? Review Lesson 9.

## 5.

Joe started the day with a tank of gas 1/2 full. Each hour, he burned three gallons of gas. After driving for 2 hours, Joe's tank was empty. How many gallons of gas can his tank hold when it's full?

a. 16   **b. 12**   c. 8   d. 20

**The correct answer is B.**
We know that Joe burned 3 gallons per hour * 2 hours = 6 gallons of gas. 6 gallons of gas = 1/2 of a tank. We can solve this as a proportion or as an algebra problem. 6 = (1/2)x. Multiply both sides by 2. x = 12. Missed this question? Review Lesson 11.

## 6.

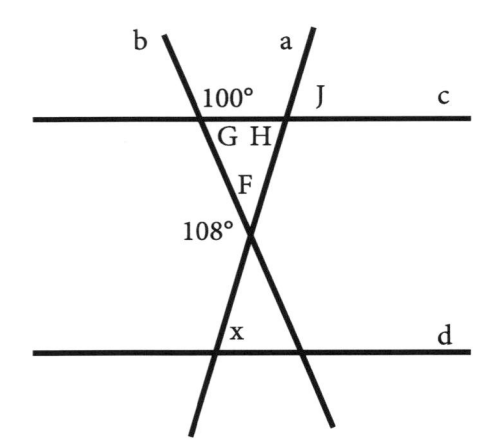

Lines c and d are parallel. Angle x = ?

**a. 28°**   b. 108°   c. 100°   d. 80°

**The correct answer is A.**
Angle F = 180 - 108 = 72°. Angle G = 180 - 100 = 80°. Angle H = 180 - 72 - 80 = 28°. Angle J = 28° because it's opposite and therefore identcal to Angle H. Therefore, x = 28° because the angles created by the intersection of lines a and c are identical to the angles created by the intersection of lines a and d, since c and d are parallel.
Missed this question? Review Lesson 14.

# Lesson 15 - Review

## 7.

Dominique and Jared own a sandwich shop. They offer 8 kinds of bread, 7 kinds of meat, and 9 kinds of cheese. Each type of sandwich on their menu has a combination of 1 bread, 1 meat, and 1 cheese. A "Value Deal" consists of one sandwich and one drink. There are 9 drink options. How many different "Value Deal" combinations are possible?

a. 23896   b. 2437   c. 4536   d. 2936

## 8.

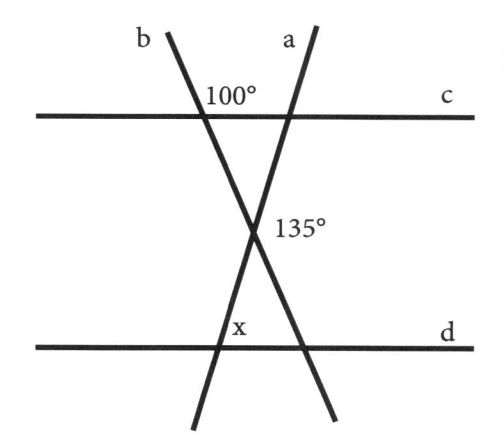

Lines c and d are parallel. Angle x = ?

a. 50°   b. 65°   c. 45°   d. 55°

## 9.

What is the next number in the pattern? 1/3, 1/9, 1/27, 1/81, …?

a. 27
b. 243
c. 1/243
d. 1/27

# 7.

Dominique and Jared own a sandwich shop. They offer 8 kinds of bread, 7 kinds of meat, and 9 kinds of cheese. Each type of sandwich on their menu has a combination of 1 bread, 1 meat, and 1 cheese. A "Value Deal" consists of one sandwich and one drink. There are 9 drink options. How many different "Value Deal" combinations are possible?

a. 23896   b. 2437   **c. 4536**   d. 2936

**The correct answer is C.**
There are 8 breads x 7 meats x 9 cheeses x 9 drinks = 4536 combinations.
8 x 7 x 9 x 9 = 4536. Use your calculator for problems like this!
Missed this question? Review Lesson 4.

# 8.

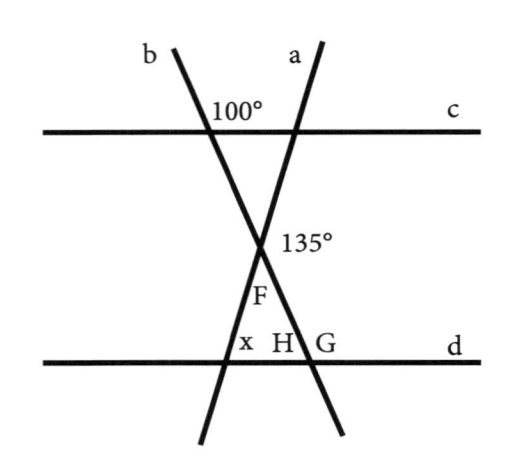

Lines c and d are parallel. Angle x = ?

a. 50°   b. 65°   c. 45°   **d. 55°**

**The correct answer is D.**
The angle we've labeled F = 180 - 135 = 45°. The angle we've labeled G = 100° because it is identical to the angle created by the intersection of lines b and c. Angle H = 180 - 100 = 80°. Therefore Angle x = 180 - 80 - 45 = 55°.
Missed this question? Review Lesson 14.

# 9.

What is the next number in the pattern? 1/3, 1/9, 1/27, 1/81, ...?

a. 27
b. 243
**c. 1/243**
d. 1/27

**The correct answer is C.**
Each term is being multiplied by 1/3. 1/3 * 1/3 = 1/9. 1/9 * 1/3 = 1/27. 1/27 * 1/3 = 1/81. To find the next number in the pattern, we apply the rule to the last term. 1/81 * 1/3 = 1/243.
Missed this question? Review Lesson 12.

# 10.

If twelve shirts cost $120, how much do 3 shirts cost?

a. $30.00
b. $35.00
c. $300
d. $3.00

# 11.

Dominique and Jared own a sandwich shop. They offer 8 kinds of bread, 2 kinds of meat, and 2 kinds of cheese. Each type of sandwich on their menu has a combination of 1 bread, 1 meat, and 1 cheese. A "Value Deal" consists of one sandwich and one drink. There are 4 drink options. How many different "Value Deal" combinations are possible?

a. 24   b. 128   c. 48   d. 96

# 12.

Darryl's friend randomly selects a shirt from a catalog as a present for Darryl's birthday. He has the choice of the colors red, blue, green, or purple; he also has the choice of short sleeve or long sleeve. Darryl wants a green long sleeve shirt for his birthday. What is the probability that Darryl's friend selected the shirt that Darryl wants?

a. 1/10   b. 1/8   c. 1/6   d. 1/2

# 10.

If twelve shirts cost $120, how much do 3 shirts cost?

a. $30.00
b. $35.00
c. $300
d. $3.00

**The correct answer is A.**
$120 divided by 12 shirts = $10.00. $10.00 per shirt times 3 shirts = $30.00.
120 / 12 = 10.00. 10.00 x 3 = 30.00. You have to figure out the value of one shirt, then you can figure out how much more than one shirt costs.

# 11.

Dominique and Jared own a sandwich shop. They offer 8 kinds of bread, 2 kinds of meat, and 2 kinds of cheese. Each type of sandwich on their menu has a combination of 1 bread, 1 meat, and 1 cheese. A "Value Deal" consists of one sandwich and one drink. There are 4 drink options. How many different "Value Deal" combinations are possible?

a. 24  **b. 128**  c. 48  d. 96

**The correct answer is B.**
There are 8 breads x 2 meats x 2 cheeses x 4 drinks = 128 combinations.
8 x 2 x 2 x 4 = 128
Missed this question? Review Lesson 4.

# 12.

Darryl's friend randomly selects a shirt from a catalog as a present for Darryl's birthday. He has the choice of the colors red, blue, green, or purple; he also has the choice of short sleeve or long sleeve. Darryl wants a green long sleeve shirt for his birthday. What is the probability that Darryl's friend selected the shirt that Darryl wants?

a. 1/10  **b. 1/8**  c. 1/6  d. 1/2

**The correct answer is B.**
4 colors * 2 sleeves = 8 combinations. There is 1 desired outcome (blue long sleeve) divided by 8 possible outcomes. 1/8
Missed this question? Review Lessons 3 & 4.

Lesson 15 - Review

# 13.

In the figure below, all line segments are either horizontal or vertical and the dimensions are in inches. What is the perimeter, in inches, of the figure?

a. 32 in   b. 64 in   c. 45 in   d. 30 in

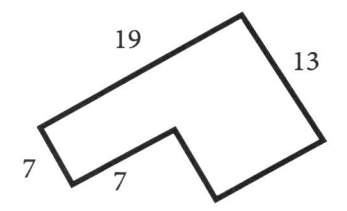

```
       19
           13
  7
    7
```

# 14.

Joe started the day with a full tank of gas. Each hour, he burned two gallons of gas. After driving for five hours, Joe had four gallons of gas left. How many gallons of gas did he start with?

a. 16   b. 18   c. 1   d. 14

# 15.

What is the next number in the pattern? 64, 32, 16, 8 … ?

a. 8
b. 6
c. 4
d. 48

# 13.

In the figure below, all line segments are either horizontal or vertical and the dimensions are in inches. What is the perimeter, in inches, of the figure?

a. 32 in   **b. 64 in**   c. 45 in   d. 30 in

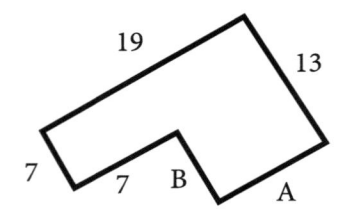

**The correct answer is B.**
First figure out the lengths of the missing sides. Write on the shape as you follow along. The side we labeled A + 7 = 19. So A = 12. The side we labeled B + 7 = 13. So B = 6. Now we can add up all of the sides. 12 + 6 +13 + 19 + 7 + 7 = 64 in.
Missed this question? Review Lesson 13.

# 14.

Joe started the day with a full tank of gas. Each hour, he burned two gallons of gas. After driving for five hours, Joe had four gallons of gas left. How many gallons of gas did he start with?

a. 16   b. 18   c. 1   **d. 14**

**The correct answer is D.**
We know that Joe burned 2 gallons of gas per hour * 5 hours = 10 gallons of gas. He was left with 4 gallons of gas + 10 gallons burned = 14 gallons started with.
Missed this question? Review Lesson 11.

# 15.

What is the next number in the pattern? 64, 32, 16, 8 … ?

a. 8
b. 6
**c. 4**
d. 48

**The correct answer is C.**
Each term in the pattern is being divided by 2. 64 / 2 = 32. 32 / 2 = 16. 16 / 2 = 8. To figure out the next number in the pattern, we apply the rule: 8 / 2 = 4.
Missed this question? Review Lesson 12.

# Lesson 16
# Pythagorean Theorem

The Pythagorean Theorem is a math formula that lets you figure out the length of the sides of a RIGHT TRIANGLE.

A RIGHT TRIANGLE is a triangle that has a RIGHT ANGLE, or one that is 90°.

When you are solving a problem with a right triangle, the Pythagorean Theorem applies:

$a^2 + b^2 = c^2$

For example, if A = 3 and B = 4, then:

$3^2 + 4^2 = c^2$

$c^2 = 25$

$c = \sqrt{25} = 5$

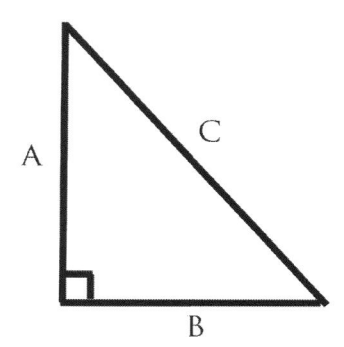

Remember that to simplify your variable when it's squared ($^2$) you have to find the SQUARE ROOT of both sides ($\sqrt{}$).

On the ACT, there is always at least one question that asks you to determine the length of the side of a right triangle. To do this, you have to apply the Pythagorean Theorem.

Lesson 16 - Pythagorean Theorem

# 1.

Length x = ?

a. 4   b. 5   c. 6   d. 7

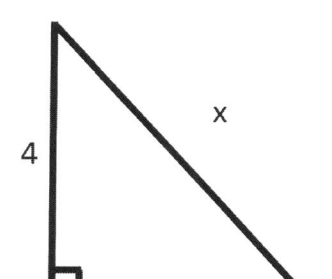

# 2.

Length x = ?

a. 6   b. $\sqrt{34}$   c. $\sqrt{41}$   d. 9

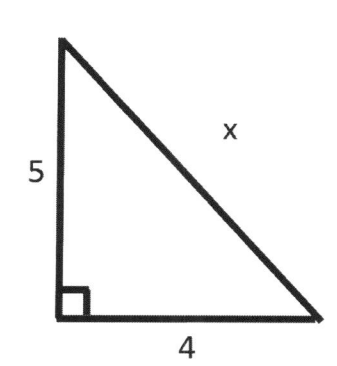

# 3.

Length x = ?

a. $\sqrt{37}$   b. $10\sqrt{5}$   c. 14   d. 30

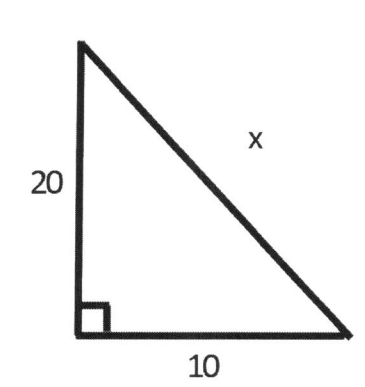

Math Mastery - Level 1

# 1.

Length x = ?

a. 4   **b. 5**   c. 6   d. 7

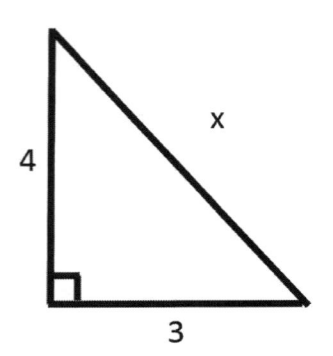

**The correct answer is B.**
$4^2 + 3^2 = x^2$
$16 + 9 = x^2$
$x^2 = 25$
$x = \sqrt{25} = 5$

# 2.

Length x = ?

a. 6   b. $\sqrt{34}$   **c. $\sqrt{41}$**   d. 9

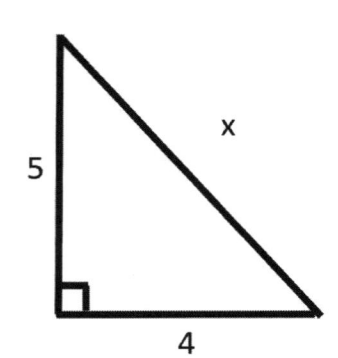

**The correct answer is C.**
$5^2 + 4^2 = x^2$
$25 + 16 = x^2$
$x^2 = 41$
$x = \sqrt{41}$

Having trouble with square roots? Refer to *Math Basics*.

# 3.

Length x = ?

a. $\sqrt{37}$   **b. $10\sqrt{5}$**   c. 14   d. 30

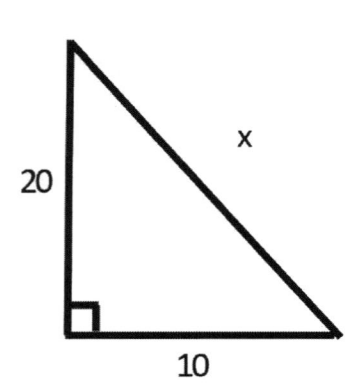

**The correct answer is B.**
$10^2 + 20^2 = x^2$
$100 + 400 = x^2$
$x^2 = 500$
$x = \sqrt{500} = 10\sqrt{5}$

Lesson 16 - Pythagorean Theorem

# 4.

Length x = ?

**a.** 10√5   b. 10   c. 50   d. √50

# 5.

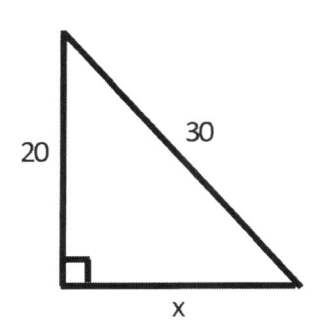

Length x = ?

a. 6√2   b. 9√2   c. 9   d. 4

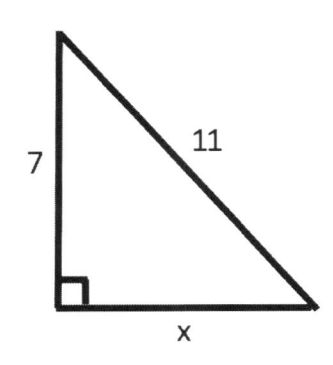

# 6.

Length x = ?

a. 2   b. 6√2   c. 6   d. 7

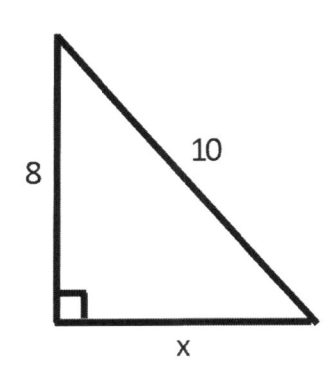

## 4.

Length x = ?

a. **10√5**   b. 10   c. 50   d. √50

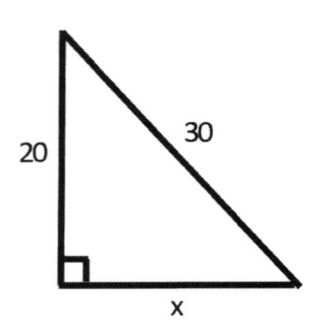

**The correct answer is A.**
$20^2 + x^2 = 30^2$
$400 + x^2 = 900$
$x^2 = 900 - 400 = 500$
$x = \sqrt{500} = 10\sqrt{5}$

## 5.

Length x = ?

a. **6√2**   b. 9√2   c. 9   d. 4

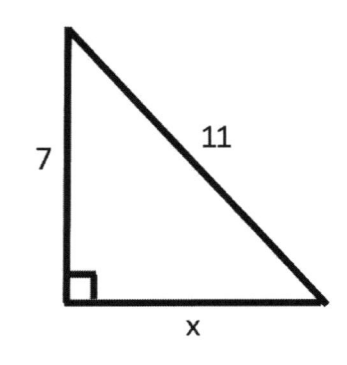

**The correct answer is A.**
$7^2 + x^2 = 11^2$
$49 + x^2 = 121$
$x^2 = 121 - 49 = 72$
$x = \sqrt{72} = 6\sqrt{2}$

## 6.

Length x = ?

a. 2   b. 6√2   c. **6**   d. 7

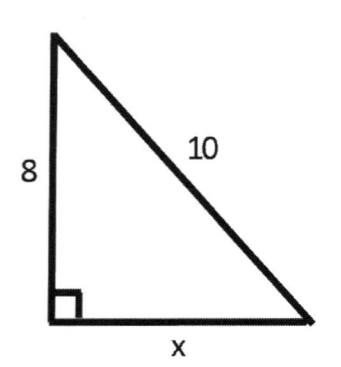

**The correct answer is C.**
$8^2 + x^2 = 10^2$
$64 + x^2 = 100$
$x^2 = 100 - 64 = 36$
$x = \sqrt{36} = 6$

## 7.

Length x = ?

a. 10   b. √85   c. 17   d. 5√3

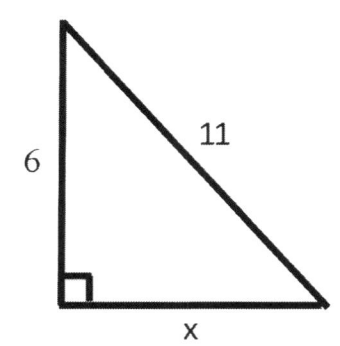

## 8.

Length x = ?

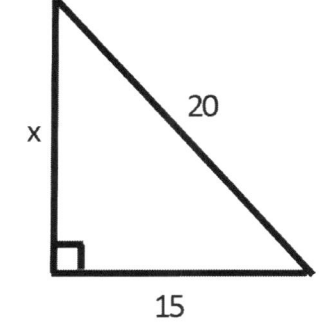

a. 5√7   b. 5√6   c. 18   d. 25

## 9.

Length x = ?  Round your answer to the nearest hundredth.

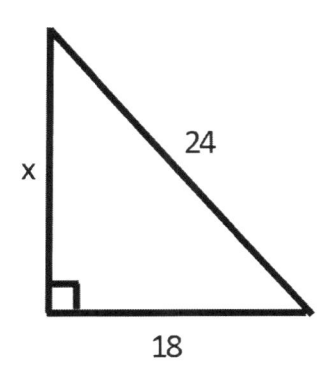

a. 17.23   b. 15.87   c. 14.21   d. 14.71

# 7.

Length x = ?

a. 10   **b. √85**   c. 17   d. 5√3

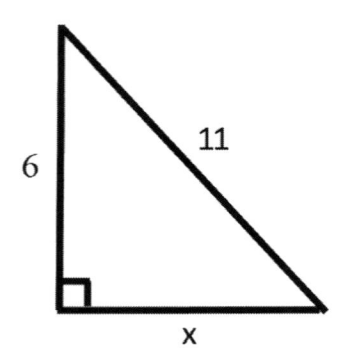

**The correct answer is B.**
$6^2 + x^2 = 11^2$
$36 + x^2 = 121$
$x^2 = 121 - 36 = 85$
$x = \sqrt{85}$

# 8.

Length x = ?

**a. 5√7**   b. 5√6   c. 18   d. 25

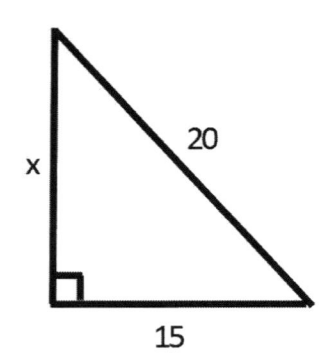

**The correct answer is A.**
$x^2 + 15^2 = 20^2$
$x^2 + 225 = 400$
$x^2 = 400 - 225 = 175$
$x = \sqrt{175} = 5\sqrt{7}$

# 9.

Length x = ?  Round your answer to the nearest hundredth.

a. 17.23   **b. 15.87**   c. 14.21   d. 14.71

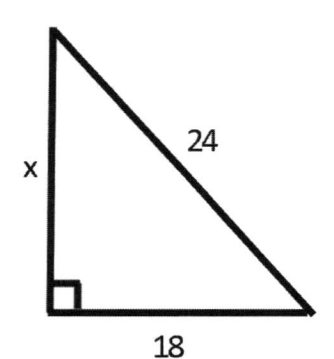

**The correct answer is B.**
$x^2 + 18^2 = 24^2$
$x^2 + 324 = 576$
$x^2 = 576 - 324 = 252$
$x = \sqrt{252} \approx 15.87$

## 10.

Length x = ?  Round your answer to the nearest hundredth.

a. 13.55   b. 13.56   c. 12.45   d. 22.32

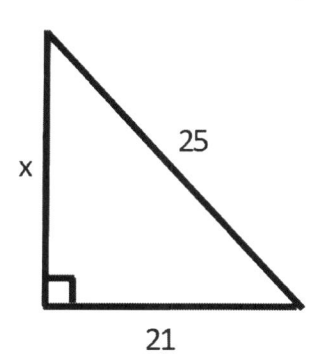

## 11.

Length x = ?  Round your answer to the nearest hundredth.

a. 7.32   b. 6.70   c. 6.71   d. 6.72

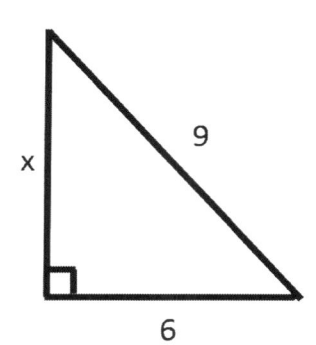

## 12.

What is the circumference of the circle with tangent ABC and line BD running through its center, rounded to the nearest 100th?

a. 14.06   b. 14.05   c. 14.03   d. 12.01

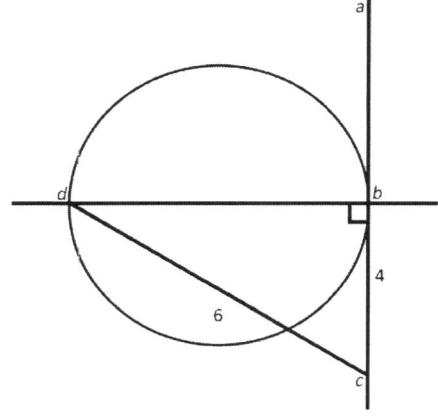

Lesson 16 - Pythagorean Theorem

# 10.

Length x = ?  Round your answer to the nearest hundredth.

a. 13.55   **b. 13.56**   c. 12.45   d. 22.32

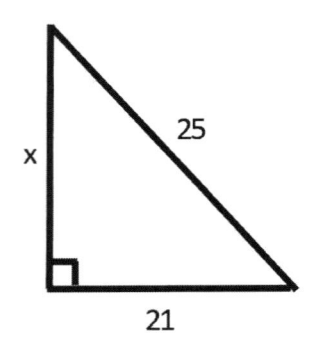

**The correct answer is B.**
$x^2 + 21^2 = 25^2$
$x^2 + 441 = 625$
$x^2 = 625 - 441 = 184$
$x = \sqrt{184} \approx 13.56$

# 11.

Length x = ?  Round your answer to the nearest hundredth.

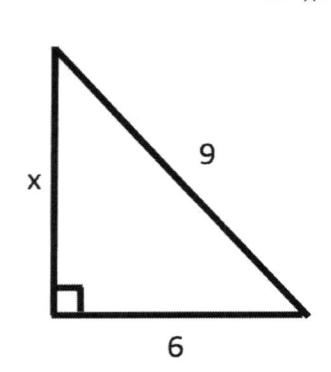

a. 7.32   b. 6.70   **c. 6.71**   d. 6.72

**The correct answer is C.**
$x^2 + 6^2 = 9^2$
$x^2 + 36 = 81$
$x^2 = 81 - 36 = 45$
$x = \sqrt{45} \approx 6.71$

# 12.

What is the circumference of the circle with tangent ABC and line BD running through its center, rounded to the nearest 100th?

a. 14.06   **b. 14.05**   c. 14.03   d. 12.01

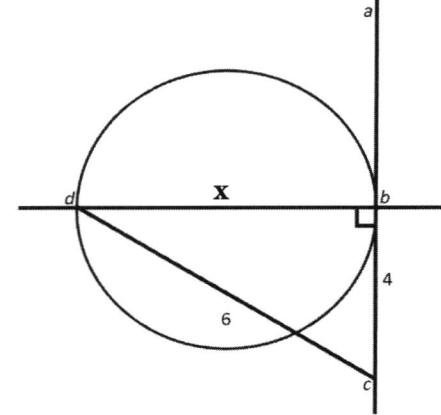

**The correct answer is B.**
First we must find the diameter of the circle, line segment DB.
We've labeled this x.
$x^2 + 4^2 = 6^2$
$x^2 + 16 = 36$
$x^2 = 36 - 16 = 20$
$x = \sqrt{20}$
Circumference = $\pi\sqrt{20} \approx 14.05$

## 13.

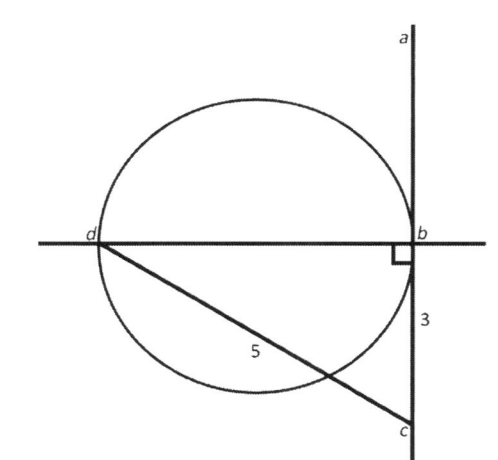

What is the circumference of the circle with tangent ABC and line BD running through its center, rounded to the nearest 100th?

a. 16.33   b. 13.25   c. 12.57   d. 12.55

## 14.

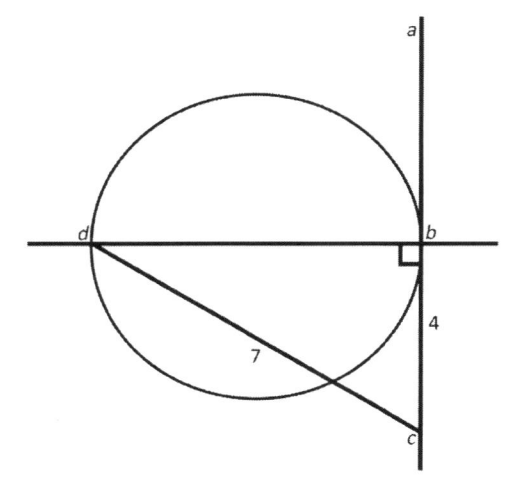

What is the circumference of the circle with tangent ABC and line BD running through its center, rounded to the nearest 100th?

a. 18.05   b. 18.04   c. 12.45   d. 12.46

## 15.

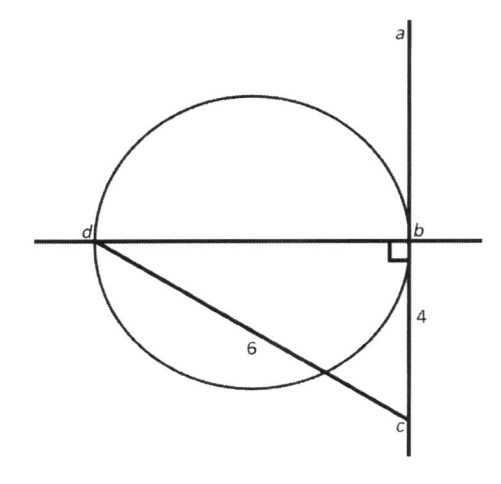

What is the area of the circle with tangent ABC and line BD running through its center, rounded to the nearest 100th?

a. 11.31   b. 15.71   c. 17.71   d. 12.22

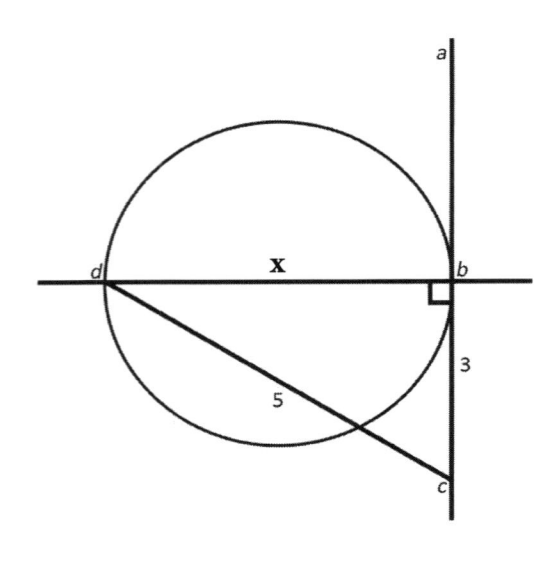

# 13.

What is the circumference of the circle with tangent ABC and line BD running through its center, rounded to the nearest 100th?

a. 16.33   b. 13.25   **c. 12.57**   d. 12.55

**The correct answer is C.**
First we must find the diameter of the circle, line segment DB.
We've labeled this x.
$x^2 + 3^2 = 5^2$
$x^2 + 9 = 25$
$x^2 = 25 - 9 = 16$
$x = \sqrt{16} = 4$
Circumference = $4\pi \approx 12.57$

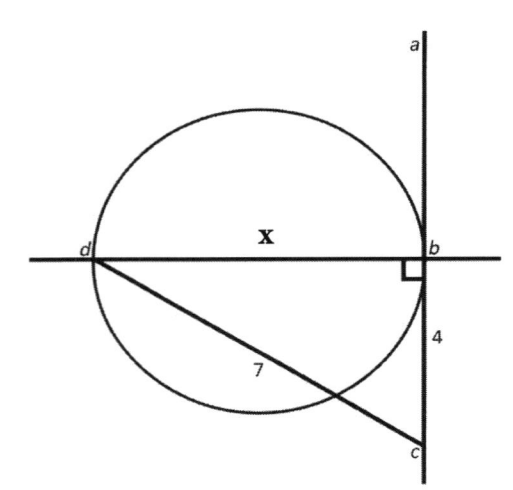

# 14.

What is the circumference of the circle with tangent ABC and line BD running through its center, rounded to the nearest 100th?

**a. 18.05**   b. 18.04   c. 12.45   d. 12.46

**The correct answer is A.**
First we must find the diameter of the circle, line segment DB.
We've labeled this x.
$x^2 + 4^2 = 7^2$
$x^2 + 16 = 49$
$x^2 = 49 - 16 = 33$
$x = \sqrt{33}$
Circumference = $\pi \sqrt{33} \approx 18.05$

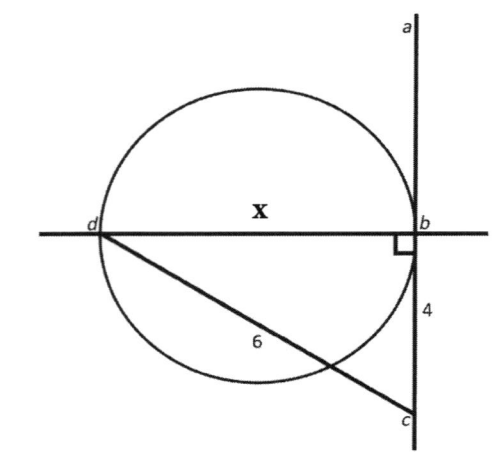

# 15.

What is the area of the circle with tangent ABC and line BD running through its center, rounded to the nearest 100th?

a. 11.31   **b. 15.71**   c. 17.71   d. 12.22

**The correct answer is B.**
First we must find the diameter of the circle, line segment DB.
We've labeled this x.
$x^2 + 4^2 = 6^2$
$x^2 + 16 = 36$
$x^2 = 36 - 16 = 20$
$x = \sqrt{20}$. Radius = $\sqrt{20} / 2$
Area = $\pi(\sqrt{20} / 2)^2 \approx 15.71$

## Lesson 17
# Area

There will always be a few questions on the ACT Math section that require you to find an area. The basic area formula is

length * height = area

However, on the ACT you'll often be asked to find, for example, how many tiles are needed to cover a certain area. The trick is to draw it all out to make it easier on yourself, and to make sure that you are comparing the same units of measure.

For example, in this question:

Ellen is planning to put in a new tile floor. Each tile is 12 inches by 12 inches. The area is 7 feet wide by 11 feet long. What is the minimum number of tiles needed to completely cover the area?

First you need to convert the tiles to feet. 12 inches = 1 foot, so each tile is 1 foot by 1 foot. The area of the tile is 1 sq. foot. Now you can calculate the area of the floor: 7 * 11 = 77 sq. feet. Now we divide 77 square feet by 1 sq. ft. tiles: 77 / 1 = 77 tiles are needed!

# Lesson 17 - Area

# 1.

George is planning to tile a rectangular kitchen countertop that is 30 inches wide and 60 inches long. He figured out that he will need one tile for each 3 inch by 3 inch region. What is the minimum number of tiles needed to completely cover the countertop to its edges?

a. 1800  b. 300  c. 200  d. 100

# 2.

George is planning to tile a rectangular kitchen countertop that is 36 inches wide and 54 inches long. He figured out that he will need one tile for each 3 inch by 3 inch region. What is the minimum number of tiles needed to completely cover the countertop to its edges?

a. 1944  b. 200  c. 224  d. 216

# 3.

George is planning to tile a rectangular kitchen countertop that is 20 inches wide and 40 inches long. He figured out that he will need one tile for each 2 inch by 2 inch region. What is the minimum number of tiles needed to completely cover the countertop to its edges?

a. 100  b. 200  c. 300  d. 800

# 1.

George is planning to tile a rectangular kitchen countertop that is 30 inches wide and 60 inches long. He figured out that he will need one tile for each 3 inch by 3 inch region. What is the minimum number of tiles needed to completely cover the countertop to its edges?

a. 1800   b. 300   **c. 200**   d. 100

**The correct answer is C.**
First we have to figure out the area of the countertop. 30 inches * 60 inches = 1800 in$^2$
Each tile is 3 inches * 3 inches = 9 in$^2$.
George needs 1800 in$^2$ / 9 in$^2$ = 200 tiles.

# 2.

George is planning to tile a rectangular kitchen countertop that is 36 inches wide and 54 inches long. He figured out that he will need one tile for each 3 inch by 3 inch region. What is the minimum number of tiles needed to completely cover the countertop to its edges?

a. 1944   b. 200   c. 224   **d. 216**

**The correct answer is D.**
First we have to figure out the area of the countertop. Use your calculator.
36 inches * 54 inches = 1944 in$^2$
Each tile is 3 inches * 3 inches = 9 in$^2$.
George needs 1944 in$^2$ / 9 in$^2$ = 216 tiles.

# 3.

George is planning to tile a rectangular kitchen countertop that is 20 inches wide and 40 inches long. He figured out that he will need one tile for each 2 inch by 2 inch region. What is the minimum number of tiles needed to completely cover the countertop to its edges?

a. 100   **b. 200**   c. 300   d. 800

**The correct answer is B.**
First we have to figure out the area of the countertop. 20 inches * 40 inches = 800 in$^2$
Each tile is 2 inches * 2 inches = 4 in$^2$.
George needs 800 in$^2$ / 4 in$^2$ = 200 tiles.

# Lesson 17 - Area

## 4.

George is planning to tile a rectangular kitchen countertop that is 90 inches wide and 60 inches long. He figured out that he will need one tile for each 3 inch by 3 inch region. What is the minimum number of tiles needed to completely cover the countertop to its edges?

a. 600   b. 700   c. 540   d. 5400

## 5.

George is planning to tile a rectangular kitchen countertop that is 20 inches wide and 20 inches long. He figured out that he will need one tile for each 1 inch by 1 inch region. What is the minimum number of tiles needed to completely cover the countertop to its edges?

a. 400   b. 300   c. 500   d. 40

## 6.

George is planning to tile a rectangular kitchen countertop that is 15 inches wide and 21 inches long. He figured out that he will need one tile for each 3 inch by 3 inch region. What is the minimum number of tiles needed to completely cover the countertop to its edges?

a. 30   b. 33   c. 35   d. 37

## 4.

George is planning to tile a rectangular kitchen countertop that is 90 inches wide and 60 inches long. He figured out that he will need one tile for each 3 inch by 3 inch region. What is the minimum number of tiles needed to completely cover the countertop to its edges?

**a. 600**   b. 700   c. 540   d. 5400

**The correct answer is A.**
First we have to figure out the area of the countertop. 90 inches * 60 inches = 5400 in²
Each tile is 3 inches * 3 inches = 9 in².
George needs 5400 in² / 9 in² = 600 tiles.

## 5.

George is planning to tile a rectangular kitchen countertop that is 20 inches wide and 20 inches long. He figured out that he will need one tile for each 1 inch by 1 inch region. What is the minimum number of tiles needed to completely cover the countertop to its edges?

**a. 400**   b. 300   c. 500   d. 40

**The correct answer is A.**
First we have to figure out the area of the countertop. 20 inches * 20 inches = 400 in²
Each tile is 1 inch * 1 inch = 1 in².
George needs 400 in² / 1 in² = 400 tiles.

## 6.

George is planning to tile a rectangular kitchen countertop that is 15 inches wide and 21 inches long. He figured out that he will need one tile for each 3 inch by 3 inch region. What is the minimum number of tiles needed to completely cover the countertop to its edges?

a. 30   b. 33   **c. 35**   d. 37

**The correct answer is C.**
First we have to figure out the area of the countertop. 15 inches * 21 inches = 315 in²
Each tile is 3 inches * 3 inches = 9 in².
George needs 315 in² / 9 in² = 35 tiles.

# Lesson 17 - Area

## 7.

Ellen is planning to put in a new tile floor. Each tile is 12 inches by 12 inches. The area is 7 feet wide by 11 feet long. What is the minimum number of tiles needed to completely cover the area?

a. 77   b. 75   c. 80   d. 4

## 8.

Ellen is planning to put in a new tile floor. Each tile is 12 inches by 12 inches. The area is 12 feet wide by 11 feet long. What is the minimum number of tiles needed to completely cover the area?

a. 1   b. 144   c. 124   d. 132

## 9.

Ellen is planning to put in a new tile floor. Each tile is 18 inches by 18 inches. The area is 10 feet wide by 11 feet long. What is the minimum number of tiles needed to completely cover the area?

a. 30   b. 40   c. 50   d. 49

# 7.

Ellen is planning to put in a new tile floor. Each tile is 12 inches by 12 inches. The area is 7 feet wide by 11 feet long. What is the minimum number of tiles needed to completely cover the area?

**a. 77**   b. 75   c. 80   d. 4

**The correct answer is A.**
First we have to convert the measure of the tile from inches to feet. 12 in = 1 ft, so the tile measures 1 ft * 1 ft = 1 ft². The area of the floor is 7 ft * 11 ft = 77 ft².
Ellen needs 77 ft² / 1 ft² = 77 tiles.

# 8.

Ellen is planning to put in a new tile floor. Each tile is 12 inches by 12 inches. The area is 12 feet wide by 11 feet long. What is the minimum number of tiles needed to completely cover the area?

a. 1   b. 144   c. 124   **d. 132**

**The correct answer is D.**
First we have to convert the measure of the tile from inches to feet. 12 in = 1 ft, so the tile measures 1 ft * 1 ft = 1 ft². The area of the floor is 12 ft * 11 ft = 132 ft².
Ellen needs 132 ft² / 1 ft² = 132 tiles.

# 9.

Ellen is planning to put in a new tile floor. Each tile is 18 inches by 18 inches. The area is 10 feet wide by 11 feet long. What is the minimum number of tiles needed to completely cover the area?

a. 30   b. 40   c. 50   **d. 49**

**The correct answer is D.**
First we have to convert the measure of the tile from inches to feet. 12 in = 1 ft, so each tile measures 18 / 12 = 1.5 feet on each side. The area of the tile is 1.5 ft * 1.5 ft = 2.25 ft². The area of the floor is 10 ft * 11 ft = 110 ft².
Ellen needs 110 ft² / 2.25 ft² ≈ 48.89 tiles. Since we can't have a fraction of a tile, we need a minimum of 49 tiles.

# Lesson 17 - Area

# 10.

Ellen is planning to put in a new tile floor. Each tile is 18 inches by 18 inches. The area is 4 feet wide by 7 feet long. What is the minimum number of tiles needed to completely cover the area?

a. 28   b. 4   c. 13   d. 12

# 11.

Ellen is planning to put in a new tile floor. Each tile is 6 inches by 6 inches. The area is 7 feet wide by 11 feet long. What is the minimum number of tiles needed to completely cover the area?

a. 325   b. 300   c. 250   d. 308

# 12.

Danielle has a new classroom floor that she is planning on covering with carpet samples. Each carpet sample is 24 inches wide by 12 inches long. If the classroom is 8 feet wide by 12 feet long, what is the minimum number of carpet samples needed to completely cover the area?

a. 288   b. 46   c. 48   d. 50

Math Mastery - Level 1

# 10.

Ellen is planning to put in a new tile floor. Each tile is 18 inches by 18 inches. The area is 4 feet wide by 7 feet long. What is the minimum number of tiles needed to completely cover the area?

a. 28  b. 4  **c. 13**  d. 12

**The correct answer is C.**
First we have to convert the measure of the tile from inches to feet. 12 in = 1 ft, so each tile measures 18 / 12 = 1.5 feet on each side. The area of the tile is 1.5 ft * 1.5 ft = 2.25 ft². The area of the floor is 4 ft * 7 ft = 28 ft².
Ellen needs 28 ft² / 2.25 ft² ≈ 12.44 tiles. Since we can't have a fraction of a tile, we need a minimum of 13 tiles.

# 11.

Ellen is planning to put in a new tile floor. Each tile is 6 inches by 6 inches. The area is 7 feet wide by 11 feet long. What is the minimum number of tiles needed to completely cover the area?

a. 325  b. 300  c. 250  **d. 308**

**The correct answer is D.**
First we have to convert the measure of the tile from inches to feet. 12 in = 1 ft, so each tile measures 6 / 12 = .5 feet on each side. The area of the tile is .5 ft * .5 ft = .25 ft². The area of the floor is 7 ft * 11 ft = 77 ft².
Ellen needs 77 ft² / .25 ft² = 308 tiles.

# 12.

Danielle has a new classroom floor that she is planning on covering with carpet samples. Each carpet sample is 24 inches wide by 12 inches long. If the classroom is 8 feet wide by 12 feet long, what is the minimum number of carpet samples needed to completely cover the area?

a. 288  b. 46  **c. 48**  d. 50

**The correct answer is C.**
First we have to convert the measure of the tile from inches to feet. 12 in = 1 ft, so each carpet sample measures 24 / 12 = 2 feet wide and 12 / 12 = 1 foot long. The area of the carpet sample is 2 ft * 1 ft = 2 ft². The area of the floor is 8 ft * 12 ft = 96 ft².
Ellen needs 96 ft² / 2 ft² = 48 carpet samples.

# Lesson 17 - Area

# 13.

Danielle has a new classroom floor that she is planning on covering with carpet samples. Each carpet sample is 24 inches wide by 12 inches long. If the classroom is 12 feet wide by 20 feet long, what is the minimum number of carpet samples needed to completely cover the area?

a. 180   b. 120   c. 60   d. 240

# 14.

Danielle has a new classroom floor that she is planning on covering with carpet samples. Each carpet sample is 24 inches wide by 12 inches long. If the classroom is 16 feet wide by 20 feet long, what is the minimum number of carpet samples needed to completely cover the area?

a. 180   b. 80   c. 160   d. 240

# 15.

Danielle has a new classroom floor that she is planning on covering with carpet samples. Each carpet sample is 24 inches wide by 12 inches long. If the classroom is 14 feet wide by 11 feet long, what is the minimum number of carpet samples needed to completely cover the area?

a. 80   b. 77   c. 67   d. 154

# 13.

Danielle has a new classroom floor that she is planning on covering with carpet samples. Each carpet sample is 24 inches wide by 12 inches long. If the classroom is 12 feet wide by 20 feet long, what is the minimum number of carpet samples needed to completely cover the area?

a. 180   **b. 120**   c. 60   d. 240

**The correct answer is B.**
First we have to convert the measure of the tile from inches to feet. 12 in = 1 ft, so each carpet sample measures 24 / 12 = 2 feet wide and 12 / 12 = 1 foot long. The area of the carpet sample is 2 ft * 1 ft = 2 ft². The area of the floor is 12 ft * 20 ft = 240 ft².
Ellen needs 240 ft² / 2 ft² = 120 carpet samples.

# 14.

Danielle has a new classroom floor that she is planning on covering with carpet samples. Each carpet sample is 24 inches wide by 12 inches long. If the classroom is 16 feet wide by 20 feet long, what is the minimum number of carpet samples needed to completely cover the area?

a. 180   b. 80   **c. 160**   d. 240

**The correct answer is C.**
First we have to convert the measure of the tile from inches to feet. 12 in = 1 ft, so each carpet sample measures 24 / 12 = 2 feet wide and 12 / 12 = 1 foot long. The area of the carpet sample is 2 ft * 1 ft = 2 ft². The area of the floor is 16 ft * 20 ft = 320 ft².
Ellen needs 320 ft² / 2 ft² = 160 carpet samples.

# 15.

Danielle has a new classroom floor that she is planning on covering with carpet samples. Each carpet sample is 24 inches wide by 12 inches long. If the classroom is 14 feet wide by 11 feet long, what is the minimum number of carpet samples needed to completely cover the area?

a. 80   **b. 77**   c. 67   d. 154

**The correct answer is B.**
First we have to convert the measure of the tile from inches to feet. 12 in = 1 ft, so each carpet sample measures 24 / 12 = 2 feet wide and 12 / 12 = 1 foot long. The area of the carpet sample is 2 ft * 1 ft = 2 ft². The area of the floor is 14 ft * 11 ft = 154 ft².
Ellen needs 154 ft² / 2 ft² = 77 carpet samples.

# Lesson 18
# Y-Intercepts

The definition of Y intercept is the point on a line that crosses the Y axis on a graph.

A line on a graph is expressed with this equation:

$y = mx + b$

m is called the slope. b is called the y-intercept. This is because when x = 0 (which is the point where the line crosses the y axis), y = b. So b is always the y intercept.
In order to figure out what the slope and y intercept of a graph are, you have to get your equationinto the format y = mx + b using your algebra skills.

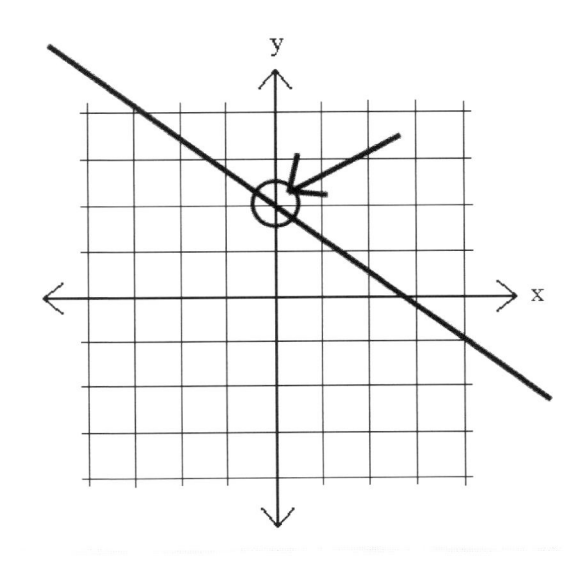

The formula for slope is:

m = Change in y / Change in x.  $m = (y_2 - y_1) / (x_2 - x_1)$

Sometimes you are given two coordinates and asked to find the y-intercept. First you have to figure out m using the slope formula, then plug in one of the coordinates as the X and Y values to find what b is.

For example, in this question:

What is the y intercept of the line in the standard (x,y) coordinate plane that goes through the points (-4,7) and (4,1)?

209

First you find the slope.

m = (1 - 7) / (4 - (-4)) = -6 / 8 = -3/4

Now you have the equation:

y = -3/4x + b

Now let's plug in the x,y coordinates (4,1):

1 = (-3/4)*4 + b

1 = -3 + b

1 + 3 = b

b = 4

*Note: This graphing system is referred to as the Cartesian Coordinate Plane, the Cartesian Coordinate System, or simply "the coordinate plane." If the ACT specifically uses this language, the test is simply referring to the two-dimensional graph with the x and y axes as shown on the previous page.*

# Lesson 18 - Y-Intercepts

## 1.

What is the y intercept of the line 3x + 2y = 5?

a. 1   b. 1.5   c. 3   d. 2.5

## 2.

What is the y intercept of the line 5x + 2y = 1?

a. 1   b. 4/5   c. 2/3   d. 1/2

## 3.

What is the y intercept of the line y = 4x +3?

a. 3   b. 2   c. 4   d. 1

# 1.

What is the y intercept of the line 3x + 2y = 5?

a. 1   b. 1.5   c. 3   **d. 2.5**

**The correct answer is D.**
2y = -3x + 5
y = (-3/2)x + 5/2
The y intercept is 5/2 = 2.5

# 2.

What is the y intercept of the line 5x + 2y = 1?

a. 1   b. 4/5   c. 2/3   **d. 1/2**

**The correct answer is D.**
2y = -5x + 1
y = (-5/2)x + 1/2
The y intercept is 1/2.

# 3.

What is the y intercept of the line y = 4x +3?

**a. 3**   b. 2   c. 4   d. 1

**The correct answer is A.**
The line equation is y = mx + b, where b is the y-intercept. Therefore the y-intercept for this line is 3. Note that this question is easier than the questions before it. ACT questions are not ordered by difficulty. On the test you'll find easy, simple questions right after very difficult ones, and difficult questions after a run of easy ones. If you're having trouble with a math problem on the ACT, skip it and go to the next one. You can always go back to it later.

# 4.

What is the y intercept of the line 9x + 3y = -8?

a. 8/3   b. -8/3   c. 3   d. -3

# 5.

What is the y intercept of the line 14x + 17y = -13?

a. 13/17   b. -13/17   c. 17   d. -13

# 6.

What is the y intercept of the line 7x - 6y = -4?

a. 3/4   b. 2/3   c. 7/6   d. -4

# 4.

What is the y intercept of the line 9x + 3y = -8?

a. 8/3   **b. -8/3**   c. 3   d. -3

**The correct answer is B.**
3y = -9x - 8
y = -3x - 8/3
The y intercept is -8/3.

# 5.

What is the y intercept of the line 14x + 17y = -13?

a. 13/17   **b. -13/17**   c. 17   d. -13

**The correct answer is B.**
17y = -14x - 13
y = (-14/17)x - 13/17
The y intercept is -13/17.

# 6.

What is the y intercept of the line 7x - 6y = -4?

a. 3/4   **b. 2/3**   c. 7/6   d. -4

**The correct answer is B.**
-6y = -7x - 4
y = (7/6)x + 4/6
The y intercept is 4/6 = 2/3

# Lesson 18 - Y-Intercepts

## 7.

What is the y intercept of the line 3x - 2y = 4?

a. 2    b. 1    c. -2    d. -3

## 8.

What is the y intercept of the line 11x + 4y = -15?

a. -15/4    b. 15/4    c. 11/4    d. -11/4

## 9.

What is the y intercept of the line in the standard (x,y) coordinate plane that goes through the points (-4,7) and (4,1)?

a. -4/3    b. 4/3    c. -19/3    d. 4

# 7.

What is the y intercept of the line 3x - 2y = 4?

a. 2   b. 1   **c. -2**   d. -3

**The correct answer is C.**
-2y = -3x + 4
y = (3/2)x - 2
The y intercept is -2.

# 8.

What is the y intercept of the line 11x + 4y = -15?

**a. -15/4**   b. 15/4   c. 11/4   d. -11/4

**The correct answer is A.**
4y = -11x - 15
y = (-11/4)x - 15/4
The y intercept is -15/4.

# 9.

What is the y intercept of the line in the standard (x,y) coordinate plane that goes through the points (-4,7) and (4,1)?

a. -4/3   b. 4/3   c. -19/3   **d. 4**

**The correct answer is D.**
First we have to find the slope using our slope equation.  m = (1 - 7) / (4 - (-4)) = -6 / 8 = -3/4
y = (-3/4)x + b.  Plug in one of the coordinates.
1 = (-3/4)(4) + b
1 = -3 + b
b = 3 + 1 = 4

# Lesson 18 - Y-Intercepts

## 10.

What is the y intercept of the line in the standard (x,y) coordinate plane that goes through the points (-2,7) and (5,3)?

a. 31/7   b. 41/7   c. -41   d. 41

## 11.

What is the y intercept of the line in the standard (x,y) coordinate plane that goes through the points (-6,7) and (-4,-1)?

a. -17/6   b. 17/6   c. -17   d. 17

## 12.

What is the y intercept of the line in the standard (x,y) coordinate plane that goes through the points (-15,6) and (-6,-1)?

a. -17/3   b. 17/3   c. -15/3   d. 15/3

# 10.

What is the y intercept of the line in the standard (x,y) coordinate plane that goes through the points (-2,7) and (5,3)?

a. 31/7   **b. 41/7**   c. -41   d. 41

**The correct answer is B.**
First we have to find the slope using our slope equation.  m = (3 - 7) / (5 - (-2)) = -4 / 7 = -4/7
y = (-4/7)x + b.  Plug in one of the coordinates.
3 = (-4/7)(5) + b
3 = -20/7 + b
b = 20/7 + 3 = 41/7

# 11.

What is the y intercept of the line in the standard (x,y) coordinate plane that goes through the points (-6,7) and (-4,-1)?

a. -17/6   b. 17/6   **c. -17**   d. 17

**The correct answer is C.**
First we have to find the slope using our slope equation.  m = (-1 - 7) / (-4 - (-6)) = -8 / 2 = -4
y = -4x + b.  Plug in one of the coordinates.
-1 = (-4)(-4) + b
-1 = 16 + b
b = -1 - 16 = -17

# 12.

What is the y intercept of the line in the standard (x,y) coordinate plane that goes through the points (-15,6) and (-6,-1)?

**a. -17/3**   b. 17/3   c. -15/3   d. 15/3

**The correct answer is A.**
First we have to find the slope using our slope equation.  m = (-1 - 6) / (-6 - (-15)) = -7 / 9 = -7/9
y = (-7/9)x + b.  Plug in one of the coordinates.
-1 = (-7/9)(-6) + b
-1 = 42/9 + b
b = -1 - 42/9 = -51/9 = -17/3

# Lesson 18 - Y-Intercepts

# 13.

What is the y intercept of the line in the standard (x,y) coordinate plane that goes through the points (-2,5) and (-4,2)?

a. -5/2   b. 4/3   c. -8   d. 8

# 14.

What is the y intercept of the line in the standard (x,y) coordinate plane that goes through the points (-7,7) and (4,21), rounded to the nearest tenth?

a. -15.9   b. 15.9   c. -7   d. 1.3

# 15.

What is the y intercept of the line in the standard (x,y) coordinate plane that goes through the points (-15,7) and (21,27), rounded to the nearest tenth?

a. -15.3   b. 15.3   c. 18.2   d. -18.2

# 13.

What is the y intercept of the line in the standard (x,y) coordinate plane that goes through the points (-2,5) and (-4,2)?

a. -5/2   b. 4/3   c. -8   **d. 8**

**The correct answer is D.**
First we have to find the slope using our slope equation.  m = (2 - 5) / (-4 - (-2)) = -3 / -2 = 3/2
y = (3/2)x + b.  Plug in one of the coordinates.
2 = (3/2)(-4) + b
2 = -6 + b
b = 2 + 6 = 8

# 14.

What is the y intercept of the line in the standard (x,y) coordinate plane that goes through the points (-7,7) and (4,21), rounded to the nearest tenth?

a. -15.9   **b. 15.9**   c. -7   d. 1.3

**The correct answer is B.**
First we have to find the slope using our slope equation.  m = (21 - 7) / (4 - (-7)) = 14 / 11 = 14/11
y = (14/11)x + b.  Plug in one of the coordinates.
7 = (14/11)(-7) + b
7 = -98/11 + b
b = 7 + 98/11 = 175/11 ≈ 15.9

# 15.

What is the y intercept of the line in the standard (x,y) coordinate plane that goes through the points (-15,7) and (21,27), rounded to the nearest tenth?

a. -15.3   **b. 15.3**   c. 18.2   d. -18.2

**The correct answer is B.**
First we have to find the slope using our slope equation.  m = (27 - 7) / (21 - (-15)) = 20 / 36 = 5/9
y = (5/9)x + b.  Plug in one of the coordinates.
27 = (5/9)(21) + b
27 = 105/9 + b
b = 27 - 105/9 = 138/9 ≈ 15.3

# Lesson 19
# Rates

Some ACT math questions will ask you to figure out how long it will take for two things working at different rates to become equal.

For example, you might get a question like this:

The depth of a swimming pool is 195 cm. Every week, evaporation causes it to be reduced in depth by 1 cm. The depth of a second swimming pool is 189 cm. Every week, evaporation causes it to be reduced in depth by ½ cm per week. If the depths of both swimming pools continue to be reduced at these constant rates, in about how many weeks will the swimming pools have the same depths?

The key to solving this problem, and solving many problems like it, is to convert the word problem into an ALGEBRAIC EQUATION. An algebraic equation is one that has a variable, like x, and tells us that one side EQUALS another side.

In this case, we are trying to figure out how many weeks it will take for the swimming pools to have the same depths.

So we'll call the number of weeks x.

The depth of the first swimming pool is:

195 - 1x

The depth of the second swimming pool is:

189 - (1/2)x

We want to find out how many weeks it will take for these two pools to be equal, so we set it up as an equation:

$195 - 1x = 189 - (1/2)x$

Now solve for x. Add 1x to both sides, so that we get x on only one side.

$195 = 189 + (1/2)x$

Subtract 189 from both sides.

$6 = (1/2)x$

Multiply both sides by 2.

$x = 12$

It will take twelve weeks for both pools to be equal.

You can solve a lot of word problems by turning them into algebraic equations. The trick is to figure out how to express the question as an algebra problem, then solve for x!

NOTE: When in doubt, you can always plug the answers given to you in the multiple choices as potential solutions into your equation and see which one works. This is often quicker than figuring it out, and in any event is a good way to check your answers!

# Lesson 19 - Rates

## 1.

The depth of a swimming pool is 180 cm. Every week, evaporation causes it to be reduced in depth by 1 cm. The depth of a second swimming pool is 175 cm. Every week, evaporation causes it to be reduced in depth by ½ cm per week. If the depths of both swimming pools continue to be reduced at these constant rates, in about how many weeks will the swimming pools have the same depths?

a. 15   b. 12   c. 5   d. 10

## 2.

The depth of a swimming pool is 160 cm. Every week, evaporation causes it to be reduced in depth by 3 cm. The depth of a second swimming pool is 130 cm. Every week, evaporation causes it to be reduced in depth by 2 cm per week. If the depths of both swimming pools continue to be reduced at these constant rates, in about how many weeks will the swimming pools have the same depths?

a. -3   b. 40   c. 30   d. 20

## 3.

The depth of a swimming pool is 200 cm. Every week, evaporation causes it to be reduced in depth by 5 cm. The depth of a second swimming pool is 180 cm. Every week, evaporation causes it to be reduced in depth by 4 cm per week. If the depths of both swimming pools continue to be reduced at these constant rates, in about how many weeks will the swimming pools have the same depths?

a. 20   b. 30   c. 40   d. 10

# Math Mastery - Level 1

# 1.

The depth of a swimming pool is 180 cm. Every week, evaporation causes it to be reduced in depth by 1 cm. The depth of a second swimming pool is 175 cm. Every week, evaporation causes it to be reduced in depth by ½ cm per week. If the depths of both swimming pools continue to be reduced at these constant rates, in about how many weeks will the swimming pools have the same depths?

a. 15   b. 12   c. 5   **d. 10**

**The correct answer is D.**
The depth of the first pool is expressed 180 - 1x.
The depth of the second pool is expressed 175 - (1/2)x.
180 - 1x = 175 - (1/2)x
Solve for x.  x = 10.  See Lesson Eight for more help on solving for x.

# 2.

The depth of a swimming pool is 160 cm. Every week, evaporation causes it to be reduced in depth by 3 cm. The depth of a second swimming pool is 130 cm. Every week, evaporation causes it to be reduced in depth by 2 cm per week. If the depths of both swimming pools continue to be reduced at these constant rates, in about how many weeks will the swimming pools have the same depths?

a. -3   b. 40   **c. 30**   d. 20

**The correct answer is C.**
The depth of the first pool is expressed 160 - 3x.
The depth of the second pool is expressed 130 - 2x
160 - 3x = 130 - 2x
Solve for x.  x = 30.  See Lesson Eight for more help on solving for x.

# 3.

The depth of a swimming pool is 200 cm. Every week, evaporation causes it to be reduced in depth by 5 cm. The depth of a second swimming pool is 180 cm. Every week, evaporation causes it to be reduced in depth by 4 cm per week. If the depths of both swimming pools continue to be reduced at these constant rates, in about how many weeks will the swimming pools have the same depths?

**a. 20**   b. 30   c. 40   d. 10

**The correct answer is A.**
The depth of the first pool is expressed 200 - 5x.
The depth of the second pool is expressed 180 - 4x
200 - 5x = 180 - 4x
Solve for x.  x = 20.  See Lesson Eight for more help on solving for x.

# Lesson 19 - Rates

## 4.

The depth of a swimming pool is 300 cm. Every week, evaporation causes it to be reduced in depth by 10 cm. The depth of a second swimming pool is 275 cm. Every week, evaporation causes it to be reduced in depth by 8 cm per week. If the depths of both swimming pools continue to be reduced at these constant rates, in about how many weeks will the swimming pools have the same depths?

a. 13   b. 12.5   c. 11   d. 11.5

## 5.

The depth of a swimming pool is 250 cm. Every week, evaporation causes it to be reduced in depth by 1 cm. The depth of a second swimming pool is 220 cm. Every week, evaporation causes it to be reduced in depth by ½ cm per week. If the depths of both swimming pools continue to be reduced at these constant rates, in about how many weeks will the swimming pools have the same depths?

a. 50   b. 60   c. 70   d. 40

## 6.

Car A has 15 gallons of gas in its tank and burns a gallon of gas for every 20 miles it travels. Car B has 12 gallons of gas in its tank and burns a gallon of gas for every 30 miles it travels. Both cars begin their journey at the same time with full tanks of gas. About how many miles would the cars have to travel before both cars have the same amount of gasoline in their tanks?

a. 180   b. 240   c. 300   d. 360

## 4.

The depth of a swimming pool is 300 cm. Every week, evaporation causes it to be reduced in depth by 10 cm. The depth of a second swimming pool is 275 cm. Every week, evaporation causes it to be reduced in depth by 8 cm per week. If the depths of both swimming pools continue to be reduced at these constant rates, in about how many weeks will the swimming pools have the same depths?

a. 13   **b. 12.5**   c. 11   d. 11.5

**The correct answer is B.**
The depth of the first pool is expressed 300 - 10x.
The depth of the second pool is expressed 275 - 8x.
300 - 10x = 275 - 8x
Solve for x.  x = 25/2 = 12.5 weeks.  See Lesson Eight for more help on solving for x.

## 5.

The depth of a swimming pool is 250 cm. Every week, evaporation causes it to be reduced in depth by 1 cm. The depth of a second swimming pool is 220 cm. Every week, evaporation causes it to be reduced in depth by ½ cm per week. If the depths of both swimming pools continue to be reduced at these constant rates, in about how many weeks will the swimming pools have the same depths?

a. 50   **b. 60**   c. 70   d. 40

**The correct answer is B.**
The depth of the first pool is expressed 250 - 1x.
The depth of the second pool is expressed 220 - (1/2)x.
250 - 1x = 220 - (1/2)x
Solve for x.  x = 60 weeks.  See Lesson Eight for more help on solving for x.

## 6.

Car A has 15 gallons of gas in its tank and burns a gallon of gas for every 20 miles it travels. Car B has 12 gallons of gas in its tank and burns a gallon of gas for every 30 miles it travels. Both cars begin their journey at the same time with full tanks of gas. About how many miles would the cars have to travel before both cars have the same amount of gasoline in their tanks?

**a. 180**   b. 240   c. 300   d. 360

**The correct answer is A.**
The first car's gas tank is expressed 15 - (1/20)x.
The second car's gas tank is expressed 12 - (1/30)x.
15 - (1/20)x = 12 - (1/30)x
Solve for x.  3 = (1/60)x.  x = 180.

# Lesson 19 - Rates

# 7.

Car A has 16 gallons of gas in its tank and burns a gallon of gas for every 20 miles it travels. Car B has 12 gallons of gas in its tank and burns a gallon of gas for every 32 miles it travels. Both cars begin their journey at the same time with full tanks of gas. About how many miles would the cars have to travel before both cars have the same amount of gasoline in their tanks, rounded to the nearest mile?

a. 213   b. 190   c. 252   d. 384

# 8.

Car A has 10 gallons of gas in its tank and burns a gallon of gas for every 30 miles it travels. Car B has 7 gallons of gas in its tank and burns a gallon of gas for every 60 miles it travels. Both cars begin their journey at the same time with full tanks of gas. About how many miles would the cars have to travel before both cars have the same amount of gasoline in their tanks?

a. 240   b. 180   c. 120   d. 300

# 9.

Car A has 20 gallons of gas in its tank and burns a gallon of gas for every 20 miles it travels. Car B has 14 gallons of gas in its tank and burns a gallon of gas for every 30 miles it travels. Both cars begin their journey at the same time with full tanks of gas. About how many miles would the cars have to travel before both cars have the same amount of gasoline in their tanks?

a. 280   b. 320   c. 360   d. 400

# 7.

Car A has 16 gallons of gas in its tank and burns a gallon of gas for every 20 miles it travels. Car B has 12 gallons of gas in its tank and burns a gallon of gas for every 32 miles it travels. Both cars begin their journey at the same time with full tanks of gas. About how many miles would the cars have to travel before both cars have the same amount of gasoline in their tanks, rounded to the nearest mile?

a. **213**   b. 190   c. 252   d. 384

**The correct answer is A.**
The first car's gas tank is expressed 16 - (1/20)x.
The second car's gas tank is expressed 12 - (1/32)x.
16 - (1/20)x = 12 - (1/32)x
Solve for x.  4 = (3/160)x.  x = 640/3.  x ≈ 213.

# 8.

Car A has 10 gallons of gas in its tank and burns a gallon of gas for every 30 miles it travels. Car B has 7 gallons of gas in its tank and burns a gallon of gas for every 60 miles it travels. Both cars begin their journey at the same time with full tanks of gas. About how many miles would the cars have to travel before both cars have the same amount of gasoline in their tanks?

a. 240   **b. 180**   c. 120   d. 300

**The correct answer is B.**
The first car's gas tank is expressed 10 - (1/30)x.
The second car's gas tank is expressed 7 - (1/60)x.
10 - (1/30)x = 7 - (1/60)x
Solve for x.  3 = (1/60)x.  x = 180

# 9.

Car A has 20 gallons of gas in its tank and burns a gallon of gas for every 20 miles it travels. Car B has 14 gallons of gas in its tank and burns a gallon of gas for every 30 miles it travels. Both cars begin their journey at the same time with full tanks of gas. About how many miles would the cars have to travel before both cars have the same amount of gasoline in their tanks?

a. 280   b. 320   **c. 360**   d. 400

**The correct answer is C.**
The first car's gas tank is expressed 20 - (1/20)x.
The second car's gas tank is expressed 14 - (1/30)x.
20 - (1/20)x = 14 - (1/30)x
Solve for x.  6 = (1/60)x.  x = 360

Lesson 19 - Rates

# 10.

Car A has 15 gallons of gas in its tank and burns a gallon of gas for every 20 miles it travels. Car B has 12 gallons of gas in its tank and burns a gallon of gas for every 30 miles it travels. Both cars begin their journey at the same time with full tanks of gas. About how many miles would the cars have to travel before both cars have the same amount of gasoline in their tanks?

a. 360   b. 300   c. 240   d. 180

# 11.

Car A has 16 gallons of gas in its tank and burns a gallon of gas for every 20 miles it travels. Car B has 14 gallons of gas in its tank and burns a gallon of gas for every 30 miles it travels. Both cars begin their journey at the same time with full tanks of gas. About how many miles would the cars have to travel before both cars have the same amount of gasoline in their tanks?

a. 200   b. 160   c. 120   d. 80

# 12.

Car A has 8 gallons of gas in its tank and burns a gallon of gas for every 20 miles it travels. Car B has 6 gallons of gas in its tank and burns a gallon of gas for every 30 miles it travels. Both cars begin their journey at the same time with full tanks of gas. About how many miles would the cars have to travel before both cars have the same amount of gasoline in their tanks?

a. 150   b. 120   c. 600   d. 48

## 10.

Car A has 15 gallons of gas in its tank and burns a gallon of gas for every 20 miles it travels. Car B has 12 gallons of gas in its tank and burns a gallon of gas for every 30 miles it travels. Both cars begin their journey at the same time with full tanks of gas. About how many miles would the cars have to travel before both cars have the same amount of gasoline in their tanks?

a. 360   b. 300   c. 240   **d. 180**

**The correct answer is D.**
The first car's gas tank is expressed 15 - (1/20)x.
The second car's gas tank is expressed 12 - (1/30)x.
15 - (1/20)x = 12 - (1/30)x
Solve for x.  3 = (1/60)x.  x = 180

## 11.

Car A has 16 gallons of gas in its tank and burns a gallon of gas for every 20 miles it travels. Car B has 14 gallons of gas in its tank and burns a gallon of gas for every 30 miles it travels. Both cars begin their journey at the same time with full tanks of gas. About how many miles would the cars have to travel before both cars have the same amount of gasoline in their tanks?

a. 200   b. 160   **c. 120**   d. 80

**The correct answer is C.**
The first car's gas tank is expressed 16 - (1/20)x.
The second car's gas tank is expressed 14 - (1/30)x.
16 - (1/20)x = 14 - (1/30)x
Solve for x.  2 = (1/60)x.  x = 120

## 12.

Car A has 8 gallons of gas in its tank and burns a gallon of gas for every 20 miles it travels. Car B has 6 gallons of gas in its tank and burns a gallon of gas for every 30 miles it travels. Both cars begin their journey at the same time with full tanks of gas. About how many miles would the cars have to travel before both cars have the same amount of gasoline in their tanks?

a. 150   **b. 120**   c. 600   d. 48

**The correct answer is B.**
The first car's gas tank is expressed 8 - (1/20)x.
The second car's gas tank is expressed 6 - (1/30)x.
8 - (1/20)x = 6 - (1/30)x
Solve for x.  2 = (1/60)x.  x = 120

# Lesson 19 - Rates

# 13.

Car A has 15 gallons of gas in its tank and burns half of a gallon of gas for every 12 miles it travels. Car B has 13 gallons of gas in its tank and burns a gallon of gas for every 28 miles it travels. Both cars begin their journey at the same time with full tanks of gas. About how many miles would the cars have to travel before both cars have the same amount of gasoline in their tanks?

a. 336   b. 326   c. 195   d. 4

# 14.

Car A has 15 gallons of gas in its tank and burns a third of a gallon of gas for every 7 miles it travels. Car B has 13 gallons of gas in its tank and burns a fourth of a gallon of gas for every 8 miles it travels. Both cars begin their journey at the same time with full tanks of gas. About how many miles would the cars have to travel before both cars have the same amount of gasoline in their tanks?

a. 122   b. 132   c. 112   d. 180

# 15.

Car A has 18 gallons of gas in its tank and burns a gallon of gas for every 40 miles it travels. Car B has 16 gallons of gas in its tank and burns a gallon of gas for every 75 miles it travels. Both cars begin their journey at the same time with full tanks of gas. About how many miles would the cars have to travel before both cars have the same amount of gasoline in their tanks?

a. 150   b. 171   c. 175   d. 161

# 13.

Car A has 15 gallons of gas in its tank and burns half of a gallon of gas for every 12 miles it travels. Car B has 13 gallons of gas in its tank and burns a gallon of gas for every 28 miles it travels. Both cars begin their journey at the same time with full tanks of gas. About how many miles would the cars have to travel before both cars have the same amount of gasoline in their tanks?

a. 336   b. 326   c. 195   d. 4

**The correct answer is A.**
1/2 a gallon per 12 miles = 1 gallon per 24. The first car's gas tank is expressed 15 - (1/24)x.
The second car's gas tank is expressed 13 - (1/28)x.
15 - (1/24)x = 13 - (1/28)x
Solve for x.  2 = (1/168)x.  x = 336

# 14.

Car A has 15 gallons of gas in its tank and burns a third of a gallon of gas for every 7 miles it travels. Car B has 13 gallons of gas in its tank and burns a fourth of a gallon of gas for every 8 miles it travels. Both cars begin their journey at the same time with full tanks of gas. About how many miles would the cars have to travel before both cars have the same amount of gasoline in their tanks?

a. 122   b. 132   c. 112   d. 180

**The correct answer is A.**
1/3 a gallon per 7 miles = 1 gallon per 21 miles. The first car's gas tank is expressed 15 - (1/21)x.
1/4 gallon per 8 miles = 1 gallon per 32 miles. The second car's gas tank is expressed 13 - (1/32)x.
15 - (1/21)x = 13 - (1/32)x
Solve for x.  2 = (11/672)x.  x ≈ 122

# 15.

Car A has 18 gallons of gas in its tank and burns a gallon of gas for every 40 miles it travels. Car B has 16 gallons of gas in its tank and burns a gallon of gas for every 75 miles it travels. Both cars begin their journey at the same time with full tanks of gas. About how many miles would the cars have to travel before both cars have the same amount of gasoline in their tanks?

a. 150   b. 171   c. 175   d. 161

**The correct answer is B.**
The first car's gas tank is expressed 18 - (1/40)x.
The second car's gas tank is expressed 16 - (1/75)x.
18 - (1/40)x = 16 - (1/75)x
Solve for x.  2 = (7/600)x.  x = 171

# Lesson 20
# Review

This lesson provides review questions for everything you've covered so far in this book.

Remember: if you miss a question, be sure to go back and re-do the lesson that goes with it!

At this point, you may want to try the "plug-in" method to arrive at answers to questions you are having difficulty with.

To do this, simply plug in each multiple choice answer into the question and see which one works best.

Note that if you do this and get the answer correct, you still may want to go back and review the lesson that the question corresponded to. You want to know how to solve these problems backwards and forward, so that you can maximize your score on the ACT!

# Lesson 20 - Review

## 1.

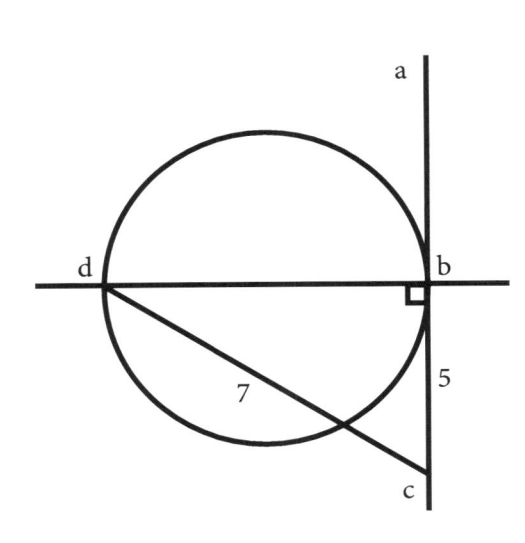

What is the circumference of the circle with tangent ABC and line BD running through its center, rounded to the nearest 100th?

a. 15.39   b. 15.4   c. 12.45   d. 12.46°

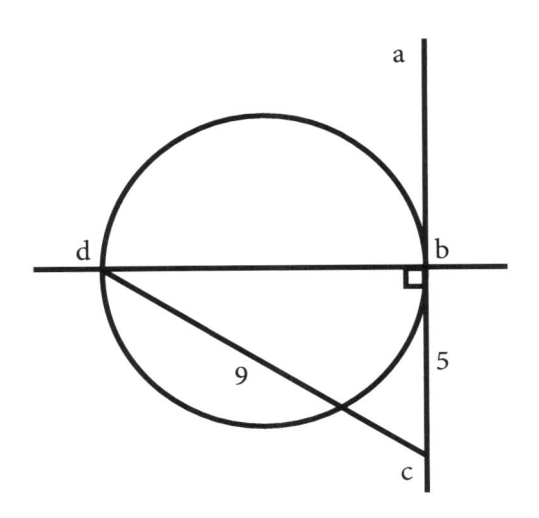

## 2.

What is the area of the circle with tangent ABC and line BD running through its center, rounded to the nearest 100th?

a. 43.99   b. 43.98   c. 42.17   d. 87.96

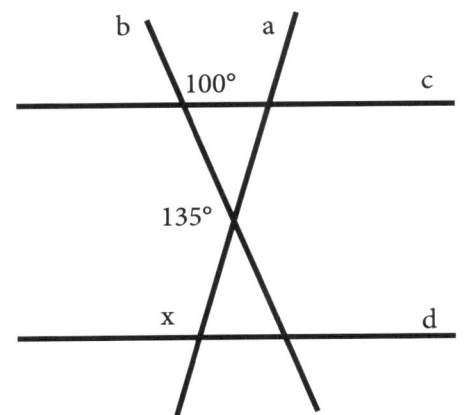

## 3.

Lines c and d are parallel.  Angle x = ?

a. 125°   b. 45°   c. 105°   d. 35°

235

Math Mastery - Level 1

## 1.

What is the circumference of the circle with tangent ABC and line BD running through its center, rounded to the nearest 100th?

    **a. 15.39**   b. 15.4   c. 12.45   d. 12.46°

**The correct answer is A.**
First we must find the diameter of the circle, line segment DB.
We've labeled this x.
$$x^2 + 5^2 = 7^2$$
$$x^2 + 25 = 49$$
$$x^2 = 49 - 25 = 24$$
$x = \sqrt{24}$. Circumference = $\pi \sqrt{24} \approx 15.39$
Missed this question? Review Lesson 16.

## 2.

What is the area of the circle with tangent ABC and line BD running through its center, rounded to the nearest 100th?

    a. 43.99   **b. 43.98**   c. 42.17   d. 87.96

**The correct answer is B.**
First we must find the diameter of the circle, line segment DB.
We've labeled this x.
$$x^2 + 5^2 = 9^2 \mid x^2 + 25 = 81$$
$$x^2 = 81 - 25 = 56$$
$x = \sqrt{56}$. Radius = $\sqrt{56}/2$
Area = $\pi(\sqrt{56}/2)^2 \approx 43.98$
Missed this question? Review Lesson 16.

## 3.

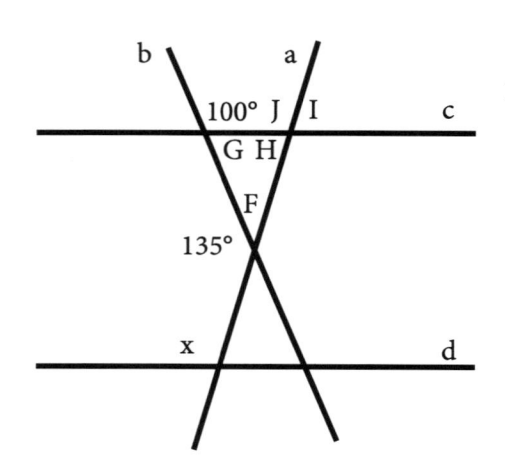

Lines c and d are parallel. Angle x = ?

    **a. 125°**   b. 45°   c. 105°   d. 35°

**The correct answer is A.**
Angle F = 180 - 135 = 45°. Angle G = 180 - 100 = 80°. Angle H = 180 - 45 - 80 = 55°. Angle I = 55° because it's opposite to Angle H and therefore identical to it. Angle J = 180 - 55 = 125°. Therefore, x = 125° because the angles created by the intersection of lines a and c are identical to the angles created by the intersection of lines a and d because c and d are parallel.
Missed this question? Review Lesson 14.

# Lesson 20 - Review

## 4.

Jim is trying to save up for a car over the summer. The car costs $2650.00. He has started a job where he earns $9.50 per hour. If the summer lasts ten weeks, what is the minimum average number of hours per week that he needs to work in order to earn enough for the car, rounded to the nearest hour?

a. 31   b. 32   c. 34   d. 28

## 5.

In the figure below, all line segments are either horizontal or vertical and the dimensions are in inches. What is the perimeter, in inches, of the figure?

a. 50 in   b. 70 in   c. 62 in   d. 65 in

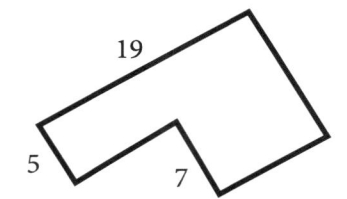

## 6.

If eight shirts cost $150, how much do 5 shirts cost?

a. $93.75
b. $50.00
c. $450
d. $22.50

## 4.

Jim is trying to save up for a car over the summer. The car costs $2650.00. He has started a job where he earns $9.50 per hour. If the summer lasts ten weeks, what is the minimum average number of hours per week that he needs to work in order to earn enough for the car, rounded to the nearest hour?

a. 31   b. 32   c. 34   **d. 28**

**The correct answer is D.**
Jim needs to work $2650 divided by $9.50 per hour = 278.95 hours. The average number of hours per week he needs to work is 278.95 hours divided into 10 weeks = 27.895 hours. We round this up to the nearest hour for our answer, 28. Missed this question? Review Lesson 2.

## 5.

In the figure below, all line segments are either horizontal or vertical and the dimensions are in inches. What is the perimeter, in inches, of the figure?

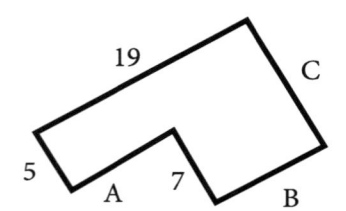

a. 50 in   b. 70 in   **c. 62 in**   d. 65 in

**The correct answer is C.**
First figure out the lengths of the missing sides. Write on the shape as you follow along. The line segments we labeled A & B = 19. The line segment we labeled C = 7 + 5 = 12. Now we can add all of our sides. 12 + 19 + 19 + 5 + 7 = 62 in.
Missed this question? Review Lesson 13.

## 6.

If eight shirts cost $150, how much do 5 shirts cost?

**a. $93.75**
b. $50.00
c. $450
d. $22.50

**The correct answer is A.**
$150 divided by 8 shirts = $18.75. $18.75 per shirt times 5 shirts = $93.75. 150 / 8 = 18.75. 18.75 x 5 = 93.75. You have to figure out the value of one shirt, then you can figure out how much more than one shirt costs. Missed this question? Review Lesson 1.

# Lesson 20 - Review

# 7.

What is the y intercept of the line in the standard (x,y) coordinate plane that goes through the points (-7,7) and (4,14), rounded to the nearest tenth?

a. -14.6   b. 11.5   c. -7   d. 1.3

# 8.

Danielle has a new classroom floor that she is planning on covering with carpet samples. Each carpet sample is 24 inches wide by 24 inches long. If the classroom is 16 feet wide by 20 feet long, what is the minimum number of carpet samples needed to completely cover the area?

a. 80   b. 180   c. 160   d. 40

# 9.

Car A has 14 gallons of gas in its tank and burns a third of a gallon of gas for every 7 miles it travels. Car B has 13 gallons of gas in its tank and burns a fourth of a gallon of gas for every 8 miles it travels. Both cars begin their journey at the same time with full tanks of gas. About how many miles would the cars have to travel before both cars have the same amount of gasoline in their tanks?

a. 61   b. 42   c. 85   d. 135

# 7.

What is the y intercept of the line in the standard (x,y) coordinate plane that goes through the points (-7,7) and (4,14), rounded to the nearest tenth?

a. -14.6   **b. 11.5**   c. -7   d. 1.3

**The correct answer is B.**
First we have to find the slope using our slope equation.  m = (14 - 7) / (4 - (-7)) = 7 / 11
y = (7/11)x + b.  Plug in one of the coordinates.
7 = (7/11)(-7) + b
7 = -49/11 + b
b = 7 + 49/11 = 126/11 ≈ 11.5.  Missed this question?  Review Lesson 18.

# 8.

Danielle has a new classroom floor that she is planning on covering with carpet samples.  Each carpet sample is 24 inches wide by 24 inches long.  If the classroom is 16 feet wide by 20 feet long, what is the minimum number of carpet samples needed to completely cover the area?

**a. 80**   b. 180   c. 160   d. 40

**The correct answer is A.**
First we have to convert the measure of the tile from inches to feet.  12 in = 1 ft, so each carpet sample measures 24 / 12 = 2 feet wide and 24 / 12 = 2 feet long.  The area of the carpet sample is 2 ft * 2 ft = 4 ft².  The area of the floor is 16 ft * 20 ft = 320 ft².
Ellen needs 320 ft² / 4 ft² = 80 carpet samples.  Missed this question?  Review Lesson 17.

# 9.

Car A has 14 gallons of gas in its tank and burns a third of a gallon of gas for every 7 miles it travels.  Car B has 13 gallons of gas in its tank and burns a fourth of a gallon of gas for every 8 miles it travels.  Both cars begin their journey at the same time with full tanks of gas.  About how many miles would the cars have to travel before both cars have the same amount of gasoline in their tanks?

**a. 61**   b. 42   c. 85   d. 135

**The correct answer is A.**
1/3 a gallon per 7 miles = 1 gallon per 21 miles.  The first car's gas tank is expressed 14 - (1/21)x.
1/4 gallon per 8 miles = 1 gallon per 32 miles.  The second car's gas tank is expressed 13 - (1/32)x.
14 - (1/21)x = 13 - (1/32)x
Solve for x.  1 = (11/672)x.  x ≈ 61.  Missed this question?  Review Lesson 19.

# Lesson 20 - Review

# 10.

Danielle has a new classroom floor that she is planning on covering with carpet samples. Each carpet sample is 24 inches wide by 18 inches long. If the classroom is 14 feet wide by 12 feet long, what is the minimum number of carpet samples needed to completely cover the area?

a. 65   b. 56   c. 42   d. 168

# 11.

What is the y intercept of the line in the standard (x,y) coordinate plane that goes through the points (1,7) and (11,27), rounded to the nearest tenth?

a. 5   b. -5   c. 3.2   d. -3.2

# 12.

Car A has 17 gallons of gas in its tank and burns a gallon of gas for every 40 miles it travels. Car B has 16 gallons of gas in its tank and burns a gallon of gas for every 75 miles it travels. Both cars begin their journey at the same time with full tanks of gas. About how many miles would the cars have to travel before both cars have the same amount of gasoline in their tanks?

a. 80   b. 86   c. 90   d. 171

# 10.

Danielle has a new classroom floor that she is planning on covering with carpet samples. Each carpet sample is 24 inches wide by 18 inches long. If the classroom is 14 feet wide by 12 feet long, what is the minimum number of carpet samples needed to completely cover the area?

a. 65   **b. 56**   c. 42   d. 168

**The correct answer is B.**
First we have to convert the measure of the tile from inches to feet. 12 in = 1 ft, so each carpet sample measures 24 / 12 = 2 feet wide and 18 / 12 = 1.5 feet long. The area of the carpet sample is 2 ft * 1.5 ft = 3 ft². The area of the floor is 14 ft * 12 ft = 168 ft².
Ellen needs 168 ft² / 3 ft² = 56 carpet samples. Missed this question? Review Lesson 17.

# 11.

What is the y intercept of the line in the standard (x,y) coordinate plane that goes through the points (1,7) and (11,27), rounded to the nearest tenth?

**a. 5**   b. -5   c. 3.2   d. -3.2

**The correct answer is A.**
First we have to find the slope using our slope equation. m = (27 - 7) / (11 - 1) = 20 / 10 = 2
y = 2x + b. Plug in one of the coordinates.
7 = 2(1) + b
b = 5
Missed this question? Review Lesson 18.

# 12.

Car A has 17 gallons of gas in its tank and burns a gallon of gas for every 40 miles it travels. Car B has 16 gallons of gas in its tank and burns a gallon of gas for every 75 miles it travels. Both cars begin their journey at the same time with full tanks of gas. About how many miles would the cars have to travel before both cars have the same amount of gasoline in their tanks?

a. 80   **b. 86**   c. 90   d. 171

**The correct answer is B.**
The first car's gas tank is expressed 17 - (1/40)x.
The second car's gas tank is expressed 16 - (1/75)x.
17 - (1/40)x = 16 - (1/75)x
Solve for x. 1 = (7/600)x. x ≈ 86. Missed this question? Review Lesson 19.

# Lesson 20 - Review

## 13.

The depth of a swimming pool is 285 cm. Every week, evaporation causes it to be reduced in depth by 10 cm. The depth of a second swimming pool is 275 cm. Every week, evaporation causes it to be reduced in depth by 8 cm per week. If the depths of both swimming pools continue to be reduced at these constant rates, in about how many weeks will the swimming pools have the same depths?

a. 6   b. 5   c. 4   d. 10

## 14.

Ellen is planning to put in a new tile floor. Each tile is 18 inches by 18 inches. The area is 3 feet wide by 9 feet long. What is the minimum number of tiles needed to completely cover the area?

a. 28   b. 4   c. 12   d. 13

## 15.

Length x = ? (Rounded to the nearest hundredth.)

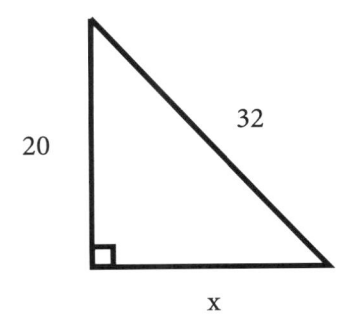

a. 24.98   b. 24.99   c. 24.97   d. 25

# 13.

The depth of a swimming pool is 285 cm. Every week, evaporation causes it to be reduced in depth by 10 cm. The depth of a second swimming pool is 275 cm. Every week, evaporation causes it to be reduced in depth by 8 cm per week. If the depths of both swimming pools continue to be reduced at these constant rates, in about how many weeks will the swimming pools have the same depths?

a. 6   **b. 5**   c. 4   d. 10

**The correct answer is B.**
The depth of the first pool is expressed 285 - 10x.
The depth of the second pool is expressed 275 - 8x.
285 - 10x = 275 - 8x
Solve for x.  x = 5 weeks.  Missed this question?  Review Lesson 19.

# 14.

Ellen is planning to put in a new tile floor. Each tile is 18 inches by 18 inches. The area is 3 feet wide by 9 feet long. What is the minimum number of tiles needed to completely cover the area?

a. 28   b. 4   **c. 12**   d. 13

**The correct answer is C.**
First we have to convert the measure of the tile from inches to feet. 12 in = 1 ft, so each tile measures 18 / 12 = 1.5 feet on each side. The area of the tile is 1.5 ft * 1.5 ft = 2.25 ft². The area of the floor is 3 ft * 9 ft = 27 ft².
Ellen needs 27 ft² / 2.25 ft² = 12 tiles.
Missed this question?  Review Lesson 17.

# 15.

Length x = ? (Rounded to the nearest hundredth.)

**a. 24.98**   b. 24.99   c. 24.97   d. 25

**The correct answer is A.**
$20^2 + x^2 = 32^2$
$400 + x^2 = 1024$
$x^2 = 1024 - 400 = 624$
$x = \sqrt{624} \approx 24.979 \approx 24.98$
Missed this question?  Review Lesson 16.

# Lesson 21
# Slope

There will always be at least one or two questions on the ACT that ask you to find the slope of a line.

Remember that, as we covered in the lesson on Y-intercepts, in the equation for the line:

$y = mx + b$

m is the slope and b is the y-intercept.

To figure out the slope of a line, you have to get the y all by itself on one side of the equation. Whatever number is multiplying the X is your slope!

If a question asked you for slope of a line PARALLEL to a line that is described, the slope of the parallel line is the same as the slope of the first line. The reason for this is that PARALLEL LINES ALWAYS HAVE THE SAME SLOPE. Otherwise they eventually would bump into each other and for that reason wouldn't be parallel.

Remember the slope formula. If you have two coordinates $(x_1, y_1)$, $(x_2, y_2)$ then you can use it:

Slope = $(y_2 - y_1) / (x_2 - x_1)$

# Lesson 21 - Slope

## 1.

What is the slope of any line parallel to the line 6x + 9y = 12?

a. -3/2   b. -2/3   c. 3/2   d. 2/3

## 2.

What is the slope of any line parallel to the line -2x + 5y = 15?

a. 5/2   b. 2/5   c. -2/5   d. -5/2

## 3.

What is the slope of any line parallel to the line ½x + 3y = -5?

a. -6   b. 6   c. 1/6   d. -1/6

# 1.

What is the slope of any line parallel to the line 6x + 9y = 12?

a. -3/2   **b. -2/3**   c. 3/2   d. 2/3

**The correct answer is B.**
9y = -6x + 12
y = (-6/9)x + 12/9
The slope of any line parallel is -6/9 = -2/3.

# 2.

What is the slope of any line parallel to the line -2x + 5y = 15?

a. 5/2   **b. 2/5**   c. -2/5   d. -5/2

**The correct answer is B.**
5y = 2x + 15
y = (2/5)x + 3
The slope of any line parallel is 2/5.

# 3.

What is the slope of any line parallel to the line ½x + 3y = -5?

a. -6   b. 6   c. 1/6   **d. -1/6**

**The correct answer is D.**
3y = -(1/2)x - 5
y = (-1/6)x - 5/3
The slope of any line parallel is -1/6.

# Lesson 21 - Slope

## 4.

What is the slope of any line parallel to the line 4x + 9y = 20?

a. -4/9   b. 4/9   c. 9/4   d. -9/4

## 5.

What is the slope of any line parallel to the line 30x + 9y = 14?

a. -3/10   b. 3/10   c. -10/3   d. 10/3

## 6.

What is the slope of any line parallel to the line x + y = 12?

a. -1   b. 0   c. 1   d. 12

## 4.

What is the slope of any line parallel to the line 4x + 9y = 20?

a. **-4/9**   b. 4/9   c. 9/4   d. -9/4

**The correct answer is A.**
9y = -4x + 20
y = (-4/9)x + 20/9
The slope of any line parallel is -4/9.

## 5.

What is the slope of any line parallel to the line 30x + 9y = 14?

a. -3/10   b. 3/10   **c. -10/3**   d. 10/3

**The correct answer is C.**
9y = -30x + 14
y = (-30/9)x + 14/9
The slope of any line parallel is -30/9 = -10/3.

## 6.

What is the slope of any line parallel to the line x + y = 12?

a. **-1**   b. 0   c. 1   d. 12

**The correct answer is A.**
y = -x + 12
The slope of any line parallel is -1.
Note that there is no number next to x. The 1 is assumed, so watch out for this.

# 7.

What is the slope of any line parallel to the line 2x - y = 12?

a. 1/2   b. 2   c. -2   d. -12

# 8.

What is the slope of the line passing through the points (6, 3) and (5, 1)?

a. -1/2   b. 1/2   c. 2   d. -2

# 9.

What is the slope of the line passing through the points (4, 3) and (-5, 1)?

a. -9/2   b. 9/2   c. -2/9   d. 2/9

# 7.

What is the slope of any line parallel to the line 2x - y = 12?

a. 1/2  **b. 2**  c. -2  d. -12

**The correct answer is B.**
2x = 12 + y
y = 2x - 12
The slope of any line parallel is 2.

# 8.

What is the slope of the line passing through the points (6, 3) and (5, 1)?

a. -1/2  b. 1/2  **c. 2**  d. -2

**The correct answer is C.**
Use the slope formula.  (1 - 3) / (5 - 6) = -2 / -1 = 2

# 9.

What is the slope of the line passing through the points (4, 3) and (-5, 1)?

a. -9/2  b. 9/2  c. -2/9  **d. 2/9**

**The correct answer is D.**
Use the slope formula.  (1 - 3) / (-5 - 4) = -2 / -9 = 2/9

# Lesson 21 - Slope

## 10.

What is the slope of the line passing through the points (5, 3) and (-2, 4)?

a. -1/7   b. 1/7   c. -7   d. 7

## 11.

What is the slope of the line passing through the points (1, 3) and (3, 1)?

a. -1/3   b. 1/3   c. 1   d. -1

## 12.

What is the slope of the line passing through the points (10, 4) and (-5, -1)?

a. 1/3   b. -1/3   c. 1/2   d. -1/2

# 10.

What is the slope of the line passing through the points (5, 3) and (-2, 4)?

a. **-1/7**  b. 1/7  c. -7  d. 7

**The correct answer is A.**
Use the slope formula. (4 - 3) / (-2 - 5) = 1 / -7 = -1/7

# 11.

What is the slope of the line passing through the points (1, 3) and (3, 1)?

a. -1/3  b. 1/3  c. 1  **d. -1**

**The correct answer is D.**
Use the slope formula. (1 - 3) / (3 - 1) = -2 / 2 = -1

# 12.

What is the slope of the line passing through the points (10, 4) and (-5, -1)?

**a. 1/3**  b. -1/3  c. 1/2  d. -1/2

**The correct answer is A.**
Use the slope formula. (-1 - 4) / (-5 - 10) = -5 / -15 = 1/3

# Lesson 21 - Slope

## 13.

What is the slope of the line passing through the points (-6, 3) and (-5, -1)?

a. -1/4   b. -4   c. 1/4   d. 4

## 14.

What is the slope of the line passing through the points (16, 3) and (-4, 4)?

a. 1/20   b. -1/20   c. 20   d. -20

## 15.

What is the slope of the line passing through the points (-6, 7) and (12, 1)?

a. 1/3   b. -1/3   c. 3   d. -3

# 13.

What is the slope of the line passing through the points (-6, 3) and (-5, -1)?

a. -1/4   **b. -4**   c. 1/4   d. 4

**The correct answer is B.**
Use the slope formula.  (-1 - 3) / (-5 - (-6)) = -4 / 1 = -4

# 14.

What is the slope of the line passing through the points (16, 3) and (-4, 4)?

a. 1/20   **b. -1/20**   c. 20   d. -20

**The correct answer is B.**
Use the slope formula.  (4 - 3) / (-4 - 16) = 1 / -20 = -1/20

# 15.

What is the slope of the line passing through the points (-6, 7) and (12, 1)?

a. 1/3   **b. -1/3**   c. 3   d. -3

**The correct answer is B.**
Use the slope formula.  (1 - 7) / (12 - (-6)) = -6 / 18 = -1/3

# Lesson 22
# Systems of Equations

We've already covered how to solve for *x*. But what if you need to solve for *x* when there is both an *x* and a *y* in the equation?

The answer, if there are two variables and two equations, is to solve the system of equations (algebra involving two or more variables and two or more equations).

For example, in the question:

$2x + 3y = 4$

$5x + 6y = 7$

What does x = ?

There are several ways you can solve this problem. You can subtract the equations from one another. This works because $2x + 3y = 4$. So you can subtract $2x + 3y$ from $5x + 6y$ on one side, and subtract 4 from 7 on the other side: you're subtracting the same amount from both sides, because your first equation tells us that $2x + 3y$ and 4 are equal.

Now we're left with:

$3x + 3y = 3$

Now we subtract $2x + 3y = 4$ again.

$x = -1$

We've arrived at our answer.

To make your problem solving go faster, you can first multiply both sides of one of the equations to make the number of y's match up. That way you can subtract one time and cancel out the y's.

For example, in the same problem, you could have multiplied both sides of 2x + 3y = 4 by 2.

4x + 6y = 8.

When you subtract that from 5x + 6y = 7 you end up with the same answer.

Lesson 22 - Systems of Equations

# 1.

$3x + 2y = 5$
$5x + y = -1$
$x = ?$

a. -1   b. 1   c. 3   d. -3

# 2.

$4x + 3y = 5$
$2x + y = -5$
$x = ?$

a. -5   b. 5   c. -10   d. 10

# 3.

$3x + 2y = 5$
$4x + 3y = 22$
$x = ?$

a. -3   b. 3   c. 29   d. -29

# 1.

$3x + 2y = 5$
$5x + y = -1$
$x = ?$

a. **-1**   b. 1   c. 3   d. -3

**The correct answer is A.**
Multiply $5x + y = -1$ by 2 and then subtract that from $3x + 2y = 5$.
$(3x + 2y) - (10x + 2y) = 5 - (-2)$
$-7x = 7$
$x = -1$

# 2.

$4x + 3y = 5$
$2x + y = -5$
$x = ?$

a. -5   b. 5   **c. -10**   d. 10

**The correct answer is C.**
Multiply the equation $2x + y = -5$ by 3 and then subtract that from $4x + 3y = 5$.
$(4x + 3y) - (6x + 3y) = 5 - (-15)$
$-2x = 20$
$x = -10$

# 3.

$3x + 2y = 5$
$4x + 3y = 22$
$x = ?$

a. -3   b. 3   c. 29   **d. -29**

**The correct answer is D.**
Multiply the equation $3x + 2y = 5$ by 3/2 and then subtract that from $4x + 3y = 22$
$(4x + 3y) - (9/2x + 3y) = 22 - 15/2$
$-1/2x = 29/2$
$x = -29$

## 4.

$$x + 2y = 8$$
$$7x - 5y = -1$$
$$y = ?$$

a. -3   b. 3   c. 2   d. -2

## 5.

$$4x + 5y = 11$$
$$2x - y = -5$$
$$y = ?$$

a. 2   b. 3   c. -2   d. 4

## 6.

$$8x - 2y = -2$$
$$5x - 2y = 10$$
$$3x + 6y = ?$$

a. -6   b. 6   c. -102   d. 102

## 4.

$$x + 2y = 8$$
$$7x - 5y = -1$$
$$y = ?$$

a. -3   **b. 3**   c. 2   d. -2

**The correct answer is B.**
Multiply both sides of $x + 2y = 8$ by 7, then subtract that from $7x - 5y = -1$.
$$(7x - 5y) - (7x + 14y) = -1 - 56$$
$$-19y = -57$$
$$y = 3$$

## 5.

$$4x + 5y = 11$$
$$2x - y = -5$$
$$y = ?$$

a. 2   **b. 3**   c. -2   d. 4

**The correct answer is B.**
Multiply both sides of $2x - y = -5$ by 2, then subtract that from $4x + 5y = 11$.
$$(4x + 5y) - (4x - 2y) = 11 - (-10)$$
$$7y = 21$$
$$y = 3$$

## 6.

$$8x - 2y = -2$$
$$5x - 2y = 10$$
$$3x + 6y = ?$$

a. -6   b. 6   **c. -102**   d. 102

**The correct answer is C.**
You have to solve for both x and y to answer the question.
First subtract $5x - 2y = 10$ from $8x - 2y = -2$.
$3x = -12$.  $x = -4$.  Now plug in x to one of the equations and solve for y.  $y = -15$.
$$3(-4) + 6(-15) = -12 - 90 = -102$$

# 7.

$8x - 5y = 4$
$5y + 3x = 7$
$4x + 5y = ?$

a. -7   b. 7   c. -8   d. 8

# 8.

$3x + 2y = 5$
$6x + 3y = 20$
$6x + 5y = ?$

a. 11   b. 25   c. -25   d. 0

# 9.

$7x - 4y = -7$
$9x - 5y = 7$
$3x + 6y = ?$

a. 861   b. 9   c. 348   d. 927

# 7.

$$8x - 5y = 4$$
$$5y + 3x = 7$$
$$4x + 5y = ?$$

a. -7   b. 7   c. -8   **d. 8**

**The correct answer is D.**
First add $8x - 5y = 4$ to $5y + 3x = 7$.
$11x = 11$. $x = 1$. Then plug this answer into one of the equations and solve for y. $y = 4/5$.
$4(1) + 5(4/5) = 4 + 4 = 8$.

# 8.

$$3x + 2y = 5$$
$$6x + 3y = 20$$
$$6x + 5y = ?$$

a. 11   b. 25   c. -25   **d. 0**

**The correct answer is D.**
First multiply $3x + 2y = 5$ by 2, then subtract it from $6x + 3y = 20$.
$(6x + 3y) - (6x + 4y) = 20 - 10$. $-y = 10$. $y = -10$. Then plug this answer into one of the equations and solve for x. $x = 25/3$.
$6(25/3) + 5(-10) = 50 - 50 = 0$

# 9.

$$7x - 4y = -7$$
$$9x - 5y = 7$$
$$3x + 6y = ?$$

**a. 861**   b. 9   c. 348   d. 927

**The correct answer is A.**
First multiply $7x - 4y = -7$ by 5, and $9x - 5y = 7$ by 4. Then subtract one from another.
$(35x - 20y) - (36x - 20y) = -35 - 28$. $-x = -63$. $x = 63$. Then plug in this answer into one of the equations and solve for y. $y = 112$.
$3(63) + 6(112) = 861$

# Lesson 22 - Systems of Equations

# 10.

x - y = 3
2x + 4y = 18
5x + 9y = ?

a. -42   b. 43   c. 17   d. 59

# 11.

Two trains are traveling at different constant speeds. When train A travels 3 hours, and train B travels 2 hours, together they cover a distance of 300 miles. When train A travels 4 hours, and train B travels 4 hours, they cover a distance of 400 miles. What is the speed of train A, rounded to the nearest mile per hour?

a. 150 mph   b. 104 mph   c. 75 mph   d. 100 mph

# 12.

Two trains are traveling at different constant speeds. When train A travels 3 hours, and train B travels 2 hours, together they cover a distance of 200 miles. When train A travels 1 hour, and train B travels 4 hours, they cover a distance of 300 miles. What is the speed of train B, rounded to the nearest mile per hour?

a. 80   b. 70   c. 56   d. 72

## 10.

$$x - y = 3$$
$$2x + 4y = 18$$
$$5x + 9y = ?$$

a. -42    **b. 43**    c. 17    d. 59

**The correct answer is B.**
Multiply $x - y = 3$ by 2 and subtract that from $2x + 4y = 18$.
$(2x + 4y) - (2x - 2y) = 18 - 6$.  $6y = 12$.  $y = 2$.  Then plug in the answer into one of the equations and solve for x.  $x = 5$.
$5(5) + 9(2) = 25 + 18 = 43$

## 11.

Two trains are traveling at different constant speeds. When train A travels 3 hours, and train B travels 2 hours, together they cover a distance of 300 miles. When train A travels 4 hours, and train B travels 4 hours, they cover a distance of 400 miles. What is the speed of train A, rounded to the nearest mile per hour?

a. 150 mph    b. 104 mph    c. 75 mph    **d. 100 mph**

**The correct answer is D.**
Convert this into two double variable equations. Let x = the speed of train A and y = the speed of train B.
$3x + 2y = 300$    |    $4x + 4y = 400$.  Now solve for x.  $x = 100$.

## 12.

Two trains are traveling at different constant speeds. When train A travels 3 hours, and train B travels 2 hours, together they cover a distance of 200 miles. When train A travels 1 hour, and train B travels 4 hours, they cover a distance of 300 miles. What is the speed of train B, rounded to the nearest mile per hour?

a. 80    **b. 70**    c. 56    d. 72

**The correct answer is B.**
Convert this into two double variable equations. Let x = the speed of train A and y = the speed of train B.
$3x + 2y = 200$    |    $1x + 4y = 300$.  Now solve for y.  $y = 70$.

# Lesson 22 - Systems of Equations

## 13.

Two trains are traveling at different constant speeds. When train A travels 5 hours, and train B travels 2 hours, together they cover a distance of 450 miles. When train A travels 2 hours, and train B travels 2 hours, they cover a distance of 250 miles. What is the speed of train B, rounded to the nearest mile per hour?

a. 58 mph   b. 55 mph   c. 65 mph   d. 63 mph

## 14.

Two trains are traveling at different constant speeds. When train A travels 3 hours, and train B travels 2 hours, together they cover a distance of 200 miles. When train A travels 1 hour, and train B travels 4 hours, they cover a distance of 300 miles. How far would they travel if they both traveled for five hours, rounded to the nearest mile?

a. 500   b. 400   c. 450   d. 350

## 15.

Two trains are traveling at different constant speeds. When train A travels 2 hours, and train B travels 4 hours, together they cover a distance of 100 miles. When train A travels 1 hour, and train B travels 3 hours, they cover a distance of 60 miles. How far would they travel if they both traveled for six hours, rounded to the nearest mile?

a. 253   b. 180   c. 240   d. 300

# 13.

Two trains are traveling at different constant speeds. When train A travels 5 hours, and train B travels 2 hours, together they cover a distance of 450 miles. When train A travels 2 hours, and train B travels 2 hours, they cover a distance of 250 miles. What is the speed of train B, rounded to the nearest mile per hour?

**a. 58 mph**  b. 55 mph  c. 65 mph  d. 63 mph

**The correct answer is A.**
Convert this into two double variable equations. Let x = the speed of train A and y = the speed of train B.
5x + 2y = 450  |  2x + 2y = 250. Now solve for y. y = 350/6 ≈ 58

# 14.

Two trains are traveling at different constant speeds. When train A travels 3 hours, and train B travels 2 hours, together they cover a distance of 200 miles. When train A travels 1 hour, and train B travels 4 hours, they cover a distance of 300 miles. How far would they travel if they both traveled for five hours, rounded to the nearest mile?

a. 500  b. 400  **c. 450**  d. 350

**The correct answer is C.**
Convert this into two double variable equations. Let x = speed of train A and y = speed of train B.
3x + 2y = 200  |  1x + 4y = 300. Solve for x & y, then plug these values in for 5x + 5y.
x = 20. y = 70. 5x + 5y = 5(20) + 5(70) = 450

# 15.

Two trains are traveling at different constant speeds. When train A travels 2 hours, and train B travels 4 hours, together they cover a distance of 100 miles. When train A travels 1 hour, and train B travels 3 hours, they cover a distance of 60 miles. How far would they travel if they both traveled for six hours, rounded to the nearest mile?

a. 253  b. 180  **c. 240**  d. 300

**The correct answer is C.**
Convert this into two double variable equations. Let x = speed of train A and y = speed of train B.
2x + 4y = 100  |  1x + 3y = 60. Solve for x & y, then plug these values in for 6x + 6y.
x = 30. y = 10. 6x + 6y = 6(30) + 6(10) = 240

## Lesson 23
# Review of Lessons 1-10

You've come a long way. Now we'll review the material you covered in the first half of the book, in Lessons 1 - 10, including division, multiplication, algebra, combinations, and probability.

Remember to go back to the corresponding lesson and re-do it if you miss a question here. It's important that you have mastered every concept we've covered here. There are still 3 more math levels to cover in order to achieve a complete mastery of the ACT Math section. If you neglect anything in this workbook that you don't understand, it's only going to make it harder to grasp what we'll be covering in the next workbook!

# 1.

There are 6 pieces of paper in a hat, numbered one through 6. Jeff pulls 1 piece of paper at a time out of the hat and writes down the number he drew. If each time he draws the piece of paper he leaves it outside of the hat, how many different combinations of numbers can he write if he draws a total of 3 times?

a. 80   b. 1200   c. 60   d. 120

# 2.

If 8x + 1 = 2x + 25, then x = ?

a. -4   b. 4   c. 2   d. -2

# 3.

Jim can travel 30 miles on one gallon of gas. His gas tank holds 16 gallons of gas. What is the furthest distance (in miles) he can travel without needing to refuel?

a. 480 mi
b. 240 mi
c. 46 mi
d. 960 mi

# 1.

There are 6 pieces of paper in a hat, numbered one through 6. Jeff pulls 1 piece of paper at a time out of the hat and writes down the number he drew. If each time he draws the piece of paper he leaves it outside of the hat, how many different combinations of numbers can he write if he draws a total of 3 times?

a. 80   b. 1200   c. 60   **d. 120**

**The correct answer is D.**
Jeff can write 6 x 5 x 4 = 120 different combinations of numbers. The first draw, there are 6 different possibilities. The second draw, there are only 5 possibilities (one piece of paper is left out). The third draw, there are only 4 possibilities. 6 x 5 x 4 = 120. Missed this question? Review Lesson 3.

# 2.

If $8x + 1 = 2x + 25$, then $x = ?$

a. -4   **b. 4**   c. 2   d. -2

**The correct answer is B.**
Subtract 2x from both sides.
$6x + 1 = 25$
Subtract 1 from both sides
$6x = 24$
Divide both sides by 6
$x = 4$. Missed this question? Review Lesson 8.

# 3.

Jim can travel 30 miles on one gallon of gas. His gas tank holds 16 gallons of gas. What is the furthest distance (in miles) he can travel without needing to refuel?

**a. 480 mi**
b. 240 mi
c. 46 mi
d. 960 mi

**The correct answer is A.**
Jim can travel 30 miles per gallon x 16 gallons = 480 mi. 30 x 16 = 480
Missed this question? Review Lesson 7.

## 4.

If -4x + 2 = 7x − 31, then x = ?

a. -3   b. 3   c. 1/3   d. -1/3

## 5.

Damien did an internship in the accounting department of a large corporation. He was asked to do a little math for them. The company earned a yearly profit of $8.0 million dollars for three years. For the next two years, the company earned $10 million each year. What was the average profit earned by the company in this five-year period?

a. $44 million   b. $8.2 million   c. $8.8 million   d. $7.8 million

## 6.

If 3x +2 = 4x + 7, then x = ?

a. -5   b. 5   c. -1   d. 1

## 4.

If -4x + 2 = 7x − 31, then x = ?

a. -3   **b. 3**   c. 1/3   d. -1/3

**The correct answer is B.**
Add 4x to both sides.
2 = 11x - 31
Add 31 to both sides.
33 = 11x
Divide both sides by 11.
x = 3.  Missed this question?  Review Lesson 8.

## 5.

Damien did an internship in the accounting department of a large corporation.  He was asked to do a little math for them.  The company earned a yearly profit of $8.0 million dollars for three years.  For the next two years, the company earned $10 million each year.  What was the average profit earned by the company in this five-year period?

a. $44 million   b. $8.2 million   **c. $8.8 million**   d. $7.8 million

**The correct answer is C.**
$8.0 million per x 3 years = $24 million.  $10 million per year x 2 years = $20 million.  The total amount of profit in five years is $24 million + $20 million = $44 million.  The average profit per year is $44 million divided into 5 years = $8.8 million.
Missed this question?  Review Lesson 2.

## 6.

If 3x +2 = 4x + 7, then x = ?

**a. -5**   b. 5   c. -1   d. 1

**The correct answer is A.**
Subtract 3x from both sides.
2 = x + 7
Subtract 7 from both sides.
x = -5
Missed this question?  Review Lesson 8.

# Lesson 23 - Review of Lessons 1-10

# 7.

How many miles has a car driving 70 miles per hour traveled after 135 minutes?

a. 157.5   b. 60   c. 40   d. 145.5

# 8.

How far has a car driving 40 miles per hour traveled after three and a half hours?

a. 100
b. 140
c. 120
d. 180

# 9.

$(5x - 5)^2 = ?$

a. $25x^2 - 50x - 25$
b. $-25x^2 + 50x - 25$
c. $25x^2 - 50x + 25$
d. $-25x^2 - 50x + 25$

# 7.

How many miles has a car driving 70 miles per hour traveled after 135 minutes?

a. **157.5**   b. 60   c. 40   d. 145.5

**The correct answer is A.**
To solve this problem, first you have to convert 135 minutes into hours. 135 minutes / 60 minutes per hour = 2.25 hours. 70 miles per hour x 2.25 hours = 157.5 miles. Before you multiply in these types of problems, you have to make sure the units of measure match up. You can't multiply hours and minutes together. Missed this question? Review Lesson 7.

# 8.

How far has a car driving 40 miles per hour traveled after three and a half hours?

a. 100
**b. 140**
c. 120
d. 180

**The correct answer is B.**
40 miles per hour x 3.5 hours = 140 miles. 40 x 3.5 = 140
Missed this question? Review Lesson 7.

# 9.

$(5x - 5)^2 = ?$

a. $25x^2 - 50x - 25$
b. $-25x^2 + 50x - 25$
**c. $25x^2 - 50x + 25$**
d. $-25x^2 - 50x + 25$

**The correct answer is C.**
$(5x - 5)^2 = (5x - 5)(5x - 5)$
FIRST: $5x * 5x = 25x^2$. OUTER: $5x * -5 = -25x$. INNER: $5x * -5 = -25x$. LAST: $-5 * -5 = 25$.
$25x^2 - 25x - 25x + 25 = 25x^2 - 50x + 25$. Missed this question? Review Lesson 9.

# Lesson 23 - Review of Lessons 1-10

## 10.

John went to the store and purchased nine shirts at the following prices: $9.00, $4.00, $12.00, $18.00, $36.00, $39.00, $41.00, $43.00, and $50.00.  What was the average price of the nine shirts?

- a. $24.55
- b. $30.00
- c. $28.00
- d. None of the above

## 11.

A gasoline truck can hold 950 gallons of gasoline.  Each gallon of gasoline weighs approximately 7 pounds.  About how many pounds of gasoline can a gasoline truck hold?

- a. 7650
- b. 6650
- c. 957
- d. 136

## 12.

If $41x - 1 = x - 81$, then $x = $ ?

a. 2   b. -2   c. 5   d. -5

# 10.

John went to the store and purchased nine shirts at the following prices: $9.00, $4.00, $12.00, $18.00, $36.00, $39.00, $41.00, $43.00, and $50.00. What was the average price of the nine shirts?

a. $24.55
b. $30.00
**c. $28.00**
d. None of the above

**The correct answer is C.**
The total price of the nine shirts is $9 + $4 + $12 + $18 + $36 + $39 + $41 + $43 + $50 = $252. The average price of each shirt is $252 divided by 9 shirts = $28. Missed this question? Review Lesson 2.

# 11.

A gasoline truck can hold 950 gallons of gasoline. Each gallon of gasoline weighs approximately 7 pounds. About how many pounds of gasoline can a gasoline truck hold?

a. 7650
**b. 6650**
c. 957
d. 136

**The correct answer is B.**
950 gallons x 7 pounds per gallon = 6650 pounds. 950 x 7 = 6650
Missed this question? Review Lesson 7.

# 12.

If $41x - 1 = x - 81$, then $x = ?$

a. 2   **b. -2**   c. 5   d. -5

**The correct answer is B.**
Subtract x from both sides.
$40x - 1 = -81$
Add 1 to both sides.
$40x = -80$
Divide both sides by 40.
$x = -2$. Missed this question? Review Lesson 8.

# 13.

Ellen is trying to pick out a dress, but she can't decide. Her friends finally tell her that they are going to play a game. They have numbered the dresses one through five. She has to pick a number, and that's the dress they'll buy her. One dress is red, two are green, one is blue, and one is pink. What are the odds that she will pick something else besides a red dress?

a. 2:3   b. 4:1   c. 1:4   d. 3:2

# 14.

Dominique and Jared own a sandwich shop. They offer 6 kinds of bread, 8 kinds of meat, and 5 kinds of cheese. Each type of sandwich on their menu has a combination of 1 bread, 1 meat, and 1 cheese. A "Value Deal" consists of one sandwich and one drink. There are 8 drink options. How many different "Value Deal" combinations are possible?

a. 1320   b. 1780   c. 1920   d. 3840

# 15.

$2x^2 + 10x + 8 = 0$, $x = ?$

a. -1 or -4
b. 1 or 4
c. 1 or -4
d. -1 or 4

## 13.

Ellen is trying to pick out a dress, but she can't decide. Her friends finally tell her that they are going to play a game. They have numbered the dresses one through five. She has to pick a number, and that's the dress they'll buy her. One dress is red, two are green, one is blue, and one is pink. What are the odds that she will pick something else besides a red dress?

a. 2:3  **b. 4:1**  c. 1:4  d. 3:2

### The correct answer is B.
The odds that she will pick something besides a red dress are 4 desired outcomes vs. 1 undesired outcome = 4:1. Missed this question? Review Lesson 3.

## 14.

Dominique and Jared own a sandwich shop. They offer 6 kinds of bread, 8 kinds of meat, and 5 kinds of cheese. Each type of sandwich on their menu has a combination of 1 bread, 1 meat, and 1 cheese. A "Value Deal" consists of one sandwich and one drink. There are 8 drink options. How many different "Value Deal" combinations are possible?

a. 1320  b. 1780  **c. 1920**  d. 3840

### The correct answer is C.
There are 6 breads x 8 meats x 5 cheeses x 8 drinks = 1920 combinations.
6 x 8 x 5 x 8 = 1920. Use your calculator for problems like this.
Missed this question? Review Lesson 4.

## 15.

$2x^2 + 10x + 8 = 0$, $x = ?$

**a. -1 or -4**
b. 1 or 4
c. 1 or -4
d. -1 or 4

### The correct answer is A.
We know that FIRST = $2x^2$, OUTER + INNER = $10x$, and LAST = 8. Through trial and error, we find that $(2x + 2)(x + 4)$.
$x = -1$ or $-4$. Missed this question? Review Lesson 9.

# Lesson 24
# Review of Lessons 11-20

You're almost there! This is the second-to-last lesson. This chapter reviews everything you've covered from Lessons 11 - 20. If you miss any question, be sure to go back to the corresponding lesson and go over it again.

# Lesson 24 - Review of Lessons 11-20

## 1.

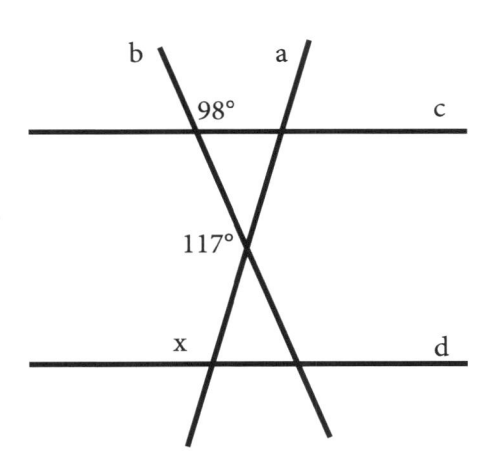

Lines c and d are parallel. Angle x = ?

**a. 145°**   b. 90°   c. 115°   d. 80°

## 2.

Joe started the day with a tank of gas 3/5 full. Each hour, he burned two gallons of gas. After driving for five hours, Joe's tank was empty. How many gallons of gas can his tank hold when it's full, rounded to the nearest gallon?

a. 16   b. 17   c. 12   d. 8

## 3.

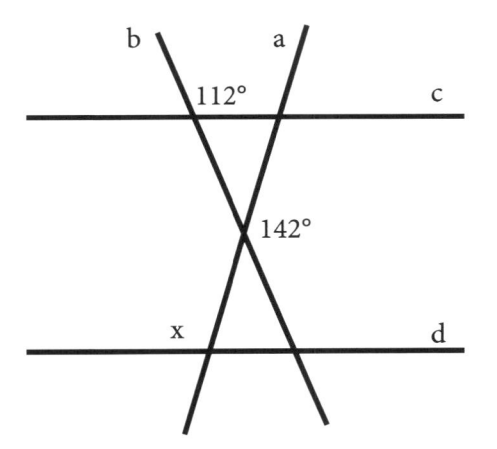

Lines c and d are parallel. Angle x = ?

a. 34°   b. 100°   c. 124°   d. 106°

## 1.

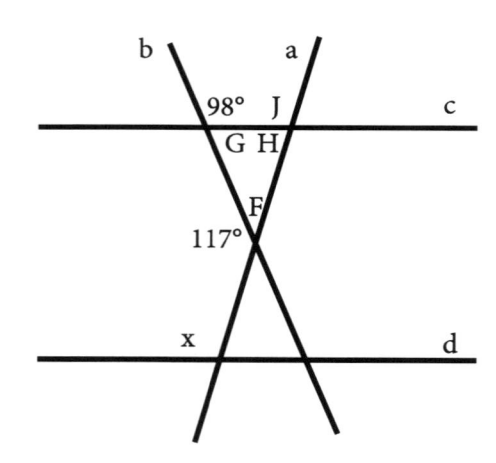

Lines c and d are parallel. Angle x = ?

**a. 145°**  b. 90°  c. 115°  d. 80°

**The correct answer is A.**
Angle F = 180 - 117 = 63°. Angle G = 180 - 98 = 82°. Angle H = 180 - 63 - 82 = 35°. Angle J = 180 - 35 = 145°. Therefore, x = 145° because the angles created by the intersection of lines a and c are identical to the angles created by the intersection of lines a and d because c and d are parallel.
Missed this question?  Review Lesson 14.

## 2.

Joe started the day with a tank of gas 3/5 full.  Each hour, he burned two gallons of gas.  After driving for five hours, Joe's tank was empty.  How many gallons of gas can his tank hold when it's full, rounded to the nearest gallon?

a. 16  **b. 17**  c. 12  d. 8

**The correct answer is B.**
We know that Joe burned 2 gallons per hour * 5 hours = 10 gallons of gas. 10 gallons of gas = 3/5 of a tank. We can solve this as a proportion or as an algebra problem. 10 = (3/5)x. Multiply both sides by 5/3. x = 50/3. x ≈ 17.
Missed this question?  Review Lesson 19.

## 3.

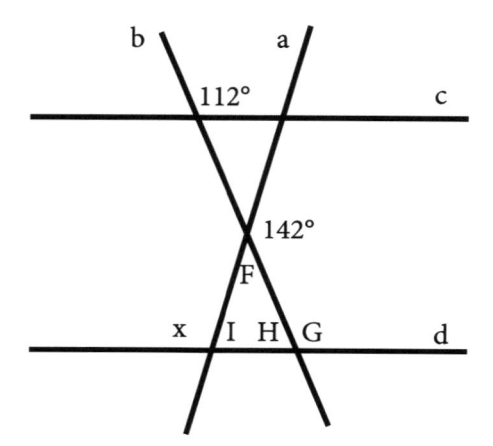

Lines c and d are parallel. Angle x = ?

a. 34°  b. 100°  c. 124°  **d. 106°**

**The correct answer is D.**
The angle we've labeled F = 180 - 142 = 38°. The angle we've labeled G = 112° because it is identical to the angle created by the intersection of lines b and c. Angle H = 180 - 112 = 68°. Therefore angle I = 180 - 38 - 68 = 74°. Therefore angle x = 180 - 74 = 106°.
Missed this question?  Review Lesson 14.

# 4.

What is the next number in the pattern? 5, 10, 20, 40, …?

       a. 1/40
       b. 40
       c. 80
       d. 60

# 5.

Joe started the day with a full tank of gas. Each hour, he burned four gallons of gas. After driving for two hours, Joe had four gallons of gas left. How many gallons of gas did he start with?

       a. 14   b. 8   c. 10   d. 12

# 6.

What is the next number in the pattern? 12, 6, 3, 3/2 … ?

       a. -3/2
       b. 1
       c. 3/4
       d. 2/3

# 4.

What is the next number in the pattern? 5, 10, 20, 40, …?

    a. 1/40
    b. 40
    **c. 80**
    d. 60

**The correct answer is C.**
Each term is being multiplied by 2. 5 * 2 = 10. 10 * 2 = 20. 20 * 2 = 40. To find the next number in the pattern, we apply the rule to the last term. 40 * 2 = 80.
Missed this question? Review Lesson 12.

# 5.

Joe started the day with a full tank of gas. Each hour, he burned four gallons of gas. After driving for two hours, Joe had four gallons of gas left. How many gallons of gas did he start with?

    a. 14  b. 8  c. 10  **d. 12**

**The correct answer is D.**
We know that Joe burned 4 gallons of gas per hour * 2 hours = 8 gallons of gas. He was left with 4 gallons of gas + 8 gallons burned = 12 gallons started with.
Missed this question? Review Lesson 11.

# 6.

What is the next number in the pattern? 12, 6, 3, 3/2 … ?

    a. -3/2
    b. 1
    **c. 3/4**
    d. 2/3

**The correct answer is C.**
Each term in the pattern is being divided by 2. 12 / 2 = 6. 6 / 2 = 3. 3 / 2 = 3/2. To figure out the next number in the pattern, we apply the rule: (3/2) / 2 = 3/4
Missed this question? Review Lesson 12.

## 7.

George is planning to tile a rectangular kitchen countertop that is 20 inches wide and 40 inches long. He figured out the he will need one tile for each 4 inch by 4 inch region. What is the minimum number of tiles needed to completely cover the countertop to its edges?

a. 25   b. 50   c. 75   d. 100

## 8.

Length x = ?
Round your answer to the nearest tenth.

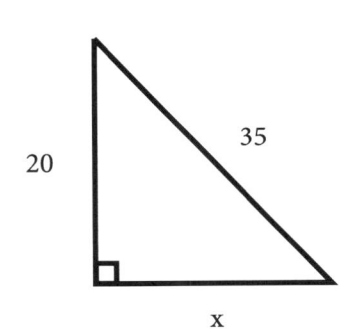

a. 28.7   b. 30.5   c. 28.2   d. 29.5

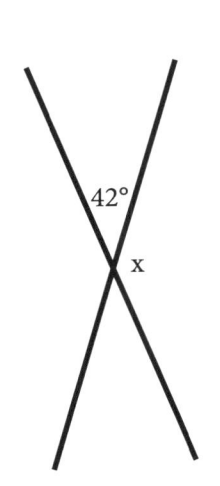

## 9.

Angle x = ?

a. 48°   b. 113°   c. 123°   d. 138°

# 7.

George is planning to tile a rectangular kitchen countertop that is 20 inches wide and 40 inches long. He figured out the he will need one tile for each 4 inch by 4 inch region. What is the minimum number of tiles needed to completely cover the countertop to its edges?

a. 25   **b. 50**   c. 75   d. 100

**The correct answer is B.**
First we have to figure out the area of the countertop. 20 inches * 40 inches = 800 in²
Each tile is 4 inches * 4 inches = 16 in².
George needs 800 in² / 16 in² = 50 tiles.
Missed this question? Review Lesson 17.

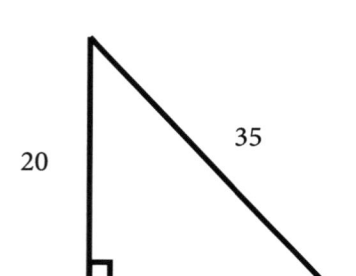

# 8.

Length x = ?
Round your answer to the nearest tenth.

**a. 28.7**   b. 30.5   c. 28.2   d. 29.5

**The correct answer is A.**
$20^2 + x^2 = 35^2$
$400 + x^2 = 1225$
$x^2 = 1225 - 400 = 825$
$x = \sqrt{825} \approx 28.7$
Missed this question? Review Lesson 16.

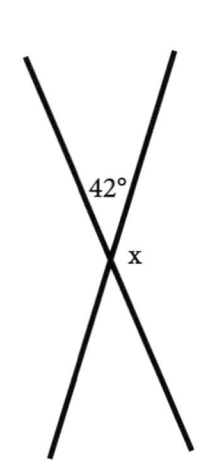

# 9.

Angle x = ?

a. 48°   b. 113°   c. 123°   **d. 138°**

**The correct answer is D.**
The angles on any one side of a line add up to 180°.
x = 180 - 42 = 138°
Missed this question? Review Lesson 14.

Lesson 24 - Review of Lessons 11-20

# 10.

What is the y intercept of the line 6x - 6y = -12?

a. -2   b. 2   c. 3   d. -3

# 11.

Sales for a business were 6 million dollars more the second year than the first, and sales for the third year were triple the sales for the second year. If sales for the third year were 30 million dollars, what were the sales, in millions of dollars, of the first year?

a. 36 million   b. 8 million   c. 4 million   d. 10 million

# 12.

Length x = ?  (Round your answer to the nearest tenth.)

a. 4.6   b. 4.2   c. 3   d. 3.9

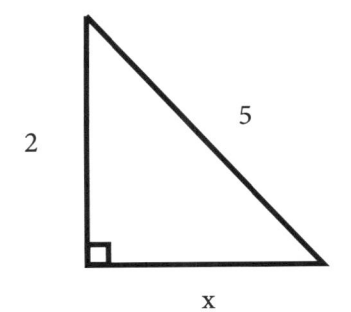

## 10.

What is the y intercept of the line 6x - 6y = -12?

a. -2   **b. 2**   c. 3   d. -3

**The correct answer is B.**
-6y = -6x - 12
y = x + 2
The y intercept is 2
Missed this question?  Review Lesson 18.

## 11.

Sales for a business were 6 million dollars more the second year than the first, and sales for the third year were triple the sales for the second year.  If sales for the third year were 30 million dollars, what were the sales, in millions of dollars, of the first year?

a. 36 million   b. 8 million   **c. 4 million**   d. 10 million

**The correct answer is C.**
Working backwards from year 3: 30 million divided by 3 = 10 million in year 2.  10 million - 6 million = 4 million in year 1.
Missed this question?  Review Lesson 11.

## 12.

Length x = ?  (Round your answer to the nearest tenth.)

**a. 4.6**   b. 4.2   c. 3   d. 3.9

**The correct answer is A.**
$2^2 + x^2 = 5^2$
$4 + x^2 = 25$
$x^2 = 25 - 4 = 21$
$x = \sqrt{21} \approx 4.6$
Missed this question?  Review Lesson 16.

# 13.

George is planning to tile a rectangular kitchen countertop that is 21 inches wide and 21 inches long. He figured out that he will need one tile for each 3 inch by 3 inch region. What is the minimum number of tiles needed to completely cover the countertop to its edges?

a. 63   b. 42   c. 49   d. 37

# 14.

A circle has a radius of 3 centimeters. What is its perimeter?

a. $9\pi$ cm
b. $4\pi$ cm
c. $6\pi$ cm
d. $(1/3)\pi$ cm

# 15.

Which of the following statements is true about the arithmetic sequence 3, 5, 7, 9, …?

a. The numbers are being increased by 4 each time.
b. The fifth term is 11.
c. The fifth term is 10.
d. The fourth term is 7.

# 13.

George is planning to tile a rectangular kitchen countertop that is 21 inches wide and 21 inches long. He figured out that he will need one tile for each 3 inch by 3 inch region. What is the minimum number of tiles needed to completely cover the countertop to its edges?

a. 63   b. 42   **c. 49**   d. 37

**The correct answer is C.**
First we have to figure out the area of the countertop. 21 inches * 21 inches = 441 in².
Each tile is 3 inches * 3 inches = 9 in².
George needs 441 in² / 9 in² = 49 tiles.
Missed this question? Review Lesson 17.

# 14.

A circle has a radius of 3 centimeters. What is its perimeter?

a. 9π cm
b. 4π cm
**c. 6π cm**
d. (1/3)π cm

**The correct answer is C.**
The formula for the perimeter of a circle is 2πr. The radius of this circle is 3 cm, so the perimeter is 2 * π * 3 = 6π cm
Missed this question? Review Lesson 13.

# 15.

Which of the following statements is true about the arithmetic sequence 3, 5, 7, 9, …?

a. The numbers are being increased by 4 each time.
**b. The fifth term is 11.**
c. The fifth term is 10.
d. The fourth term is 7.

**The correct answer is B.**
The term is being increased by 2 each time. The change between 3 and 5 is +2. The change between 5 and 7 is +2. This is the pattern. 9 + 2 = 11.
Missed this question? Review Lesson 12.

## Lesson 25
# Final Review

This is the last lesson in Math Mastery Level 1. Congratulations on getting this far!

Everything that we've covered in this book is fair game in this review.

Be sure to go back to the lesson you are directed to if you miss a question, and answer the questions in the lesson again.

Only by correctly answering problems like these over and over again will you be able to master the ACT Math section.

## Lesson 25 - Final Review

# 1.

$$2x - y = 3$$
$$2x + 4y = 18$$
$$6x + 9y = ?$$

a. -45   b. 45   c. 15   d. -15

# 2.

Two trains are traveling at different constant speeds. When train A travels 4 hours, and train B travels 3 hours, together they cover a distance of 200 miles. When train A travels 4 hours, and train B travels 2 hours, they cover a distance of 160 miles. What is the speed of train B, rounded to the nearest mile per hour?

a. 60   b. 40   c. 50   d. 45.5

# 3.

What is the slope of any line parallel to the line $x + 3y = -5$?

a. -6   b. 6   c. 1/3   d. -1/3

295

# Math Mastery - Level 1

# 1.

$$2x - y = 3$$
$$2x + 4y = 18$$
$$6x + 9y = ?$$

a. -45   **b. 45**   c. 15   d. -15

**The correct answer is B.**
Subtract $2x - y = 3$ from $2x + 4y = 18$
$(2x - y) - (2x + 4y) = 3 - 18$. $-5y = -15$. $y = 3$. Then plug in the answer into one of the equations and solve for x. $x = 3$.
$6(3) + 9(3) = 18 + 27 = 45$. Missed this question? Review Lesson 22.

# 2.

Two trains are traveling at different constant speeds. When train A travels 4 hours, and train B travels 3 hours, together they cover a distance of 200 miles. When train A travels 4 hours, and train B travels 2 hours, they cover a distance of 160 miles. What is the speed of train B, rounded to the nearest mile per hour?

a. 60   **b. 40**   c. 50   d. 45.5

**The correct answer is B.**
Convert this into two double variable equations. Let x = the speed of train A and y = the speed of train B.
$4x + 3y = 200$  |  $4x + 2y = 160$. Now solve for y. $y = 40$. Missed this question? Review Lesson 22.

# 3.

What is the slope of any line parallel to the line $x + 3y = -5$?

a. -6   b. 6   c. 1/3   **d. -1/3**

**The correct answer is D.**
Convert this equation into slope-intercept form ($y = mx + b$).
$$3y = -x - 5$$
$$y = (-1/3)x - 5/3$$
The slope $= -1/3$
Missed this question? Review Lesson 21.

# 4.

What is the slope of the line passing through the points (-3, 7) and (11, 0)?

a. 1/2   b. -1/2   c. 2   d. -2

# 5.

What is the next number in the pattern? 20, 10, 5, 5/2 ... ?

a. -5/4
b. 1
c. 5/4
d. 4/5

# 6.

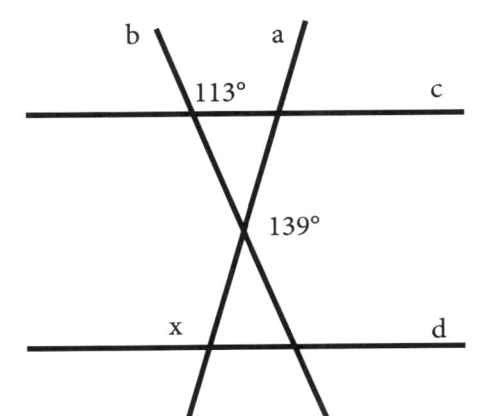

Lines c and d are parallel. Angle x = ?

a. 41°   b. 100°   c. 114°   d. 108°

# 4.

What is the slope of the line passing through the points (-3, 7) and (11, 0)?

a. 1/2    **b. -1/2**    c. 2    d. -2

**The correct answer is B.**
Use the slope formula.
(0 - 7) / (11 - (-3)) = -7 / 14 = -1/2
Missed this question? Review Lesson 21.

# 5.

What is the next number in the pattern? 20, 10, 5, 5/2 ... ?

a. -5/4
b. 1
**c. 5/4**
d. 4/5

**The correct answer is C.**
Each term in the pattern is being divided by 2. 20 / 2 = 10. 10 / 2 = 5. 5 / 2 = 5/2. To figure out the next number in the pattern, we apply the rule: (5/2) / 2 = 5/4
Missed this question? Review Lesson 12.

# 6.

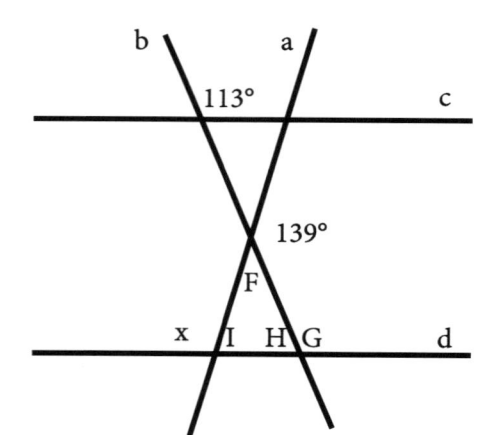

Lines c and d are parallel. Angle x = ?

a. 41°    b. 100°    c. 114°    **d. 108°**

**The correct answer is D.**
The angle we've labeled F = 180 - 139 = 41°. The angle we've labeled G = 113° because it is identical to the angle created by the intersection of lines b and c. Angle H = 180 - 113 = 67°. Therefore angle I = 180 - 41 - 67 = 72°. Therefore angle x = 180 - 72 = 108°.
Missed this question? Review Lesson 14.

# 7.

What is the next number in the pattern? 3, 6, 12, 24, ...?

      a. 25
      b. 32
      c. 48
      d. 96

# 8.

Joe started the day with a tank of gas 1/5 full. Each hour, he burned two gallons of gas. After driving for two hours, Joe's tank was empty. How many gallons of gas can his tank hold when it's full?

    a. 16   b. 20   c. 12   d. 8

# 9.

Ellen is planning to put in a new tile floor. Each tile is 6 inches by 6 inches. The area is 12 feet wide by 11 feet long. What is the minimum number of tiles needed to completely cover the area?

    a. 820   b. 132   c. 264   d. 528

# 7.

What is the next number in the pattern? 3, 6, 12, 24, …?

> a. 25
> b. 32
> **c. 48**
> d. 96

**The correct answer is C.**
Each term is being multiplied by 2.  3 * 2 = 6.  6 * 2 = 12.  12 * 2 = 24.  To find the next number in the pattern, we apply the rule to the last term.  24 * 2 = 48.
Missed this question?  Review Lesson 12.

# 8.

Joe started the day with a tank of gas 1/5 full.  Each hour, he burned two gallons of gas.  After driving for two hours, Joe's tank was empty.  How many gallons of gas can his tank hold when it's full?

> a. 16   **b. 20**   c. 12   d. 8

**The correct answer is B.**
We know that Joe burned 2 gallons per hour * 2 hours = 4 gallons of gas.  4 gallons of gas = 1/5 of a tank.  We can solve this as a proportion or as an algebra problem.  4 = (1/5)x.  Multiply both sides by 5.  x = 20.
Missed this question?  Review Lesson 19.

# 9.

Ellen is planning to put in a new tile floor.  Each tile is 6 inches by 6 inches.  The area is 12 feet wide by 11 feet long.  What is the minimum number of tiles needed to completely cover the area?

> a. 820   b. 132   c. 264   **d. 528**

**The correct answer is D.**
First we have to convert the measure of the tile from inches to feet.  12 in = 1 ft, so each tile measures 6 / 12 = .5 feet on each side.  The area of the tile is .5 ft * .5 ft = .25 ft².  The area of the floor is 12 ft * 11 ft = 132 ft².
Ellen needs 132 ft² / .25 ft² = 528 tiles.
Missed this question?  Review Lesson 17.

# Lesson 25 - Final Review

## 10.

John went to the store and purchased nine shirts at the following prices: $9.00, $13.00, $21.00, $27.00, $36.00, $39.00, $41.00, $43.00, and $50.00.  What was the average price of the nine shirts?

a. $279.00
b. $33.00
c. $31.00
d. None of the above

## 11.

A gasoline truck can hold 1150 gallons of gasoline.  Each gallon of gasoline weighs approximately 7.5 pounds.  About how many pounds of gasoline can a gasoline truck hold?

a. 7650
b. 8625
c. 657.5
d. 1157.5

## 12.

If $21x - 1 = x - 81$, then $x = ?$

a. 4   b. -4   c. 5   d. -5

Math Mastery - Level 1

# 10.

John went to the store and purchased nine shirts at the following prices: $9.00, $13.00, $21.00, $27.00, $36.00, $39.00, $41.00, $43.00, and $50.00. What was the average price of the nine shirts?

a. $279.00
b. $33.00
**c. $31.00**
d. None of the above

**The correct answer is C.**
The total price of the nine shirts is $9 + $13 + $21 + $27 + $36 + $39 + $41 + $43 + $50 = $279. The average price of each shirt is $279 divided by 9 shirts = $31. Missed this question? Review Lesson 2.

# 11.

A gasoline truck can hold 1150 gallons of gasoline. Each gallon of gasoline weighs approximately 7.5 pounds. About how many pounds of gasoline can a gasoline truck hold?

a. 7650
**b. 8625**
c. 657.5
d. 1157.5

**The correct answer is B.**
1150 gallons x 7.5 pounds per gallon = 8625 pounds. 1150 x 7.5 = 8625
Missed this question? Review Lesson 7.

# 12.

If $21x - 1 = x - 81$, then $x = ?$

a. 4   **b. -4**   c. 5   d. -5

**The correct answer is B.**
Subtract x from both sides.
$20x - 1 = -81$
Add 1 to both sides.
$20x = -80$
Divide both sides by 20.
$x = -4$. Missed this question? Review Lesson 8.

# Lesson 25 - Final Review

# 13.

There are 7 pieces of paper in a hat, numbered 1 through 7. Jeff pulls 1 piece of paper at a time out of the hat and writes down the number he drew. If each time he draws the piece of paper he leaves it outside of the hat, how many different combinations of numbers can he write if he draws a total of 7 times?

a. 10080   b. 1260   c. 2520   d. 5040

# 14.

If $4x + 1 = 2x + 25$, then $x = ?$

a. -4   b. 4   c. 12   d. -12

# 15.

Jim can travel 40 miles on one gallon of gas. His gas tank holds 15 gallons of gas. What is the furthest distance (in miles) he can travel without needing to refuel?

a. 600 mi
b. 480 mi
c. 720 mi
d. 960 mi

# 13.

There are 7 pieces of paper in a hat, numbered 1 through 7. Jeff pulls 1 piece of paper at a time out of the hat and writes down the number he drew. If each time he draws the piece of paper he leaves it outside of the hat, how many different combinations of numbers can he write if he draws a total of 7 times?

a. 10080   b. 1260   c. 2520   **d. 5040**

**The correct answer is D.**
Jeff can write 7 x 6 x 5 x 4 x 3 x 2 x 1 = 5040 different combinations of numbers. The first draw, there are 7 different possibilities. The second draw, there are only 6 possibilities (one piece of paper is left out). The third draw, there are only 5 possibilities, and so on. Missed this question?  Review Lesson 3.

# 14.

If $4x + 1 = 2x + 25$, then $x = ?$

a. -4   b. 4   **c. 12**   d. -12

**The correct answer is C.**
Subtract 2x from both sides.
$2x + 1 = 25$
Subtract 1 from both sides
$2x = 24$
Divide both sides by 2
$x = 12$. Missed this question?  Review Lesson 8.

# 15.

Jim can travel 40 miles on one gallon of gas. His gas tank holds 15 gallons of gas. What is the furthest distance (in miles) he can travel without needing to refuel?

**a. 600 mi**
b. 480 mi
c. 720 mi
d. 960 mi

**The correct answer is A.**
Jim can travel 40 miles per gallon x 15 gallons = 600 mi.  40 x 15 = 600
Missed this question?  Review Lesson 7.

# Math Mini-Practice Tests

In the next series of lessons, you'll work through ten ACT Math mini-tests which will help you improve your speed and confidence on the ACT Math test. These sets of practice questions are designed to emulate the ACT in every way.

Unlike the other ACT test sections, the math test increases in difficulty from front to back, which means that the test questions gradually become more and more difficult. If you don't push to answer the front half of the test as quickly as possible, you might find that you don't have enough time to answer the last part of the math test.

We recommend two-part approach to pacing yourself:

Move through the first 30 questions in 20 minutes.

Since the ACT gives you 60 minutes to move through 60 math questions, that leaves you 40 minutes for the last 30 questions.

It's one thing to know that's the pace. It's quite another thing to do it. That's why we practice with these mini-tests. The first two mini-tests in this book will help you find the correct pace for the front half of the math test. The next three will help you pace yourself for the back half of the test. There are questions you can answer correctly in the back of the test. You just need to give yourself enough time to have a shot at them.

Time yourself 10 minutes for this mini-test. Actually use a timer and work to complete these 15 questions under the time limit. Just like a track runner never improves his pace until he gets out on the track and does laps, you can't improve your speed on the ACT Math test until you practice.

After you complete the mini-test, read the explanations to the questions. Even if you answered correctly, review the answer. This will help you improve your certainty with ACT Math questions, which can in turn boost your speed.

## Math Test
### 60 Minutes — 60 Questions

**Directions:** *Begin by working out each problem. Once solved, choose the correct answer then color its corresponding bubble on your answer sheet.*

*Do not waste time on difficult questions. Instead, leave them; by answering as many questions as possible first, you can use the leftover time to return to the others.*

*Calculators are allowed for any problems you choose, but some may be better solved without one.*

*Note: Unless stated otherwise, the following should be assumed:*

1. *Illustrative figures used in this test are not necessarily drawn to scale.*
2. *Geometric figures lie on an X,Y coordinate plane.*
3. *The word "line" indicates a straight line.*
4. *The word "average" indicates a calculated mean.*

---

1. If $5x + 2 = 7x - 7$, then $x = ?$

   A. 1/3
   B. 2/9
   C. 9/2
   D. 3/2
   E. 2/3

2. The expression $x[(y - w) + z]$ is equivalent to:

   F. $xy - xw + xz$
   G. $xy - w + z$
   H. $xy + xw + xz$
   J. $xy - xw - xz$
   K. $xy + w + z$

3. The toxicity level of a lake is found by dividing the amount of dissolved toxins the lake water currently has per liter by the maximum safe amount of dissolved toxins that the water can hold per liter, and then converting to a percent. If the river currently has .86 milligrams of dissolved toxins per liter of water, and the maximum safe amount of dissolved toxins is 1.04 milligrams per liter, what is the toxicity level of the lake water, to the nearest percent?

   A. 84%
   B. 79%
   C. 86%
   D. 83%
   E. 80%

4. A rectangular pasture that measures 250 ft by 300 ft is completely fenced around its borders. What is the approximate length, in feet, of the surrounding fence?

   F. 75,000
   G. 550
   H. 1,100
   J. 750
   K. 600

5. So far, Michael has earned the following scores on five 100-point tests this semester: 72, 94, 85, 83, 97. What score must he earn on the sixth 100-point test of the semester if he wants to make an 88 point average for the six tests?

   A. 88
   B. 100
   C. 97
   D. 85
   E. He cannot make an average of 88

Math Mini-Test 1

6. Which 2 numbers should be placed in the blanks below so that the difference between consecutive numbers is the same?

   19, __ , __ , 55

   F. 27, 50
   G. 31, 43
   H. 30, 48
   J. 34, 42
   K. 20, 53

7. Mrs. Cook is a teacher whose salary is $23,125 for this 185 day school year. In Mrs. Cook's school district substitute teachers are paid $90 per day. If a sub is paid to teach Mrs. Cook's class in her absence one day, how much less does the school district pay in salary by paying a substitute teacher instead of paying Mrs. Cook for that day?

   A. $215
   B. $90
   C. $125
   D. $45
   E. $35

8. If a marble is randomly chosen from a bag that contains exactly 6 purple marbles, 4 blue marbles, and 10 green marbles, what is the probability that the marble will NOT be green?

   F. 3/10
   G. 1/5
   H. 1/2
   J. 3/5
   K. 1/3

9. Zach has 3 pairs of shoes, 8 shirts, and 5 pairs of jeans. How many distinct outfits, each consisting of a pair of shoes, a shirt, and a pair of jeans, can Zach select?

   A. 40
   B. 16
   C. 240
   D. 8
   E. 120

10. $4x^2y \cdot 2x^3y \cdot 3xy^2$ is equivalent to:

    F. $24x^6y^4$
    G. $24x^6y^2$
    H. $9x^6y^4$
    J. $9x^6y^2$
    K. $12xy^{10}$

11. Which of the following is a solution to the equation $x^2 - 25x = 0$ ?

    A. -5
    B. 25
    C. 5
    D. -25
    E. 125

12. Craig ran 2 ⅔ miles on Wednesday and 3 ¼ miles on Thursday. What was the total distance, in miles, Craig ran during those two days?

    F. 5 ⅗
    G. 5 3/12
    H. 5 11/12
    J. 5 ⅖
    K. 5 9/12

307

13. The ratio of the side lengths for a triangle is exactly 9:12:15. In another triangle which is similar to the first, the shortest side is 18 inches long. To the nearest hundredth of an inch, what is the length of the longest side of the other triangle?

    A. 18.25
    B. 24.00
    C. 25.50
    D. 30.00
    E. Cannot be determined from the given information

14. The formula for the volume V of a sphere with radius r is $V = \frac{4}{3}\pi r^3$. If the radius of a spherical rubber ball is 2 ¾ inches, what is its volume to the nearest cubic inch?

    F. 56
    G. 87
    H. 8
    J. 77
    K. 11

15. For the triangle ΔPQR shown below, what is sin(R)?

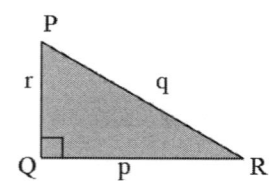

    A. r/q
    B. r/p
    C. p/r
    D. q/r
    E. p/q

Math Mastery - Level 1

# Answer Explanations

1. **The correct answer is C.** To solve for x, subtract 5x and add 7 to both sides. The resulting equation is 2x = 9. Dividing both sides of the equation by 2 yields $x = \frac{9}{2}$.

2. **The correct answer is F.** Begin by using the distributive property to multiply x to (y - w) and z, giving x(y - w) + xz. Distribute x to (y - w) again to get xy - xw + xz.

3. **The correct answer is D.** To find the toxicity level, you divide the number of milligrams of dissolved toxins per liter of water by the maximum safe amount of dissolved toxins in milligrams per liter of water, or .86 ÷ 1.04. Then you approximate the fraction as a decimal, 0.8269, then convert to a percent 82.69%, and round to 83%.

4. **The correct answer is H.** To find the length of fence needed to fence a rectangular pasture 250 ft by 300 ft, you need to find the perimeter. The formula for the perimeter of a rectangle is twice the sum of the length and width, or P = 2(l + w) = 2(250 + 300) = 2(550) = 1,100. It may help you to draw out the pasture and then solve.

5. **The correct answer is C.** Since the average for the six tests is 88, you multiply 88 by 6 to find out how many total points Michael needs to get an average of 88. 88 • 6 = 528. Then you find the composite of the scores Michael already received. 72 + 94 + 85 + 83 + 97 = 431. Then you subtract the desired score from the score Michael already has to get the score that he needs on the next exam. 528 - 431 = 97.

6. **The correct answer is G.** These 4 numbers will be an arithmetic sequence. In an arithmetic sequence, each pair of successive terms differs by the same amount. To find the difference, you can define d as the difference and let 19 be the first term and 55 be the fourth term. By definition, the second term is 19 + d and the third term is 19 + d + d. The fourth term can also be written as 19 + d + d + d. Using that expression you obtain that 55 = 19 + 3d, so d = 12. Then the second term is 19 + 12 = 31. And, the third term is 31 + 12 = 43. You may also solve this by plugging in the possible answer choices. Only G makes the *difference between the consecutive numbers the same* as it asks for in the problem.

7. **The correct answer is E.** First you need to figure out Mrs. Cook's pay per day. Divide her salary by the number of days she is paid. 23,125 ÷ 185 = $125 per day. When Mrs. Cook takes a day off without pay and the school pays a substitute teacher $90 instead, the school district saves the difference in these amounts, $125 - $90 = $35.

8. **The correct answer is H.** Probability is calculated as the number of *desired outcomes* divided by total number of *possible outcomes.* In this problem, there are 10 desired outcomes: drawing any of the 6 purple marbles or 4 blue marbles is desired. 6 + 4 = 10. The total number of possible outcomes is 6 + 4 + 10 = 20 marbles in the bag. So, the probability of the marble NOT being green is $10 \div 20 = \frac{1}{2}$.

9. **The correct answer is E.** To find the number of distinct outfits that Zach can select from, 3 pairs of shoes, 8 shirts, and 5 pairs of jeans, multiply the numbers of the 3 different clothing pieces together. Thus, there are (3)(8)(5) = 120 distinct outfits that Zach can select. Whenever you are asked to find the number of different combinations that are possible, you can take this approach.

10. **The correct answer is F.** There are at least two ways to solve this. The first is to simply multiply the like terms together. 4 • 2 • 3 = 24. $x^2 \cdot x^3 \cdot x = x^6 \cdot y \cdot y \cdot y^2 = y^4 \cdot 24x^6y^4$.

    If you are feeling a little uncomfortable with the problem, you could solve it the "long way." Remember that an exponent such as $^6$ is just telling you how many times a number or variable is multiplied by itself. For example, $x^6$ is the same as x • x • x • x • x • x. Or $5^6$ is 5 • 5 • 5 • 5 • 5 • 5.

    You can expand the expression given in the problem to get rid of the exponents:
    4 • x • x • y • 2 • x • x • x • y • 3 • x • y • y

Then group the like terms:
4 • 2 • 3 • x • x • x • x • x • x • y • y • y • y

Then multiply it all together and put your exponents back in place. Since there are 6 x's, your exponent for the x's is 6. Since there are 4 y's, your exponent for the y's is 4.

11. **The correct answer is B.** To solve the equation $x^2 - 25x = 0$, you can factor an $x$ out of both terms. This gives $x(x - 25) = 0$. Therefore $x = 0$ and $x = 25$ are solutions to the equation. Because $x = 0$ is not an available answer choice, $x = 25$ is the only possible answer.

    You may find it easier and quicker to plug in the possible answer choices, in which case you'll find that only B makes the left side of the equation equal to 0.

12. **The correct answer is H.** To find the total distance (in miles) that Craig ran, you need the sum of $2\frac{2}{3}$ and $3\frac{1}{4}$. To add mixed numbers together, each fraction must have a common denominator. Because 3 and 4 do not have any common factors besides one, the least common denominator is $(3)(4) = 12$. Multiply $\frac{3}{4}$ by $\frac{3}{3}$ and multiply $\frac{2}{3}$ by $\frac{4}{4}$ to get $2\frac{8}{12} + 3\frac{3}{12} = 5\frac{11}{12}$.

13. **The correct answer is D.** Similar triangles have sides that are in proportion to one another. For example, if the shortest side of one triangle is half the length of the shortest side of another similar triangle, then all of the other sides will be half the length as well. The easiest way to solve this is to draw an imaginary triangle that fits the description in the problem, with side lengths 9, 12, and 15. Then draw the second triangle. If its shortest side is 18, that means that it's twice the length of the first triangle's shortest side. That means the second triangle's longest side is twice the length as well. $15 \cdot 2 = 30$. Remember that the question asked for the answer to the nearest hundredth.

14. **The correct answer is G.** To find the volume, you plug in $2\frac{3}{4}$ as $r$ in your volume equation, then use your calculator to solve. First resolve the exponent $2.75^3$, then multiply out the rest.

    The problem asked for the question rounded to the nearest cubic inch, so our answer is 87.

15. **The correct answer is A.** To find sin(R), take the ratio of the length of the opposite side to the length of the hypotenuse, or $\frac{r}{q}$

    To solve most trigonometric problems on the ACT, you need to remember that the SIN of an angle equals the length OPPOSITE the angle divided by HYPOTENUSE length.

    COS(angle) = the length ADJACENT the angle divided by the HYPOTENUSE length.

    TAN(angle) = the length OPPOSITE the angle divided by the length ADJACENT to the angle.

    The abbreviation SOHCAHTOA can help you remember this.

    $$\sin\theta = \frac{o}{h} \qquad \cos\theta = \frac{a}{h} \qquad \tan\theta = \frac{o}{a}$$

# Math Mini-Test 2

In this next segment, you might notice that the questions are a little more difficult than in the mini-test you just completed. Challenge yourself to answer the questions as quickly and accurately as possible.

Use a timer and give yourself ten minutes.

If you find that you are spending too long on any one question, make your best guess and move on to the next question. It's more important that you get a chance to consider each and every question, than it is that you get that one difficult question right.

## Math Mastery - Level 1

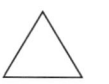

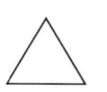

16. If x and y are positive integers such that the greatest common factor of $x^2y^2$ and $xy^3$ is 50, then which of the following could equal y?

    F. 50
    G. 2
    H. 25
    J. 10
    K. 5

17. If x is a real number such that $x^3 = 729$, then $x^2 + \sqrt{x} = ?$

    A. 732
    B. 90
    C. 738
    D. 84
    E. 12

18. A circle in the standard (x,y) coordinate plane is tangent to the x-axis at 4 and tangent to the y-axis at 4. Which of the following is an equation of the circle?

    F. $(x - 4)^2 + (y - 4)^2 = 16$
    G. $(x + 4)^2 + (y + 4)^2 = 16$
    H. $(x - 4)^2 + (y - 4)^2 = 4$
    J. $x^2 + y^2 = 16$
    K. $x^2 + y^2 = 4$

19. What expression must the center cell of the table below contain so that the sums of each row and each column are equivalent?

    | 4x | 4x | 2x |
    |----|----|----|
    | x  | ?  | 6x |
    | 5x | 3x | 2x |

    A. 3x
    B. 2x
    C. 5x
    D. 4x
    E. 6x

20. At a plant, 160,000 tons of petrochemicals are required to produce 100,000 tons of plastic. How many tons of petrochemicals are required to produce 5,000 tons of plastic?

    F. 16,000
    G. 8,000
    H. 100,000
    J. 80,000
    K. 10,000

21. A chord 20 inches long is 4 inches from the center of a circle, as shown below. What is the radius of the circle, to the nearest tenth of an inch?

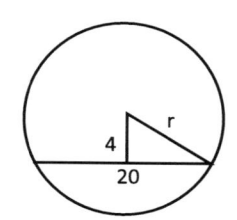

    A. 10.7
    B. 4.0
    C. 21.6
    D. 10.8
    E. 11.0

22. Members of the rescue team lean a 20-foot ladder against a building. The side of the building is perpendicular to the level ground so that the base of the ladder is 5 feet away from the base of the building. To the nearest foot, how far up the building does the ladder reach?

    F. 5
    G. 20
    H. 19
    J. 18
    K. 10

23. Point C is to be graphed in a quadrant, not on an axis, of the standard (x,y) coordinate plane below.

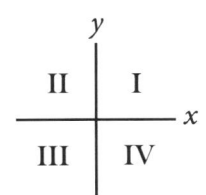

```
      y
  II  |  I
 -----+-----  x
  III | IV
```

If the x-coordinate and the y-coordinate of point C are to have the same signs, then point C must be located in:

A. Quadrant I or III
B. Quadrant I or II
C. Quadrant II or IV
D. Quadrant I or IV
E. Quadrant III or IV

24. What is the x-coordinate of the point in the standard (x,y) coordinate plane at which the two lines $y = 2x - 1$ and $y = x + 2$ intersect?

F. 1
G. 0
H. 4
J. -2
K. 3

25. A square is circumscribed about a circle of 6-foot radius, as shown below. What is the area of the square, in square feet?

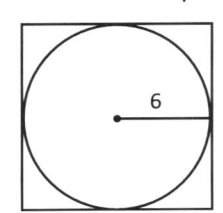

A. 144
B. 72
C. 288
D. 36
E. 12

26. If a rectangle measures 12 meters by 16 meters, what is the length, in meters, of the diagonal of the rectangle?

F. 18
G. 14
H. 28
J. 20
K. 22

27. Which of the following is a set of all real numbers x, such that $x + 1 > x + 8$ ?

A. The set containing zero
B. The set containing all real numbers
C. The set containing all positive numbers
D. The set containing all negative numbers
E. The empty set

28. For all pairs of real numbers P and Q where $P = 2Q + 9$, Q = ?

F. $2P - 9$
G. $\dfrac{P + 9}{2}$
H. $\dfrac{P}{2} + 9$
J. $\dfrac{P}{2} - 9$
K. $\dfrac{P - 9}{2}$

29. The ratio of the radii of two circles is 5:12. What is the ratio of their circumferences?

A. 5:12
B. 10π:12
C. 5:12π
D. 10:24
E. 25:144

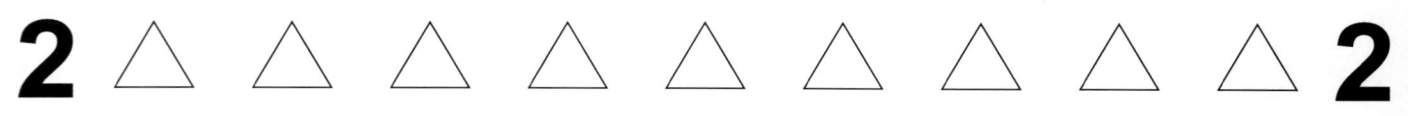

**30.** Of the 777 graduating seniors in a certain high school, approximately 1/3 are going to college and approximately 2/7 of those going to college are going to a state university. Which of the following is the closest estimate for how many of the graduating seniors are going to a state university?

F. 110
G. 256
H. 74
J. 219
K. 75

# Math Mastery - Level 1

## Answer Explanations

16. **The correct answer is K.** The definition of the *greatest common factor* is *the greatest common divisor; the highest number that divides exactly into two or more numbers.* In other words, it's the biggest number that can divide evenly into two different numbers. For example, the greatest common factor of 24 and 30 is 6. That's because the factors of 24 are 1, 2, 3, 4, 6, 8, 12, and 24, while the factors of 30 are 1, 2, 3, 5, 6, 10, 15, and 30. The largest one they have in common (the greatest) is 6.

    The easiest way to solve this is to just plug in the answer choices. It's best to start with the smallest numbers because these can be calculated the quickest, so start with 2.

    $x^2 2^2$ and $x2^3$ simplify to $4x^2$ and $8x$. It is not possible to plug in an $x$ that causes the two numbers to have a greatest common denominator of 50 (try plugging in 2, 5, 25, or 50 into $x$ to test this).

    Now let's try plugging in 5.

    $x^2 5^2$ and $x5^3$ simplifies to $25x^2$ and $125x$. Try plugging in some numbers for $x$ to get the greatest common denominator to equal 50. Substituting 2 for $x$ gives you the numbers $25(4) = 100$ and 250. The greatest common denominators of these numbers if 50, so there is your answer.

    This is the sort of problem that you circle back around to and only try once you've done everything else, as it is designed to be time-consuming. Starting with the smallest numbers can prevent this from eating all of your time.

17. **The correct answer is D.** First solve for $x$. Cube root both sides of $x^3 = 729$. Find the cube root of 729 using your calculator. $x = 9$. Then solve the second equation by substituting 9 for $x$.

18. **The correct answer is F.** Drawing a picture would be a good first step for solving this problem. The equation for a circle with center $(h, k)$ and radius $r$ is $(x - h)^2 + (y - k)^2 = r^2$. If you knew this formula, you could just deduce that the center of the circle is (4,4) and the radius is 4 from your drawing and plug in these numbers.

    If you don't remember the formula, you still know at least four coordinates of this circle: (0,4); (4,0); (8,4); and (4,8). The last two points are the opposite sides of the circle of the points that you know. If you plug these coordinates into the answer choices, you'll be able to eliminate all of the answer choices except F.

19. **The correct answer is A.** The question that you have to ask yourself to be able to solve this problem is, "What is the sum of the rows and columns?" Pick the first row. $4x + 4x + 2x = 10x$. Does that equal, say, the first column? $4x + x + 5x = 10x$. That's correct. Now what do we need to add in the middle to make the second column add up to $10x$? $4x + 3x + ? = 10x$. Subtract $7x$ from both sides. $? = 3x$.

    Now check your answer. Are all of the rows and columns equal to $10x$? Your answer is therefore correct.

20. **The correct answer is G.** Set up a proportion with ratios of tons of petrochemicals to tons of plastic.

    $$\frac{160{,}000}{100{,}000} = \frac{x}{5{,}000}$$

    Cross multiply.

    $160{,}000 \cdot 5000 = 100{,}000x$

    $800{,}000{,}000 = 100{,}000x$

    Divide both sides by 100,000.

    $x = 8{,}000$

21. **The correct answer is D.** The key to solving this problem is recognizing that there is a right triangle in the figure, with $r$ as the hypotenuse. The bottom leg of the triangle is half the length of the chord. $20 \div 2 = 10$. Use the Pythagorean Theorem: $4^2 + 10^2 = r^2$. $r^2 = 116$. Use your calculator to find the square root of 116. $r = 10.770$. We round up to the nearest tenth to arrive at our answer: 10.8.

## Math Mini-Test 2

22. **The correct answer is H.** To find out how far a 20-foot ladder 5 feet away from the base of a building reaches up the building, you can use the Pythagorean Theorem. Let the length of the ladder be the hypotenuse. Let the legs be the distance from the base of the building to the bottom of the ladder. Let the height of the building be where the ladder meets the building. This gives $20^2 = 5^2 + h^2$, where $h$ is the height of the building. Solving this equation for $h$ and rounding yields $h = 19$. The height is about 19 feet.

    $20^2 = 5^2 + h^2$

    $375 = h^2$

    $h = 19.365$

    Round down to 19.

    It can help to draw this out. Be on the lookout for questions on the ACT where the test is describing a right angle being formed. Chances are you'll need to use the Pythagorean Theorem.

23. **The correct answer is A.** Points in Quadrant I have two positive coordinates. Points in Quadrant II have negative $x$ coordinates and positive $y$ coordinates. Points in Quadrant III have two negative coordinates. Points in Quadrant IV have positive $x$ coordinates and negative $y$ coordinates. Therefore point C can be in only either Quadrant I or Quadrant III.

    If you aren't familiar with the rules governing this, you can always just make up a point or two in each quadrant and see which quadrants match what the question is looking for.

24. **The correct answer is K.** The key to solving this problem is spotting that the point where these two lines intersect will have the same $x$ and $y$ values. For that reason, you can solve these two equations as a system of equations. Since we know that $y = 2x - 1$, we can substitute $(2x - 1)$ into the second equation.

    $2x - 1 = x + 2$

    Now we solve for $x$. Subtract $x$ from both sides.

    $x - 1 = 2$

    Add 1 to both sides.

    $x = 3$

25. **The correct answer is A.** Because the circle is circumscribed in the square, it touches the square at the midpoints of its 4 sides. For that reason, the length of the side of the square is the same as the circle's diameter. The diameter of a circle is twice the radius, so the diameter of this circle is $6 \cdot 2 = 12$. This is the same as the square's length. The area of the square is therefore $12^2 = 144$ square feet.

26. **The correct answer is J.** To find the length of the diagonal of the rectangle, note that the diagonal of the rectangle and two of its sides form a right triangle. Therefore, we use the Pythagorean Theorem. Where $12^2 + 16^2 = c^2$, $c$ is the length of the diagonal. Solving this for $c$ gives $c = 20$.

    The key to solving this problem is recognizing that you can use the Pythagorean Theorem. Drawing out the word problem can help you notice this, so be sure to make a habit of sketching a diagram for this sort of problem, especially if the way to solve it isn't immediately apparent.

27. **The correct answer is E.** The immediate answer to this question is that there is no number that is greater when you add 1 to it than when you add 8 to it, so it's an empty set.

    You can also solve this algebraically: Subtract 1 from both sides and $x$ from both sides. You're left with $0 > 7$, which is never true. There is no solution to this problem and therefore it's an empty set.

    *Note*: A is not correct because "the set containing zero" doesn't mean "empty set" or "no solution." That answer is saying that the solution is the number 0, which is incorrect.

28. **The correct answer is K.** To solve the equation $P = 2Q + 9$ for $Q$, subtract 9 from both sides of the equation to get $P - 9 = 2Q$. Then, divide both sides by 2 to get $Q = \frac{P-9}{2}$. This is your answer.

This question is designed to be confusing. Normally this type of question with two variables provides you with two equations which you can solve as a system of equations. When you feel like something is missing in the question, look down at your answer choices. The answers all have $P$'s in them, so then you know that it's okay for you to solve for $Q$ and leave the $P$ in there.

29. **The correct answer is A.**

There are several ways to solve this problem, but the easiest is to draw two imaginary circles that fit the description in the question. Draw one circle with radius 5 and another circle with radius 12. Then find the circumference of each circle. Circumference = $2\pi r$, so the circumference of the smaller circle is $2\pi(5) = 10\pi$ and the circumference of the larger circle is $2\pi(12) = 24\pi$. Then find the ratio of the two circumferences. $10\pi : 24\pi$. Simplify by dividing both sides of the ratio by $\pi$. 10:24. Simplify again by dividing both sides by 2. 5:12 is the correct answer. D is not correct because the ratio is not in its simplest form; 10 and 24 have a greatest common denominator of 2.

Whenever the ACT describes the ratio between two shapes but does not give you specific dimensions, it almost always works to draw specific shapes by making up dimensions that fit the ratio in the problem and then working from there. It can make solving the problem much easier. As long as you take care to set up the shapes with the correct ratios it will all come out correctly.

30. **The correct answer is H.** To find out how many of the 768 seniors in a certain high school are going to a state university when approximately $\frac{1}{3}$ are going to college, and when approximately $\frac{2}{7}$ of those are going to a state university, first find out how many seniors are going to college. This is given by $(768)(\frac{1}{3}) = 256$. The number of those seniors going to state university is $(256)(\frac{2}{7}) = 73.14$, which rounds to 73 seniors going to state university.

# Math Mini-Test 3

The mini-test that you are about to take corresponds with questions 31 through 40 on the ACT Math test. When you start question 31 in an actual ACT Math test, you want less than 20 minutes to have already passed. If you are able to reach this goal, you'll have 40 minutes or more for the back of the test.

The questions in the back half of the ACT Math test typically require more time to solve because they might require several steps, but many of them are completely doable. Pre-algebra, Elementary Algebra, and Plane Geometry questions can be found throughout the back half of the test. It's not all trig and calculus.

In the next three mini-tests, time yourself 13 minutes per test. Your goal is to complete all of the questions in the mini-test as accurately as possible under the time limit. If you're able to accomplish this pace, you'll be able to move through the entire ACT Math test under the time limit with no problems.

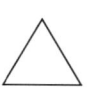

**31.** What is the slope-intercept form of $4x - y + 7 = 0$?

- A. $y = -4x + 7$
- B. $y = 4x + 7$
- C. $y = x + 4/7$
- D. $y = -4x - 7$
- E. $y = 4x - 7$

**32.** Parallelogram PQRS, with dimensions in inches, is shown in the diagram below. What is the area of the parallelogram, in square inches?

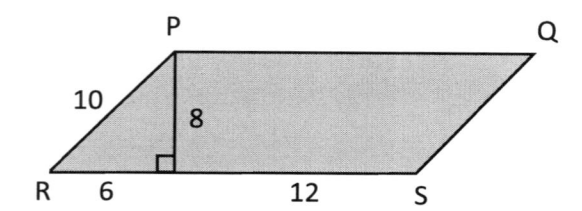

- F. 56
- G. 180
- H. 120
- J. 144
- K. 96

**33.** The length L, in meters, of a bungee cord is given by the equation $L = \frac{2}{3}F + 0.05$, where F is the applied force in newtons. What force, in newtons, must be applied for the bungee cord's length to be 0.17 meters?

- A. 0.66
- B. 0.17
- C. 0.18
- D. 0.05
- E. 0.20

**34.** If $a = b - 3$, then $(b - a)^3 = ?$

- F. 27
- G. -9
- H. 9
- J. -81
- K. -27

**35.** Points B and C lie on line segment AD as shown below. The length of line segment AD is 40 units; line segment AC is 15 units long; and line segment BD is 30 units long. How many units long, if it can be determined, is line segment BC?

- A. 20
- B. 15
- C. 10
- D. 5
- E. Cannot be determined from the given information

*The next two questions use information provided in the graph below.*

English Enrollment

| Course | Section | Period | Enrollment |
|---|---|---|---|
| Composition | A | 1 | 12 |
| English I | A | 1 | 21 |
|  | B | 4 | 19 |
|  | C | 5 | 20 |
| English II | A | 2 | 15 |
|  | B | 3 | 16 |
| English III | A | 2 | 14 |
| English IV | A | 3 | 19 |

**36.** What is the average number of students enrolled per section in English I?

- F. 18
- G. 19
- H. 21
- J. 20
- K. 17

37. The school owns 35 anthologies, which students are required to have during their English classes. There are 4 anthologies currently being re-covered, and 1 anthology is currently missing. For which of the following class periods, if any, are there NOT enough anthologies available for each student to have his or her own anthology?

   A. Period 1 & 3
   B. Period 1 & 2
   C. Period 1
   D. Period 2 & 3
   E. There are enough anthologies for each class period

38. After polling a class of 30 science students by a show of hands, you find that 12 students enjoy chemistry while 17 students enjoy biology. Given that information, what is the maximum number of students in this class who enjoy both chemistry and biology?

   F. 12
   G. 29
   H. 17
   J. 0
   K. 5

39. For all positive integers X, Y, and Z, which of the following expressions is equivalent to $\frac{Y}{Z}$?

   A. $\frac{Y}{Z} + \frac{X}{Y}$
   B. $\frac{Y \cdot Z}{Z \cdot Y}$
   C. $\frac{Y + X}{Z + X}$
   D. $\frac{Y \cdot X}{Z \cdot X}$
   E. $\frac{Y \cdot Y}{Z \cdot Z}$

40. If 120% of a number is 360, what is 50% of the number?

   F. 120
   G. 300
   H. 150
   J. 480
   K. 260

# Math Mastery - Level 1

## *Answer Explanations*

31. **The correct answer is B.** The slope-intercept form of a line is written $y = mx + b$, where $m$ is the slope of the line and $b$ is the y-intercept. To rearrange $4x - y + 7 = 0$ into slope-intercept form, add $y$ to both sides to get the $y$ by itself. $y = 4x + 7$

32. **The correct answer is J.** The area of a parallelogram is found by multiplying the length of the base times the length of the height ($A = bh$). The height of the parallelogram is 8. The base of the parallelogram is $6 + 12 = 18$. Then, $A = (18)(8) = 144$ square inches.

33. **The correct answer is C.** Don't let the scientific terms in this word problem confuse you. This is a math test so you have to assume that any science in the word problem isn't going to affect how the numbers work.

    In this problem, since you know that the length is 0.17, plug that in as $L$. Since there is only one variable left in the equation, you can then solve for $F$.

    $0.17 = \frac{2}{3}F + 0.05$

    Subtract 0.05 to both sides to get $F$ by itself.

    $0.12 = \frac{2}{3}F$

    Multiply both sides by $\frac{3}{2}$.

    $0.18 = F$

34. **The correct answer is F.** Since $a = b - 3$, substitute in $b - 3$ for $a$ in the second equation given.

    You get $[b - (b - 3)]^3 = [b - b + 3]^3$

    Since $b - b = 0$, this simplifies to:

    $(3)^3 = 27$.

35. **The correct answer is D.** Draw out the lengths as you deduce them to make solving this simpler. Since line segment AB + line segment BD = 40, and since we know line segment BD = 30, then line segment AB must be 10. Likewise, since we know that line segment AC is 15, then line segment CD is 25. Now we know what we need to solve the problem. Line segments AB + BC + CD = 40, and we know that line segment AB = 10 and line segment CD = 25, so line segment BC must = 5.

    This is the sort of problem that can be daunting at first. The key is to ask yourself, "What do I need to know to be able to solve the problem?" Working out what you can (in this case, figuring out the lengths of the other line segments) enables you to figure out what you need (the length of line segment BC).

36. **The correct answer is J.** To find an average, add up the quantities then divide by the number of quantities provided. To find the average number of students enrolled in English I, add the number of students in each English I section and divide by the number of sections. There are three sections. Section A has 21 students, Section B has 19 students, and Section C has 20 students.

    $( 19 + 20 + 21 ) \div 3 = 60 \div 3 = 20$

37. **The correct answer is A.** First you have to figure out the number of available anthologies for any period. This is 35 minus the number being re-covered or missing. $35 - 4$ re-covered $- 1$ missing $= 30$ available anthologies. Add up the number of students attending each period. Only Period 1 has more students than anthologies, since the Composition class has 12 students, while English I has 21 students. $12 + 21 = 33$, which is greater than the 30 available anthologies.

# Math Mini-Test 3

38. **The correct answer is F.** To find the maximum number of students who could enjoy both biology and chemistry, note that more students enjoy biology than chemistry. Because only 12 students enjoy chemistry, the maximum number of students who could possibly enjoy both chemistry and biology is also 12. The maximum number is limited by the number of students who enjoy chemistry, not by the number of students who enjoy biology.

    If this is a problem you skipped and came back to, and you don't feel sure about how to answer it, you could also figure it out another way. Draw a representation of the thirty students, and assign what they enjoy so as to maximize the number of students that enjoy both chemistry and biology. You'll find that after 12 students, you'll run out of students who enjoy chemistry and max out at 12.

39. **The correct answer is D.** To find which expression is equivalent to $\frac{Y}{Z}$, note that any number divided by itself is equal to 1. So, $\frac{(Y \cdot X)}{(Z \cdot X)} = \frac{YX}{ZX} = \frac{Y}{Z}$. This is the only valid answer.

    If you're not sure about the rule here, you could also just pick random numbers for $x$, $y$, and $z$ and see which works. For example, if you say that $x = 3$, $y = 4$, and $z = 5$, then only D works.

40. **The correct answer is H.** Express this word problem algebraically. First convert the percentages to decimals. 120% = 1.20, and 50% = 0.50. Then write out the first statement as an equation. Let $x$ represent the number we're trying to figure out.

    $1.2x = 360$

    Divide both sides by 1.2. Use your calculator.

    $x = 300$

    Now we just have to find out what 50% of 300 is.

    $0.50 \cdot 300 = 150$

# Math Mini-Test 4

41. The hypotenuse of the right triangle ΔLMN shown below is 18 feet long. The sine of angle L is 5/6. About how many feet long is line segment MN?

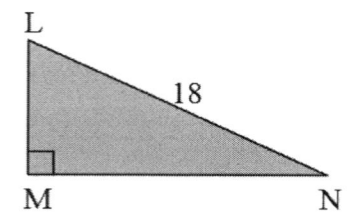

L

18

M           N

A. 12
B. 15
C. 18
D. 11
E. Cannot be determined from the given information

42. If x = 3t − 8 and y = 4 + t, which of the following equations expresses y in terms of x?

F. y = 4x − 4
G. y = (x − 20)/3
H. y = (x + 3)/20
J. y = x/(3 − 4)
K. y = (x + 20)/3

43. Hexagons have 9 diagonals, as illustrated below. How many diagonals do octagons have?

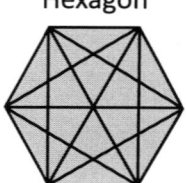

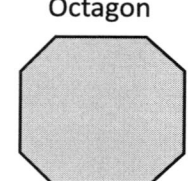

Hexagon           Octagon

A. 20
B. 8
C. 16
D. 32
E. 40

44. Jennifer wants to draw a circle graph showing the favorite candies of her friends. When she polled her friends asking each his or her favorite candy, 30% of her friends said chocolate, 25% of her friends said peppermint, 15% of her friends said licorice, 15% of her friends said gum; and the remaining friends said other than those candy types. If she groups the other candies chosen by the remaining friends in the same sector, what will the degree measure of this sector be?

F. 12°
G. 26°
H. 24°
J. 54°
K. 48°

45. The number of students participating in sports at a certain high school can be shown by the following matrix.

| Soccer | Football | Track | Basketball |
|---|---|---|---|
| [ 30 | 60 | 40 | 30 ] |

The athletics director estimates the ratio of the number of sports awards that will be earned to the number of students participating with the following matrix.

$$\begin{bmatrix} \text{Soccer} : 0.2 \\ \text{Football} : 0.3 \\ \text{Track} : 0.5 \\ \text{Basketball} : 0.4 \end{bmatrix}$$

Given this data, what is the athletic director's estimate of the number of sports awards that will be earned for these sports?

A. 60
B. 56
C. 48
D. 52
E. 36

46. After a hurricane, coastal workers removed an estimated 8,000 cubic yards of sand from the downtown area. If this sand were spread in an even layer over a rectangular segment of beach as shown below, about how many yards deep would the new layer of sand be?

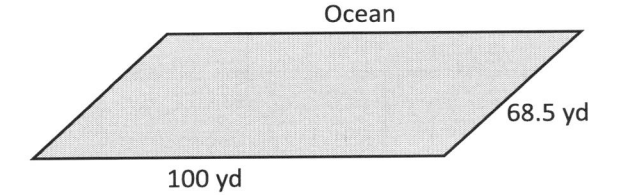

F. Less than 1
G. Between 1 and 2
H. Between 2 and 3
J. Between 3 and 4
K. More than 4

47. What is the distance in the standard (x,y) coordinate plane between the points (1,2) and (4,6)

A. 7
B. 5
C. 13
D. 4
E. 10

48. In the figure below, VWXY is a trapezoid, Z lies on line VY, and angle measures are as marked. What is the measure of ∠WYX?

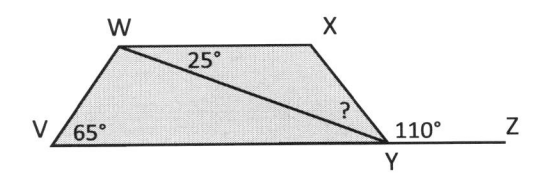

F. 25°
G. 30°
H. 65°
J. 55°
K. 45°

49. In the set of complex numbers, where $i^2 = -1$,

$$\frac{i}{i-1} \cdot \frac{i+1}{i+1} = ?$$

A. $-i$
B. $\dfrac{i}{-2}$
C. $\dfrac{i-1}{-2}$
D. $\dfrac{1}{-2}$
E. $\dfrac{i^2+i}{i^2-2i-1}$

50. If $f(x) = x^2 + x + 4$, then $f(x+h) =$

F. $x^2 + x + h^2 + h + 4$
G. $x^2 + x + 2h + 4$
H. $x^2 + 2xh + x + h^2 + h + 4$
J. $x^2 + x + h + 4$
K. $h^2 + h + 2x + 4$

Math Mastery - Level 1

# Answer Explanations

41. **The correct answer is B.** $\sin(L) = \frac{5}{6}$ means that the ratio of the OPPOSITE side length to the HYPOTENUSE side length is $\frac{5}{6}$. Set up the proportion to find the length of the OPPOSITE side length. We'll use $x$ as our unknown length.

    $\frac{5}{6} = \frac{x}{18}$

    Cross multiply.

    $5 \cdot 18 = 6x$

    $90 = 6x$

    Divide both sides by 6.

    $x = 15$.

    The abbreviation SOHCAHTOA can help you remember that SIN of an angle is the ratio of the OPPOSITE length divided by the HYPOTENUSE length in a right triangle (SOH).

42. **The correct answer is K.** The phrase "$y$ in terms of $x$" means that you are to provide an equation with $y$ all by itself, where it's expected to have the variable $x$ somewhere on the other side. In other words, you're showing what y equals using $x$.

    The first step is to get rid of the $t$ and swap that out for $x$. You can see in your answer choices that there are no $t$'s. Figure out what $t$ equals in terms of $x$.

    $x = 3t - 8$

    Add 8 to both sides to get $t$ by itself.

    $3t = x + 8$

    Divide both sides by 3.

    $t = (x + 8) \div 3$

    Substitute $(x + 8) / 3$ in for $t$ in the second equation.

    $y = 4 + (x + 8) \div 3$

    Add this together by finding the common denominator of 3, which gives

    $y = \frac{12}{3} + \frac{(x+8)}{3} = \frac{(x+20)}{3}$

43. **The correct answer is A.** The easiest way to solve this is to draw a BIG octagon on your paper and just draw all the possible diagonals. Methodically go from point to point in a clockwise direction. The first vertex has 5 diagonals coming from it (you can't connect it to the two vertexes adjacent to it). The next vertex also has 5. The next vertex already has one of its diagonals counted, so that is 4. The next vertex has 3 new ones you can count. The next vertex has 2. The final vertex only has 1 new diagonal (all the rest are already connected to it). $5 + 5 + 4 + 3 + 2 + 1 = 20$.

Math Mini-Test 4

44. **The correct answer is J.** Jennifer will count any candy other than chocolate, peppermint, licorice, and gum in the Other category. The four main candies add up to 30 + 25 + 15 + 15 = 85%, leaving 15% for the Other category. This means that 15% of the 360 degrees of the circle belong in the Other sector. This is (.15)(360) = 54 degrees.

    The space around the center of a circle is divided into 360 pieces called degrees. When you're making graphs using circles, you multiply the percentages times 360 to determine how much of the space in the circle is used by each category.

45. **The correct answer is B.** To find the number of sports awards earned, the number of participants in each sport is multiplied by the ratio for that sport and then the four products are added. This is (.2)(30) + (.3)(60) + (.5)(40) + (.4)(30) = 6 + 18 + 20 + 12 = 56.

46. **The correct answer is G.** The first trick to this problem is that even though the graphic looks like a parallelogram, it's just a 3-dimensional representation of a rectangle (as it says in the question). Therefore, the question is asking us to find the HEIGHT of a prism with a length of 100 yards, a width of 68.5 yards, and a volume of 8,000 cubic yards (because that's how much sand will be piled on to this rectangle).

    Express this algebraically using the volume formula ($V = l \cdot w \cdot h$):

    $100 \cdot 68.5 \cdot x = 8000$

    $6850x = 8000$

    Divide both sides by 6850. Use your calculator.

    $x = 1.168$

    This answer is between 1 and 2.

    Whenever the ACT gives you a volume, it's typically a clue that you'll be needing to use the volume formula to find a missing dimension (length, width, or height).

47. **The correct answer is B.** We'll show you how to solve this using the distance formula, and also to solve it in case you don't remember the distance formula during the test.

    To find the distance between two points in the standard (x, y) coordinate plane, you can use the distance formula: $d = \sqrt{(y_2 - y_1)^2 + (x_2 - x_1)^2}$. So the distance is $d = \sqrt{(6 - 2)^2 + (4 - 1)^2} = \sqrt{16 + 9} = \sqrt{25} = 5$ units.

    If you didn't remember the distance formula, you can still solve this by drawing it out on the coordinate plane and using the Pythagorean Theorem. These points give you a right triangle with side lengths 3 and 4. Using the Pythagorean Theorem ($a^2 + b^2 = c^2$):

    $3^2 + 4^2 = c^2$

    $25 = c^2$

    Find the square root of both sides.

    $c = 5$

48. **The correct answer is K.** A trapezoid always has 2 parallel line segments. To find the measure of ∠WYX in the figure below, you have to spot that line segments VY and WX are parallel and are connected by the line segment WY. So, ∠XWY and ∠VYW are alternate interior angles. So ∠VWY is also 25 degrees. ∠VYZ is a straight angle, so by definition it is 180 degrees. Therefore, 25 + 110 + ∠WYX = 180, and ∠WYX = 45 degrees.

49. **The correct answer is C.** To simplify this expression we start by multiplying out the two fractions.

    We'll start with the numerator:

    $i \times (i + 1) = i^2 + i$

    Now let's evaluate the denominator:

    $(i - 1) \times (i + 1) = i^2 - 1$.

Now we can simplify our expression.

$$\frac{i^2+i}{i^2-i} = \frac{(-1)+i}{(-1)-1} = \frac{i-1}{-2}$$

50. **The correct answer is H.** Plug in $(x + h)$ anywhere you see $x$ in the function.

    $(x + h)^2 + (x + h) + 4$

    Use the FOIL method.

    $(x + h)(x + h) + (x + h) + 4$

    $x^2 + xh + xh + h^2 + x + h + 4$

    Combine like terms.

    $x^2 + 2xh + x + h^2 + h + 4$

# Math Mini-Test 5

## Math Mastery - Level 1

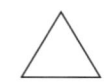

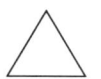

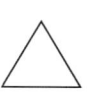

**51.** An abandoned area of town has the shape and dimensions in blocks given below. All borders run either exactly north-south or east-west. A surveyor has set up his equipment halfway between point B and point D. Which of the following is the location of the surveyor from point A?

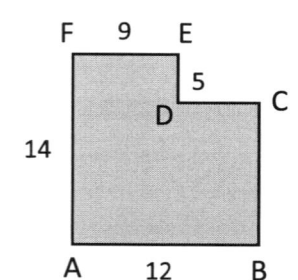

```
F    9    E
          |
     5    |
     D----C       N
              ↑
14
                  
A    12   B
```

**A.** 12 blocks east and 9 blocks north
**B.** 9 ½ blocks east and 4 ½ blocks north
**C.** 9 blocks east and 5 blocks north
**D.** 10 ½ blocks east and 4 ½ blocks north
**E.** 10 ½ blocks east and 5 ½ blocks north

**52.** Which of the following systems of inequalities is represented by the shaded region of the graph below?

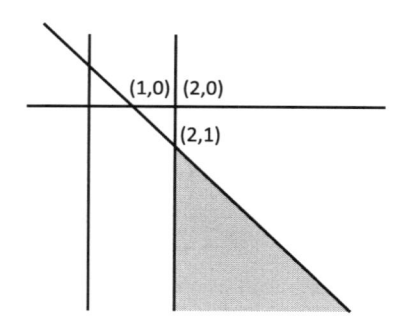

(1,0) (2,0)
(2,1)

**F.** $y \leq x$ and $x \geq 1$
**G.** $y \leq -x + 1$ and $x \geq 2$
**H.** $y \leq -x + 1$ and $x \geq 1$
**J.** $y \leq x - 1$ and $x \geq 2$
**K.** $y \leq x + 1$ and $x \geq -2$

**53.** If $\sin \theta = 4/5$ and $\pi/2 < \theta < \pi$, then $\cos \theta = ?$

**A.** $-3/4$
**B.** $3/5$
**C.** $5/3$
**D.** $-4/5$
**E.** $-3/5$

**54.** A triangle, $\triangle PQR$, is reflected across the x-axis to have the image $\triangle P'Q'R'$ in the standard (x,y) coordinate plane; thus, P reflects to P'. The coordinates of point P are (a,b). Which of the following coordinates best describe the location of point P'?

**F.** (a, -b)
**G.** (a,b)
**H.** (-a,-b)
**J.** (-a,b)
**K.** Cannot be determined from the given information

**55.** What is $\cos \pi/12$ given that $\pi/12 = \pi/3 - \pi/4$ and that $\cos(\alpha - \beta) = (\cos \alpha)(\cos \beta) - (\sin \alpha)(\sin \beta)$? (Note: You may use the following table of values.)

| $\theta$ | $\sin \theta$ | $\cos \theta$ |
|---|---|---|
| $\frac{\pi}{6}$ | $\frac{1}{2}$ | $\sqrt{\frac{3}{2}}$ |
| $\frac{\pi}{4}$ | $\frac{\sqrt{2}}{2}$ | $\frac{\sqrt{2}}{2}$ |
| $\frac{\pi}{3}$ | $\sqrt{\frac{3}{2}}$ | $\frac{1}{2}$ |

**A.** $\dfrac{\sqrt{2} + \sqrt{6}}{4}$

**B.** $\dfrac{\sqrt{2}}{2}$

**C.** $\dfrac{\sqrt{2} - \sqrt{6}}{4}$

**D.** $\dfrac{1}{2}$

**E.** $-\dfrac{1}{2}$

**56.** The larger of two numbers exceeds twice the smaller number by 6. The sum of twice the larger number and 4 times the smaller number is 70. If x is the smaller number, which equation below determines the correct value of x?

- F. $2(2x - 4) + 6x = 70$
- G. $2(2x+6) + 4x = 70$
- H. $2(2x - 6) + 4x = 70$
- J. $4(2x + 6) + 2x = 70$
- K. $4(2x - 6) + 2x = 70$

**57.** In the figure shown below, each pair of intersecting line segments meets at a right angle, and all the lengths given are in inches. What is the perimeter, in inches, of the figure?

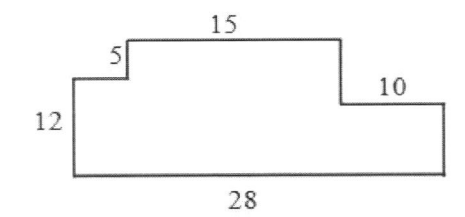

- A. 70
- B. 90
- C. 80
- D. 95
- E. 75

**58.** Which of the following statements describes the total number of dots in the first n rows of the triangular arrangement illustrated below?

1st row
2nd row
3rd row
4th row
5th row

- F. The total is equal to 2n where n is the number of rows
- G. The total is equal to $n^2$ where n is the number of rows
- H. The total is equal to n! where n equals number of rows
- J. The total is equal to $2^n$ where n is the number of rows
- K. The total is equal to $2^n - n!$ where n is the number of rows

**59.** A certain parabola in the standard (x,y) coordinate plane opens downwards and has a vertex NOT at the origin (0,0). Which of the following equations could describe the parabola?

- A. $x = 5y^2$
- B. $x = -2(y + 2)^2 + 4$
- C. $y = -3x^2$
- D. $y = -4(x +1)^2 - 3$
- E. $y = 2(x + 3)^2 + 5$

**60.** The graph below shows the 2012 estimate of the five largest cities in the United States, to the nearest 1 million. According to the graph, the population of Houston makes up what fraction of the total population living in all five cities? Key: ☺ = 1 million people.

| City | Population |
|---|---|
| New York | ☺ ☺ ☺ ☺ ☺ ☺ ☺ |
| Los Angeles | ☺ ☺ ☺ ☺ |
| Chicago | ☺ ☺ ☺ |
| Houston | ☺ ☺ |
| Philadelphia | ☺ ☺ |

**F.** 2/19
**G.** 1/10
**H.** 4/19
**J.** 3/19
**K.** 1/11

# Math Mastery - Level 1

## Answer Explanations

51. **The correct answer is D.** Draw a dotted line between B and D and place point X in the middle of that line. Since line segment AB is 12, and line segment FE is 9, then line segment DC is 3. Point X is halfway between D and C, so it's at the 1.5 mark. Therefore X is 9 + 1.5 = 10.5 blocks east of point A. You can also deduce that since line segment AF is 14, and line segment DE is 5, then line segment BC is 9. Point X is halfway between B and C, which is 4.5. Therefore X is 4.5 blocks north of point A. If this starts to get confusing as you work it out, it can help to draw a BIG version of what the test provides you and to actually make a coordinate plane with little marks for each block inside the drawing.

52. **The correct answer is G.** In order to find the correct inequality that represents the graph, we see that $y \leq -x + 1$ is satisfied for values of $y$ under the sloped line. Also note that the inequality $x \geq 2$ is satisfied by all values of $x$ to the right of the vertical line. This is the only pair of inequalities that can describe the graph.

    When solving an inequality on a graph like this, always break it down to two different inequalities that explain part of what is bounding the shaded area.

    You could also solve this by picking points inside and outside of the shaded area and seeing which answer choice works.

53. **The correct answer is E.** To find $\cos(\theta)$, create a triangle noting that the side opposite $\theta$ is length 4, and the hypotenuse is length 5. Using the Pythagorean Theorem gives that the side adjacent to $\theta$ is length 3. This then gives that $\cos(\theta) = \frac{3}{5}$ for $\theta$ between 0 and $\frac{\pi}{2}$. However, because $\theta$ is between $\frac{\pi}{2}$ and $\pi$, $\cos(\theta) = -\frac{3}{5}$.

    One way to describe angles is to use radians. There are $2\pi$ radians in a circle. If we are finding the COSINE of an angle greater than 90 degrees (or greater than $\frac{1}{2}\pi$) then the cosine comes out negative. If you are having trouble remembering this rule, it can help to plug in the different quantities into your calculator.

54. **The correct answer is F.** To find the coordinates of vertex P after it is reflected across the x-axis, notice that a reflection across the x-axis does not change the x-coordinate but does change the sign of the y-coordinate. Thus, the reflection of P $(a,b)$ across the x-axis is P' $(a,-b)$. It can help to draw this out to make sure you're not making a mistake.

    The ' symbol means PRIME and is usually used to name the first new version or copy of something. For example, you might refer to Bob's reflection in the mirror as Bob' (said "Bob Prime").

55. **The correct answer is C.** To find $\cos(\frac{\pi}{12})$ using $\cos(\alpha - \beta) = (\cos \alpha)(\cos \beta) - (\sin \alpha)(\sin \beta)$

    Given that $\frac{\pi}{12} = \frac{\pi}{3} - \frac{\pi}{4}$, substitute $\alpha = \frac{\pi}{3}$ and $\beta = \frac{\pi}{4}$ in the formula above. You then have

    $\cos(\frac{\pi}{12}) = \cos(\frac{\pi}{3})\cos(\frac{\pi}{4}) - \sin(\frac{\pi}{3})\sin(\frac{\pi}{4})$

    Then use the table to convert the values.

    $(\frac{1}{2})[\frac{\sqrt{2}}{2}] - (\frac{\sqrt{3}}{2})(\frac{\sqrt{2}}{2}) = \frac{\sqrt{2}}{4} - \frac{\sqrt{6}}{4} = \frac{\sqrt{2} - \sqrt{6}}{4}$

56. **The correct answer is G.** Express this word problem with algebraic equations. Express the first statement $y = 2x + 6$, where $y$ is the larger number. Express the second statement as $2y + 4x = 70$. Solving this as a system of equations by substituting $2x + 6$ for $y$ gives you $2(2x + 6) + 4x = 70$.

57. **The correct answer is B.** Although the shape is irregular and we are missing some information that would allow us to solve this easily, we know that the left sides add up to 12 + 5 = 17. Therefore, even though we don't know what the right sides are, we know they also add up to 17. Likewise, the bottom side is 28, therefore the top sides must add up to 28 as well. 17 + 17 + 28 + 28 = 90 inches.

58. **The correct answer is G.** If you write next to the row marker the total number of dots for that row and all the rows before it, you'll see it goes 1, 4, 9, 16, 25... This pattern is the row number squared, which is G.

    You can also test each of the given equations for consistency with the dot pattern. After inspection, $n^2$ is the only equation that represents the dot pattern for all 5 displayed, and $n$, rows.

59. **The correct answer is D.** You must use the process of elimination. The standard equation of a parabola is given by $y = 4a(x - h)^2 + k$. The parabola in question opens downward, meaning that there must be a negative sign multiplied to the equation. This eliminates A and E. Additionally, we are told it has a vertex not at the origin (0,0), meaning that $(h,k)$ does not equal (0,0). This eliminates A and C, leaving only $y = -4(x+1)^2 - 3$ as a possibility.

60. **The correct answer is F.** To find the fraction of the total population living in Houston, divide the number living in Houston by the total population in all cities. This gives $\frac{2,000,000}{19,000,000}$, which simplifies to $\frac{2}{19}$ by dividing the numerator and denominator by 1,000,000.

# Math Mini-Test 6

## Math Test
### 60 Minutes — 60 Questions

**Directions:** *Begin by working out each problem. Once solved, choose the correct answer, then fill in its corresponding bubble on your answer sheet.*

*Do not waste time on difficult questions. Instead, leave them for last; by answering as many questions as possible first, you can use the leftover time to return to the others.*

*A calculator is allowed for any problems you choose, but some may be better solved without one.*

*Note: Unless stated otherwise, the following should be assumed:*

1. *Illustrative figures used in this test are not necessarily drawn to scale.*
2. *Geometric figures lie on an X,Y coordinate plane.*
3. *The word "line" indicates a straight line.*
4. *The word "average" indicates a calculated mean.*

1. What is the value of the expression $k \cdot (k + 3)^2$ for $k = 3$ ?
    - A. 36
    - B. 243
    - C. 81
    - D. 108
    - E. 72

2. What number can you add to the numerator and denominator of $\frac{7}{15}$ to get $\frac{1}{5}$ ?
    - F. 7
    - G. -5
    - H. 15
    - J. -10
    - K. -8

3. What is the distance, in coordinate units, between points (-2,3) and (7,6) in the standard (x,y) coordinate plane?
    - A. $3\sqrt{10}$
    - B. 3
    - C. 9
    - D. $9\sqrt{10}$
    - E. $6\sqrt{5}$

4. A tether for a telephone pole is 15 feet long and reaches 12 feet up the pole, as shown below. How many feet is the bottom of the tether from the base of the telephone pole?
    - F. 9
    - G. 12
    - H. 15
    - J. $3\sqrt{3}$
    - K. $9\sqrt{3}$

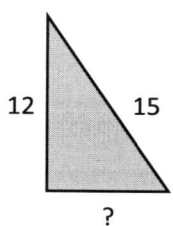

342

5. Points A and B are the endpoints of the diameter of a circle with the center at O, as shown below. Point C is on the circle, and ∠AOC measures 45°. The shortest distance along the circle from A to C is what percent of the distance along the circle from A to B?

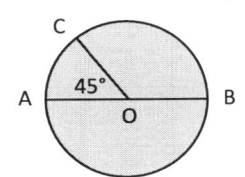

   A. 12.5%
   B. 25%
   C. 33.3%
   D. 45%
   E. 50%

6. On September 1st, a jacket was priced at $180. On October 1st, the price was reduced by 30%. On November 1st, the price was further reduced by 20% of the October 1st price and marked FINAL. What percent of the original price was the FINAL price?

   F. 50%
   G. 45%
   H. 90%
   J. 60%
   K. 56%

7. Bertrand earned 91, 86, 94, and 84 on four tests, each worth 100 points, given so far this term. How many points must he earn on his fifth test, also worth 100 points, to average at least 90 points for the five tests given this term?

   A. 95
   B. 90
   C. 100
   D. 85
   E. 80

8. When Sonny was cleaning out his refrigerator, he found 2 bottles of ranch dressing. Looking at the labels, he noticed that the capacity of the larger bottle was twice the capacity of the smaller bottle. He estimated that the smaller bottle was about $\frac{1}{2}$ full of ranch dressing and the larger bottle was about $\frac{3}{4}$ full of ranch dressing. He poured all the ranch dressing from the smaller bottle into the larger bottle. About how full was the larger bottle after this?

   F. $\frac{3}{4}$
   G. $\frac{1}{2}$
   H. $\frac{7}{8}$
   J. Completely full
   K. Overflowing

9. Isaac and Albert own an ice cream shop. They offer 12 flavors, 6 toppings, and 3 types of cones. If they use up to 1 ice cream flavor, 1 topping, and 1 type of cone for each ice cream cone they sell, how many possible combinations of ice cream cones can they make?

   A. 21
   B. 216
   C. 432
   D. 42
   E. 32

10. Traveling at approximately 186,000 miles per second, about how many miles does a beam of light travel in 3 hours?

    F. $6.70 \times 10^9$
    G. $6.70 \times 10^8$
    H. $3.35 \times 10^7$
    J. $2.01 \times 10^9$
    K. $1.12 \times 10^7$

Math Mastery - Level 1

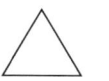

11. In the figure below, points A, C, E, and G are collinear; B, C, and D are collinear; D, E, and F are collinear. Angle measurements are as marked. What is the measurement of ∠ABC?

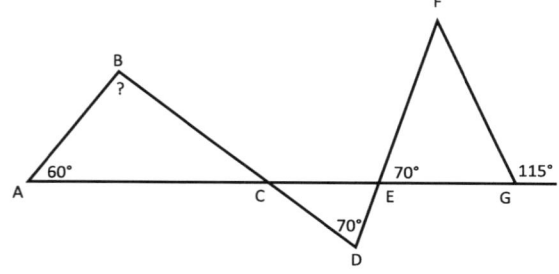

   A. 40°
   B. 60°
   C. 70°
   D. 80°
   E. 90°

12. Let $a$ equal $3b - 2c + 4$. What happens to the value of $a$ if the value of $b$ increases by 1 and the value of $c$ decreases by 2?

   F. The value of $a$ increases by 1.
   G. The value of $a$ increases by 7.
   H. The value of $a$ decreases by 3.
   J. The value of $a$ is unchanged.
   K. The value of $a$ cannot be determined.

13. In the figure below, B is on $\overline{AC}$, E is on $\overline{DF}$, $\overline{AC}$ is parallel to $\overline{DF}$, and $\overline{BE}$ is congruent to $\overline{BF}$. What is the measure of ∠FBC?

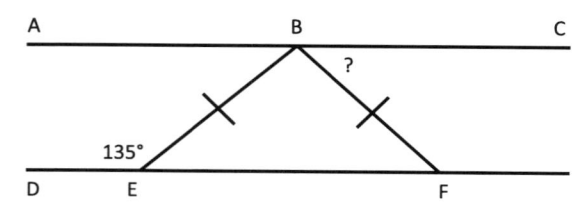

   A. 55°
   B. 35°
   C. 45°
   D. 145°
   E. 135°

14. The ratio of $a$ to $b$ is 1 to 5, and the ratio of $c$ to $b$ is 2 to 3. What is the ratio of $a$ to $c$?

   F. 3:10
   G. 1:2
   H. 5:10
   J. 2:5
   K. 3:5

15. For all real $x$, $(4x + 3)^2 = $ ?

   A. $8x^2 + 6$
   B. $8x^2 + 14x + 6$
   C. $16x^2 + 9$
   D. $16x^2 + 24x + 9$
   E. $8x^2 + 24x + 6$

344

# Math Mastery - Level 1

## Answer Explanations

1. **The correct answer is D**. Substitute 3 for *k* in the equation. 3 • (3 + 3)² = (3)(6)² = 3 • 36 = 108. Remember to resolve the exponent before multiplying.

2. **The correct answer is G**. Express this word problem algebraically. Use *x* to represent the number you're trying to figure out.

    $$\frac{(7+x)}{(15+x)} = \frac{1}{5}$$

    *Multiply both sides by 15 + x.*

    $$7 + x = \frac{(15+x)}{5}$$

    *Multiply both sides by 5.*

    35 + 5x = 15 + x

    *Solve for x by getting x by itself. Subtract x from both sides.*

    35 + 4x = 15

    *Subtract 35 from both sides.*

    4x = -20

    *Divide both sides by 4.*

    x = -5

3. **The correct answer is A**. This can be solved by using the distance formula, $d = \sqrt{(y_2 - y_1)^2 + (x_2 - x_1)^2}$. For the points (-2,3) and (7,6), this is $d = \sqrt{(6-3)^2 + [7-(-2)]^2} = \sqrt{9+81} = \sqrt{90} = 3\sqrt{10}$.

    If you didn't remember the distance formula, you can still solve this by drawing it out on the coordinate plane and using the Pythagorean Theorem. These points give you a right triangle with side lengths 3 and 9.

    Using the Pythagorean Theorem ($a^2 + b^2 = c^2$):

    $3^2 + 9^2 = c^2$

    $9 + 81 = 90 = c^2$

    *Find the square root of both sides.*

    $c = \sqrt{90} = 3\sqrt{10}$

4. **The correct answer is F**. Use the Pythagorean Theorem. Since our hypotenuse is 15, and one side length is 12, the equation is $15^2 = 12^2 + a^2$.

   $225 = 144 + a^2$

   *Subtract 144 from both sides.*

   $a^2 = 81$

   *Find the square root of both sides.*

   $a = \sqrt{81} = 9$

   A right triangle in a word problem is a good clue that you may need to use the Pythagorean Theorem.

5. **The correct answer is B**. There are 180 degrees along the circle from A to B. This means that a 45 degree angle is $\frac{1}{4}$ of the full 180 degree angle. $\frac{1}{4}$ is 25%.

6. **The correct answer is K**. Initially, the price is reduced by 30%. (30%)($180) = $54, so the new price is $180 - $54 = $126. This is then reduced by a further 20%, giving (20%)($126) = $25.20. So, the final price is $126 - $25.20 = $100.80. Divide $100.80 by $180. $100.80 is 56% of $180, so 56% is our answer.

7. **The correct answer is A**. To find the minimum score Bertrand must earn on his final test in order to receive an average grade of 90 for all of his tests, first find the sum of the first four tests.

   91 + 86 + 94 + 84 = 355. In order to have an average of 90 on each test, he must earn (90)(5) = 450 points in all. The score he needs on the final test is the difference of these two numbers. 450 - 355 = 95. Bertrand must earn a 95 on his final test in order to receive a 90 average.

8. **The correct answer is J**. Let the capacity of the larger bottle be $x$ ounces. This means that the capacity of the smaller bottle is $\frac{1}{2}$ full of ranch dressing, or $\frac{1}{2}(\frac{1}{2} \cdot x) = \frac{1}{4} \cdot x$ ounces. If the contents of the smaller bottle are poured into the larger bottle, the larger bottle will then contain $\frac{1}{4} \cdot x + \frac{3}{4} \cdot x$ ounces = $x$ ounces. So, the bottle is completely full.

9. **The correct answer is B**. For each of the 12 flavors of ice cream, there are 6 toppings and 3 cones. In order to find all combinations, multiply 12 by 6 by 3, or (12)(6)(3) = (12)(18) = 216.

10. **The correct answer is J**. In three hours, 3(60)(60) = 10,800 seconds. The speed of light is given to be 186,000 miles/sec. Multiply (10,800)(186,000) = $2.01 \times 10^9$.

11. **The correct answer is D**. Because vertical angles are equal, ∠CED is equal to ∠FEG. Therefore, ∠CED is 70 degrees. Also, because the angles of a triangle add up to 180 degrees, we can conclude that ∠DCE is 180 – 70 – 70 = 40 degrees. Again, knowing that vertical angles are equal allows us to note that ∠ACB is then 40 degrees. Finally, because interior angles add up to 180 degrees, we can say that ∠ABC is 180 – 60 – 40 = 80 degrees.

12. **The correct answer is G.** The new value of $b$ is $(b + 1)$ and the new value of $c$ is $(c - 2)$. Substituting into the given expression yields $3(b + 1) - 2(c - 2) + 4$. Rewrite this as $3b + 3 - 2c + 4 + 4 = (3b - 2c + 4) + 7$. Notice that the portion of the expression in parentheses is equal to $a$, so this expression is equal to $a + 7$. Therefore, the value of $a$ increases by 7.

    An easy way to solve this is to plug in made-up values for $a$, $b$, and $c$. Make the changes described by adding 1 to $b$ and subtracting 2 from $c$, and you'll see that $a$ increased by 7.

13. **The correct answer is C.** We are given that $\angle$DEB is 135 degrees. By supplementary angles, $\angle$BEF is 45 degrees. Because $\Delta$BEF is an isosceles triangle, we know also that $\angle$EFB is 45 degrees. Because interior angles equal 180, $\angle$EBF is 180 - 45 - 45 = 90. Because BE and BF are congruent, we know that $\angle$ABE and $\angle$CBF are equal. Lastly because straight angles are 180 degrees, we know that they share 180 - 90 degrees, and are therefore each 45 degrees.

14. **The correct answer is F.** The ratio $\frac{a}{b}$ is $\frac{1}{5}$, and the ratio $\frac{c}{b}$ is $\frac{2}{3}$. Since $\frac{a}{c} = \frac{a}{b} \cdot \frac{b}{c} = \frac{1}{5} \cdot \frac{3}{2} = \frac{3}{10}$.

    You can also plug in a number for $a$ and compare it to what you end up with at $c$. Plug in 3 at $a$. For every 1 $a$ there is 5 $b$, so in this example there is 15 $b$. For every 3 $b$ there is 2 $c$, so that means there is 10 $c$. In other words, for every 3 $a$, there is 10 $c$, so F is the best choice.

15. **The correct answer is D.** For all $x$, $(4x + 3)^2 = (4x + 3)(4x + 3)$. Using FOIL on this gives $16x^2 + 12x + 12x + 9 = 16x^2 + 24x + 9$.

# Math Mini-Test 7

16. The measure of each interior angle of a regular polygon with $n$ sides is $\frac{(n-2)\pi}{n}$ radians. What is the measure of each interior angle of a regular polygon with $n$ sides in degrees?

F. $\frac{(n+2)180}{n}$
G. $\frac{(n-1)360}{n}$
H. $\frac{(n-2)90}{n}$
J. $\frac{(n-2)180}{n}$
K. $\frac{(n-2)360}{n}$

17. If the inequality $|f| < |g|$ is true, then which of the following must be true?

A. $f < |g|$
B. $|g|$
C. $f > |g|$
D. $f \neq g$
E. $f = g$

18. Bubble Co. sells a bag of 80 pieces of bubblegum for $20.00, while Gummy Co. sells a similar bag of 50 pieces of bubblegum for $10.00. Which company's price per piece of bubble gum is cheaper, and what is that price?

F. Bubble Co. at $0.20
G. Bubble Co. at $0.25
H. Gummy Co. at $0.15
J. Gummy Co. at $0.20
K. Gummy Co. at $0.25

19. A brand of notebook costs $2.00 before sales tax is added. When you buy 4 of these notebooks, you receive one additional notebook free. What is the average cost per notebook for the 5 notebooks before sales tax is added?

A. $1.50
B. $2.00
C. $1.60
D. $2.20
E. $1.90

20. A line contains the points P, Q, R, and S. Point R is between points S and P. Point Q is between R and P. Which of the following inequalities must be true about the lengths of these segments?

F. RQ < RS
G. RQ < QP
H. SR < SQ
J. SR < RQ
K. SR < QP

21. What are the values for $x$ that satisfy the equation $(x - a)(x + b) = 0$ ?

A. $a$ and $-b$
B. $a$ and $b$
C. $-a$ and $-b$
D. $-a$ and $b$
E. $ab$ and $-ab$

22. Which of the following expressions is equivalent to $(-9x^4y^2)^3$ ?

F. $-81x^7y^5$
G. $81x^7y^5$
H. $243x^{12}y^6$
J. $-729x^{12}y^6$
K. $-243x^7y^5$

*Use the following information to answer questions 23 - 25.*

The bottom view of a cylindrical gasoline tank on its support is shown in the figure below. The interior radius of the tank's circular end is 5 feet. The interior length of the tank is 20 feet.

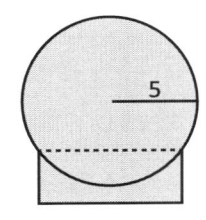

23. Which of the following is closest to the tank's volume, in cubic feet?

    A. 600
    B. 1,000
    C. 1,600
    D. 2,000
    E. 6,000

24. The tank currently holds 6,000 gallons of gasoline. Each gallon of gasoline weighs about 8 pounds. About how many pounds does this gasoline weigh?

    F. 6,000
    G. 12,000
    H. 36,000
    J. 40,000
    K. 48,000

25. The center of the circular end of the tank is 3 feet above the top level of the support. What is the width, in feet, of the support?

    A. 2
    B. 4
    C. 6
    D. 8
    E. 16

26. What is the value of $x$ that satisfies the equation $2(x - 3) = 4x + 8$ ?

    F. 5
    G. 12
    H. -8
    J. 4
    K. -7

27. A point in the standard $(x,y)$ coordinate plane has non-zero coordinates $(a,b)$. If this point is reflected about the $x$-axis, reflected about the $y$-axis, then reflected about the $x$-axis again, what will be the new coordinates of this point?

    A. $(a,b)$
    B. $(-a,b)$
    C. $(a,-b)$
    D. $(-a,-b)$
    E. $(0,0)$

28. On the real number line below, with coordinates as labeled, an object moves according to the following set of instructions:

    From point B the object moves right to D, then left to A, then right to C and continues right until it stops in its final position at E. What is the closest estimate of the total length, in coordinate units, of the movements this object makes?

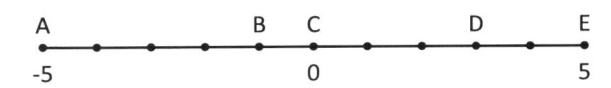

    F. 10
    G. 5
    H. 12
    J. 20
    K. 22

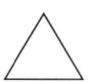

29. When Kaylee starts a math assignment, she spends 3 minutes getting out her book and a sheet of paper, sharpening her pencil, looking up the assignment in her assignment notebook, and turning to the correct page in her book. The equation $t = 12p + 3$ is a model for the time, $t$ minutes, Kaylee budgets for math assignment on $p$ problems. Which of the following statements is necessarily true according to Kaylee's model?

   A. She budgets 15 minutes per problem.
   B. She budgets 12 minutes per problem.
   C. She budgets 3 minutes per problem.
   D. She budgets 12 minutes for hard problems and 3 minutes for easy problems.
   E. She budgets 15 minutes for hard problems and 3 minutes for easy problems.

30. By definition, the determinant $\begin{bmatrix} a & c \\ b & d \end{bmatrix}$ equals $ad - bc$. What is the value of $\begin{bmatrix} x & 9x \\ 2y & 6y \end{bmatrix}$ when $x = -1$ and $y = 4$?

   F. −96
   G. −48
   H. 0
   J. 48
   K. 96

Math Mastery - Level 1

# Answer Explanations

16. **The correct answer is J.** π radians is the same as 180 degrees.

    Multiply the expression by $\frac{180}{\pi}$ to get $[(n-2)\frac{180}{n}]$.

17. **The correct answer is D.** Upon examining the expression, the only possible answer is that $f \neq g$. For each of the other answers, we can find an example that yields a false statement. You have to pick a couple numbers to see if this works, actively trying to eliminate answer choices by making them produce a false statement.

    For example, assume $f = -1$ and $g = -2$.

    Then $|f| < |g|$ is true (since $1 > 2$).

    A is incorrect because $-1 < -2$ is false.

    B is incorrect because $2 < -1$ is false.

    C is incorrect because $-1 > 2$ is false.

    D could be correct using these numbers, since it is true that $f \neq g$.

    E is incorrect because $-1 = -2$ is false.

    Therefore, through the process of elimination, D is the correct answer.

18. **The correct answer is J.** Bubble Co. sells at $20.00 for a bag of 80 pieces of gum, or $\$\frac{20}{80} = \frac{1}{4}$. Gummy Co. sells at $10.00 for a bag of 50 pieces of gum, or $\$\frac{10}{50} = \frac{1}{5}$. Bubble Co. then sells for $0.25 per piece and Gummy Co. sells for $0.20 per piece. Gummy Co. is less expensive.

19. **The correct answer is C.** A single notebook costs $2.00. However, if you buy four notebooks for 4 • $2.00 = $8.00, you will receive an additional notebook for free. This equates to five notebooks at the price of $8.00. To find the cost per notebook, divide $8.00 ÷ 5 = $1.60.

20. **The correct answer is H.** The order or the points will either be SRQP or PQRS. Although the order is given, there is no explanation of the lengths of the given segments. However, SR must be less than SQ, because SR is contained in SQ. For all other given inequalities, it is not necessarily true that one segment is larger or smaller than another.

21. **The correct answer is A.** Values for $x$ that satisfy the equation $(x - a)(x + b) = 0$ cause the left side to equal zero. When $x = a$, the equation becomes $(a - a)(a + b) = (0)(a + b) = 0$. When $x = -b$, the equation becomes $(-b - a)(-b + b) = -(a + b)(0) = 0$. So, the two values of $x$ that satisfy the equation are $x = a$ and $x = -b$.

    To solve this quickly you need to immediately start plugging in answer choices and see what works. The words *"what are the values..."* or *"which of the following..."* are clues that you may need to plug in answer choices to find the answer.

## Math Mini-Test 7

22. **The correct answer is J**. To find an equivalent expression to $(-9x^4y^2)^3$, we need to cube each term.

    $(-9)^3 = -729$, $(x^4)^3 = x^{12}$, $(y^2)^3 = y^6$. So, $(-9x^4y^2)^3 = -729x^{12}y^6$.

23. **The correct answer is C**. The volume of the cylinder is the area of the circular surface multiplied by the length of the tank. The area of the end is pi • $(5)^2 = 25\pi$. The length of the tank is 20 feet. So, the volume of the tank is $V = (20)(25)\pi = 1570.796$. Rounded up, this is 1600 ft².

24. **The correct answer is K**. The tank holds 6,000 gallons. Each gallon weighs 8 pounds. This means that the 6,000 gallons of gasoline weighs $(6,000)(8) = 48,000$ pounds.

25. **The correct answer is D**. To find the width of the tank, note that we can draw a right triangle with one side being the vertical distance from the center of the circle to the support, the hypotenuse being the radius from the center to the end of the support, and the final side being half the length of the support. This means that $3^2 + b^2 = 5^2$. Therefore $b^2 = 16$, and $b = 4$. Because $b$ represents the length of half of the support, the full length of the support is $2b = 2(4) = 8$.

26. **The correct answer is K**. To find the value of $x$ that solves the equation $2(x - 3) = 4x + 8$, we first multiply 2 to $(x - 3)$ using the distributive property. This yields $2x - 6 = 4x + 8$. Then, subtract $2x$ and 8 from both sides of the equation to get $-14 = 2x$. Dividing both sides by 2 then gives our final answer, $x = -7$.

27. **The correct answer is B**. Reflecting the point $(a,b)$ about the x-axis gives the point $(a,-b)$. Then reflecting the point about the y-axis gives $(-a,-b)$. Reflecting this point about the x-axis again places the final point at $(-a,b)$. It can help to draw this out.

28. **The correct answer is K**. Move your pencil along the line described and count up the length that your pencil point moves through as you go. From B to D is 4 units. From D to A is 8 units. From A to C is 5 units, then from C to E is another 5 units. $4 + 8 + 5 + 5 = 22$. Note that you don't just compare where your pencil started to where it ended. The question specifically asks you to estimate the total length of the movements.

29. **The correct answer is B**. In the given equation $t = 12p + 3$, the 12 represents the number of minutes required to complete a single problem; for each new problem she budgets for an additional 12 minutes. The 3 in the equations represents an initial 3 minutes she does not spend doing problems, but setting up her homework. Because this is not relevant after the initial set up, she simply budgets 12 minutes per problem.

30. **The correct answer is J**. The determinant is $(x)(6y) - (9x)(2y)$.

    For $x = -1$ and $y = 4$, this simplifies to $(-1)(6 • 4) - (9 • -1)(2 • 4) = -24 + 72 = 48$.

# Math Mini-Test 8

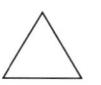

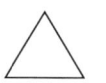

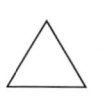

31. Clark wants to dig a circular swimming pool in his backyard. He is going to dig the pool to have a radius of either 15 feet or 20 feet. Either pool will have a depth of 6 feet. If Clark decides to dig the smaller pool, what percent of the volume of the larger pool will the volume of the smaller pool be?

   A. 100%
   B. 133%
   C. 25%
   D. 56%
   E. 75%

32. Which of the following expressions is equivalent to $2xy(3xy^2 + 3x^2y)$ ?

   F. $6x^5y^5$
   G. $12x^3y^3$
   H. $12x^5y^5$
   J. $6x^2y^3 + 6x^3y^2$
   K. $12x^2y^2 + 12x^3y^3$

33. What is the least common denominator when adding the fractions $\frac{a}{2}$, $\frac{b}{4}$, $\frac{c}{5}$, and $\frac{d}{10}$ ?

   A. 10
   B. 20
   C. 40
   D. 80
   E. 100

34. A utility company charges customers $3.00 per 1,000 gallons of water and $18.00 per month for trash pickup. Which of the following expressions gives a customer's total monthly charges, in dollars, for use of $g$ thousand gallons of water and trash pickup?

   F. $3.00g + 18.00$
   G. $21.00g$
   H. $18.00g + 3.00$
   J. $1.00g + 6.00$
   K. $3000.00g + 18.00$

35. A right triangle that has its sides measured in the same unit of length is shown below. For any such triangle, cos B • sin A is equivalent to:

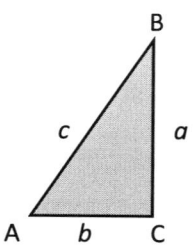

   A. $\frac{c}{a}$
   B. $\frac{a}{b}$
   C. $\frac{a^2}{b^2}$
   D. $\frac{a^2}{c^2}$
   E. $\frac{b^2}{a^2}$

36. Which real number satisfies $(4^x)(2) = 16^2$ ?

   F. $\frac{7}{4}$
   G. 3
   H. 4
   J. 2
   K. $\frac{7}{2}$

360

37. The system of equations below has at least one real solution and at most three real solutions. For which value or values of $x$ is the system satisfied?

$y = 2x - 2$
$y = x^2 - 2$
$y = |x|$

A. 0
B. 2
C. -2, 2
D. 0, 2
E. -2, 2, 0

38. The tent illustrated below is in the shape of a right triangular prism and is made of cloth. How many square feet of cloth is required for the front, rear, bottom, and 2 sides of the tent to the nearest tenth?

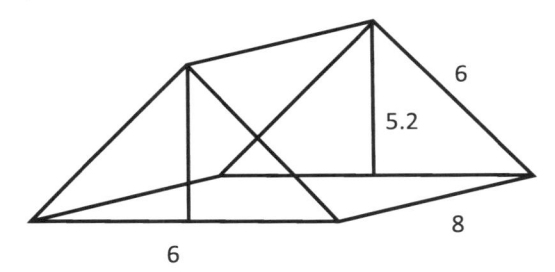

F. 175.2
G. 111.6
H. 223.2
J. 127.2
K. 254.4

39. If $a^2 = 25$ and $b^2 = 36$, which of the following CANNOT be a value of $a - b$?

A. 1
B. -1
C. -11
D. 11
E. 61

40. In a town of 1,000 people, the 550 males have an average age of 40, and the 450 females have an average age of 35. To the nearest year, what is the average age of the town's entire population?

F. 37
G. 38
H. 35
J. 40
K. 45

# Math Mastery - Level 1

## Answer Explanations

31. **The correct answer is D.** To find the percent volume of the larger pool that the smaller pool will be, we should first find both volumes. The volume of the larger pool is $V_1 = (6)(20)^2\pi$. The volume of the smaller pool is $V_2 = (6)(15)^2\pi$. The ratio of the volume of the smaller pool to the larger pool is then $\frac{V_2}{V_1} = \frac{(6)(15)^2 2\pi}{(6)(20)^2 2\pi}$ which simplifies to $\frac{225}{400} = .5625$ Convert this to a percent to get 56.25% and round to 56%.

32. **The correct answer is J.** Use the distributive property.

    $2xy(3xy^2) + 2xy(3x^2y) = 6x^2y^3 + 6x^3y^2$.

33. **The correct answer is B.** The least common denominator is the smallest possible multiple of 2, 4, 5, and 10. 2 and 5 are prime numbers, but 4 and 10 can be written as their prime factors, $2 \cdot 2 = 4$ and $2 \cdot 5 = 10$. This implies that the smallest possible multiple of all four numbers is $2 \cdot 2 \cdot 5 = 4 \cdot 5 = 20$. The least common denominator is 20.

    Another way to do this is to plug in the answer choices. 10 is not a common denominator (because 4 does not divide into it evenly) but 20 is a common denominator and it is the least of the options provided.

34. **The correct answer is F.** Each 1,000 gallons of water costs $3.00, so $g$ of these *"1,000 gallons of water"* cost $g \cdot 3$. On top of this, there is an $18.00 charge that is added for trash pickup. The resulting equation is $3.00g + $18.00.

35. **The correct answer is D.** 'Cosine' is the ratio of the length of the adjacent side to the length of the hypotenuse. So $\cos B = \frac{a}{c}$. Note, also, that 'sine' is the ratio of the length of the opposite side to the length of the hypotenuse. So, $\sin A = \frac{a}{c}$ as well. This gives $(\cos B)(\cos A) = (\frac{a}{c})(\frac{a}{c}) = \frac{a^2}{c^2}$.

    Remember the abbreviation SOHCAHTOA is you're having trouble remembering what the sin, cos, and tan functions represent.

36. **The correct answer is K.** To find the value of $x$ that satisfies $(4^x)(2) = (16)^2$, express 4 and 16 as powers of 2. $4 = 2^2$ and $16 = 2^4$. Substituting these in gives $(2^2)^x(2) = (2^4)^2$. We can rewrite these again as $(2)(2)^{2x} = 2^{2x+1} = (2)^8$. Since we now have these as expressions of the same base, we can drop the bases. $2x + 1 = 8$. Solving this for $x$ yields $x = \frac{7}{2}$.

37. **The correct answer is B.** To solve the system, first solve $2x - 2 = x^2 - 2$. Adding 2 to both sides gives $2x = x^2$, and subtracting $2x$ from both sides gives $x^2 - 2x = 0$. Factoring out $x$ from both terms $x(x - 2) = 0$. $x = 0$ or 2. This gives that the only possible answers are $x = 0$ and $x = 2$. We must also test these answers in $y = |x|$. For $x = 0$, $y = |0| = 0$, which should give the same value for $y$ in the two previous equations. However, these both yield $y = -2$. For $x = 2$, $y = |2| = 2$. $y = 2^2 - 2 = 2$ and $y = 2(2) - 2 = 2$. $x = 2$ is the only value that solves the system.

38. **The correct answer is F.** Find the area of each component of the tent. The front of the tent has a width of 6 and a height of 5.2. The area formula of a triangle is $\frac{1}{2} \cdot$ width $\cdot$ height, so the front of the tent $= 6 \cdot 5.2 \cdot \frac{1}{2} = 15.6$. The rear of the tent is identical to the front. The bottom of the tent is $6 \cdot 8 = 48$. Each side of the tent is also $6 \cdot 8 = 48$. Therefore the total surface area of the tent is $15.6 + 15.6 + 48 + 48 + 48 = 175.2$.

39. **The correct answer is E.** The values of $a$ that satisfy $a^2 = 25$ are $a = 5$ and $a = -5$. The values of $b$ that satisfy $b^2 = 36$ are $b = 6$ and $b = -6$. The possible values of $a - b$ are then 1, -1, 11, -11. 61 is not a possible value of the expression.

40. **The correct answer is G.** Because 550 males have an average age of 40, the sum of their ages is approximately (550)(40) = 22,000. Because 450 females have an average age of 35, the sum of their ages is approximately (450)(35) = 15,750. Sum the ages and then divide this value by the number of people in the town. This gives $\frac{(22,000 + 15,750)}{1,000} = 37.75$, or about 38.

# Math Mini-Test 9

## Math Mastery - Level 1

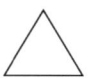

**41.** On the real number line, what is the midpoint of -4 and 12 ?

A. 8
B. 6
C. 4
D. 2
E. 0

**42.** A brackish water aquarium tank that is already partially full is having a combination of salt water and fresh water added in order to balance the salt content of the water. The graph below shows the salt content of the water over time as salt water and fresh water are poured into the tank.

Until the tank is completely full, either salt water, fresh water, or an equal combination of salt water and fresh water will be poured into the tank. The tank is completely filled at time $c$. Which of the following describes what occurred on the intervals $[0,a]$, $[a,b]$, and $[b,c]$.

F. $[0,a]$: Fresh, $[a,b]$: Salt, $[b,c]$: Fresh
G. $[0,a]$: Salt, $[a,b]$: Fresh, $[b,c]$: Equal
H. $[0,a]$: Salt, $[a,b]$: Fresh, $[b,c]$: Salt
J. $[0,a]$: Equal, $[a,b]$: Fresh, $[b,c]$: Salt
K. $[0,a]$: Equal, $[a,b]$: Salt, $[b,c]$: Fresh

**43.** What is the slope of the line given by the equation $9x + 15y - 25 = 0$ ?

A. $\frac{3}{5}$
B. $-\frac{3}{5}$
C. $\frac{25}{9}$
D. $\frac{5}{3}$
E. $-\frac{5}{3}$

**44.** If $4\frac{1}{4} = y + 2\frac{2}{5}$, then $y = $ ?

F. $6\frac{13}{20}$
G. $\frac{20}{37}$
H. $1\frac{17}{20}$
J. $-\frac{20}{37}$
K. $-6\frac{13}{20}$

**45.** If $(x - 6)$ is a factor of $3x^2 - 11x + k$, what is the value of $k$ ?

A. -21
B. 21
C. 42
D. -42
E. 36

**46.** Which of the following inequalities represents the graph on the real number line below?

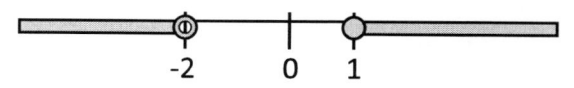

F. $-2 \geq x \geq 1$
G. $x \geq 1, x \leq -2$
H. $-2 > x \geq 1$
J. $x \geq 1, x < -2$
K. $x > 1, x < -2$

**47.** A system of linear equations is shown below:

   $5x - 6y = 15$
   $-10x + 12y = 30$

   Which of the following describes the graph of this system of linear equations in the standard $(x,y)$ coordinate plane?

   **A.** Two distinct intersecting lines
   **B.** Two parallel lines
   **C.** Two perpendicular lines
   **D.** One line with positive slope
   **E.** One line with negative slope

**48.** Tera drove 300 miles in 6 hours of actual driving time. By driving an average of 10 miles per hour faster, Tera could have saved how many hours of actual driving time?

   **F.** 2 hours
   **G.** $\frac{1}{2}$ hour
   **H.** 1 hour
   **J.** $\frac{1}{4}$ hour
   **K.** $\frac{1}{3}$ hour

**49.** Iris is going to cover a rectangular area 12 feet by 9 feet with rectangular paving blocks that are 6 inches by 4 inches by 2 inches to make a flat deck. What is the minimum number of paving blocks she will need if all the paving blocks will face the same direction?

   *Note: She will not cut any of the paving blocks.*

   **A.** 648
   **B.** 972
   **C.** 1296
   **D.** 1944
   **E.** 3888

**50.** Which of the following is a value of $x$ that satisfies $\log_x 81 = 2$ ?

   **F.** 9
   **G.** 81
   **H.** 3
   **J.** 0
   **K.** 27

## Answer Explanations

41. **The correct answer is C.** In order to find the midpoint of -4 and 12 on the real number line, take the average of the two points $\frac{(-4+12)}{2} = \frac{8}{2} = 4$. You could also just draw the number line out and find the midpoint visually.

42. **The correct answer is G.** From time 0 to time $a$, the salt content of the water seems to be increasing, meaning they are pouring in salt water. From time $a$ to time $b$, the salt content begins to decrease, meaning they are pouring in fresh water. From time $b$ to time $c$, the salt content remains constant, meaning that they are pouring in an equal combination of salt and fresh water. This gives [0,$a$]: Salt, [$a$,$b$]: Fresh, [$b$,$c$]: Equal.

43. **The correct answer is B.** One way to find the slope of the line is to place the equation $9x + 15y - 25 = 0$ into slope-intercept form, $y = mx + b$. Begin by subtracting $9x$ and adding 25 to both sides of the equation. This gives $15y = -9x + 25$. Dividing both sides by 15 gives the equation in slope-intercept form, $y = -\frac{3}{5}x + \frac{5}{3}$. In this equation, slope is given by $m = -\frac{3}{5}$.

44. **The correct answer is H.** To solve the equation $4\frac{1}{4} = y + 2\frac{2}{5}$, for $y$, subtract $2\frac{2}{5}$ from both sides. So, $y = 4\frac{1}{4} - 2\frac{2}{5}$. To subtract two mixed numbers, the fraction portions must have common denominators, so we will multiply $\frac{1}{4}$ by $\frac{5}{5}$ and $\frac{2}{5}$ by $\frac{4}{4}$, giving $y = 4\frac{5}{20} - 2\frac{8}{20} = 1\frac{17}{20}$.

45. **The correct answer is D.** If $(x - 6)$ is a factor of $3x^2 - 11x + k$, then there must be another factor such that $(x - 6)(3x + a) = 3x^2 - 11x + k$.

    Use the FOIL Method:

    $3x^2 - 18x + ax - 6a = 3x^2 = 11x + k$

    So, $-18x + ax = -11x$ and $-6a = k$.

    If $-18x + ax = -11x$, then $ax = 18x - 11x = 7x$. So, $a = 7$. If $a = 7$, then $-6(7) = k = -42$.

46. **The correct answer is J.** In order to find the inequalities that describe the graph, it is important to note that a solid dot represents *"or equal to"* while an open dot implies *"strictly greater or less than."* The left side of the number line shows that values less than -2 satisfy the inequality and the right side shows that numbers greater than or equal to 1 satisfy it. Therefore, our answer is $x \geq 1, x < -2$.

47. **The correct answer is B.** To make this determination, you need to place both equations into slope-intercept form by getting $y$ all by itself on one side of the equation. Placing these in slope-intercept form gives $y = -\frac{5}{6} - \frac{15}{6}$ and $y = -\frac{5}{6}x + \frac{15}{6}$. From here, we can see that these are two parallel lines with different $y$-intercepts. Two lines with the same slope and different $y$-intercepts are always parallel. Graph the lines if you are unsure of the rule.

48. **The correct answer is H.** Because Tera drove 300 miles in 6 hours, she was averaging $300 \div 6 = 50$ miles per hour. If she drove 10 miles faster, that would be 60 miles per hour. Driving 300 miles at 60 miles per hour would take 5 hours. So she would save 1 hour.

## Math Mini-Test 9

49. **The correct answer is A.** To minimize the number of blocks used, she needs to face the side with the maximum area upwards. This is the 6" by 4" side. A 1' by 1' square of the deck can be covered by 6 blocks, as 2 • 6" = 12" = 1' and 3 • 4 = 12" = 1'. Therefore, the minimum number of blocks necessary to cover the deck is (6)(12)(9) = 648 blocks.

    You can also solve this by converting the measure of the area to inches, since there are 12 inches in a foot. 12 ft = 144 inches, and 9 ft = 108 inches. Our rectangular area is 108 • 144 = 15552 sq inches. Our paving blocks are 6 • 4 = 24 sq inches, so we need 15552 ÷ 24 = 648 paving blocks.

    Drawing this out can simplify the question for you.

50. **The correct answer is F.** According to the definition of the log function, $\log_x(81) = 2$ is equivalent to the expression $x^2 = 81$. This implies $x = 9$ or -9. Because 9 is the only available answer, this must be the answer.

# Math Mini-Test 10

**51.** Consider the 3 statements below to be true:

*1. All frogs that jump on lily pads are green.*
*2. Frog F is not green.*
*3. Frog G jumps on lily pads.*

Which of the following statements is necessarily true?

- A. Frog F jumps on lily pads.
- B. Frog G does not jump on lily pads.
- C. Frog F is green.
- D. Frog G is green.
- E. Frog G is not green.

**52.** A large cube has edges that are three times as long as those of a small cube. The volume of the large cube is how many times the volume of the small cube?

- F. 3
- G. 9
- H. 27
- J. 81
- K. 243

**53.** Shown below is the graph of the equation $y = 3x + 1$ for values of $x$ such that $0 =< x =< 3$

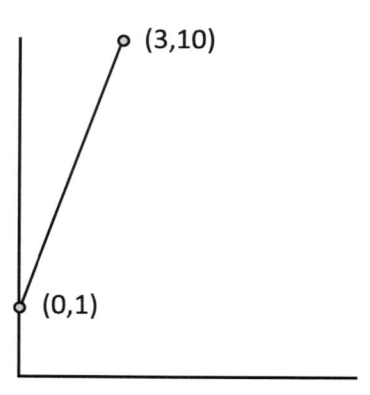

Which of the following statements is (are) true?

I. The graph has a constant slope 3.
II. The point (2,6) exists on the graph.
III. The range of the graph consists of all values of $y$ such that $1 \leq y \leq 10$.

- A. I only
- B. I and II
- C. I and III
- D. I, II, and III
- E. None of the above

**54.** The △ABC has the following side lengths:

$a = 4, b = 17, c = 29$

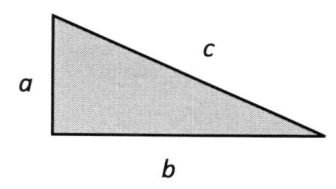

Determine if △ABC is a valid triangle.

- F. It is invalid because $b + c > a$.
- G. It is invalid because $a + b < c$.
- H. It is invalid because $b > a - c$.
- J. It is invalid because $a < b + c$.
- K. It is valid.

## Math Mini-Test 10

**55.** Which of the following inequalities defines the solution set for the inequality $14 - 7x > 6$ ?

A. $x > -\frac{20}{7}$
B. $x > \frac{20}{7}$
C. $x < \frac{20}{7}$
D. $x > \frac{8}{7}$
E. $x < \frac{8}{7}$

**56.** The electrical resistance, $r$ ohms, of 1,000 feet of solid copper wire at 77 °F can be approximated by the model $r = \frac{10,770}{d^2} - 0.37$ for any wire diameter $d$ mils (1 mil = 0.001 inch), such that $5 < d < 100$. What is the resistance, in ohms, for such a wire with a diameter of 75 mils to the nearest tenth?

F. 1.0
G. 1.5
H. 1.6
J. 2.0
K. 2.3

**57.** The amplitude of the cosine function is given by $|A|$ when $f(\theta) = A \cdot \cos \theta$.

$-4 = A \cdot \cos \frac{\pi}{3}$

What is the amplitude of the cosine function $f(\theta)$?

*You may use the chart below to find your answer.*

| $\theta$ | $\cos \theta$ |
|---|---|
| 0 | 1 |
| $\frac{\pi}{6}$ | $\frac{\sqrt{3}}{2}$ |
| $\frac{\pi}{4}$ | $\frac{1}{\sqrt{2}}$ |
| $\frac{\pi}{3}$ | $\frac{1}{2}$ |
| $\frac{\pi}{2}$ | 0 |

A. $-4$
B. $4$
C. $-8$
D. $8$
E. $16$

**58.** If $\sin A = \frac{a}{c}$, $a > 0$, $c > 0$, and $0 < A < \frac{\pi}{2}$, then what is $\tan A$ ?

F. $\frac{a}{c}$
G. $\frac{c}{a}$
H. $\frac{\sqrt{c^2 - a^2}}{c}$
J. $\frac{a}{\sqrt{c^2 - a^2}}$
K. $\frac{a}{\sqrt{c^2 + a^2}}$

373

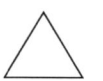

59. Pierre is cutting out lengths of an aluminum ring for an art project. He cuts out one arc with an angle of $\frac{\pi}{2}$, another with an angle of $\frac{\pi}{3}$, and one more with an angle of $\frac{\pi}{4}$. If the aluminum ring Pierre is cutting has a radius of 3 feet, what will be the total length, in feet, of the three arcs he cut from the aluminum ring?

   A. $\frac{13\pi}{4}$
   B. $3\pi$
   C. $2\pi$
   D. $\frac{7\pi}{2}$
   E. $13\pi$

60. The solution set of $\sqrt{x+2} > 3$ is the set of all real numbers x such that:

   F. $x > 5$
   G. $x > 7$
   H. $x > 13$
   J. $x > 11$
   K. $x > 9$

# Math Mastery - Level 1

## Answer Explanations

51. **The correct answer is D.** If a statement is necessarily true, it cannot be false, given the information provided. The first statement says that all frogs that jump on lily pads must be green, but this does not necessarily mean that all frogs that are green jump on lily pads. A, B, C, and E are necessarily false; they argue directly with the premises above. However, D follows directly from the above premises. Premise 1 states that if a frog has the characteristic of jumping on lily pads, then it must have a characteristic of being green. Premise 3 states that Frog G has the characteristic of jumping on lily pads, so it must also have the characteristic of being green.

52. **The correct answer is H.** The volume of a cube is given by $V = b^3$, where $b$ is the length of any of its edges (cubes have equal edges). So, if a small cube has edge length $a$, then its volume is $V = a^3$. If a large cube has edge length $3a$, then its volume is $V = (3a)^3 = 27a^3$. Its volume is 27 times that of the small cube.

    You can also solve this by selecting a length for the small cube and comparing the actual volume of the small cube to that of the larger cube. For example, if the length of the small cube is 3, then its volume is 3 • 3 • 3 = 27. The volume of the larger cube in this case would be 9 • 9 • 9 = 729. Divide the volume of the larger cube by the smaller cube: 729 ÷ 27 = 27.

53. **The correct answer is C.** Statement I is true. The slope of the graph is constant because it is a linear function; it has slope $m = 3$. Statement II is false. If the point (2,6) existed on the graph, then 6 = 3(2) + 1 = 7, which is false. Statement III is true. The range is the set of all $y$-values between 1 and 10. Therefore, Statements I & III are true.

54. **The correct answer is G.** For any triangle, the sum of the lengths of any two sides must be greater than the length of the third remaining side. For $a = 4$, $b = 17$, and $c = 29$, $a + b < c$ gives $4 + 17 < 29$, $21 < 29$. Triangle ABC cannot be valid because the sum of the lengths of $a$ and $b$ is less than the length of $c$.

    (You can try this rule out by trying to draw a triangle with a ruler with side lengths 2 inches, 3 inches, and 9 inches.)

55. **The correct answer is E.** To find the solution set that describes the inequality $14 - 7x > 6$, solve the inequality for $x$. First, add $7x$ to both sides of the equation and subtract 6 from both sides. This gives $7x < 8$. Divide both sides to get $x < \frac{8}{7}$.

56. **The correct answer is G.** Here, $d$ is given as 75 mils and $r = \frac{10{,}770}{(75)^2} - 0.37$, which is approximately 1.5 ohms.

57. **The correct answer is D.** To find amplitude, note that in $-4 = A \cdot \cos(\frac{\pi}{3})$, $\cos(\frac{\pi}{3}) = \frac{1}{2}$. This implies that $-4 = A(\frac{1}{2})$, or $A = -8$. Because amplitude is $|A|$, amplitude is then $|-8| = 8$.

58. **The correct answer is J.** If $\sin A = \frac{a}{c}$, then the side opposite A is $a$, and the hypotenuse is $c$. The side adjacent to A is then given by $\sqrt{(c^2 - a^2)}$ by using the Pythagorean Theorem.

    This means that $\tan A = \frac{opposite}{adjacent} = \frac{a}{\sqrt{(c^2-a^2)}}$

    It can help to draw this out in order to simplify solving it.

Math Mini-Test 10

59. **The correct answer is A**. Arc Length is given by $s = r(\theta)$. Pierre cut from a circle of $r = 3$, three pieces with angles $\frac{\pi}{2}, \frac{\pi}{3}$, and $\frac{\pi}{4}$. So total length of the pieces he cut was $s = 3(\frac{\pi}{2} + \frac{\pi}{3} + \frac{\pi}{4}) = 3(\frac{13\pi}{12}) = \frac{13\pi}{4}$.

60. **The correct answer is G**. To find the solution set of $\sqrt{[x+2]} > 3$, first square both sides of the equation. This yields $x + 2 > 9$, and subtracting 2 from both sides gives $x > 7$. This is our answer.

# Math Glossary

Not knowing the meaning of certain words can stop you from solving a math question on the ACT. Refer to this as you are answering questions on this test whenever you reach a math word you don't understand.

If you've finished Math Mastery Level 1, the final thing you should do in this book is read through these definitions. Even if you aced the whole book, some of these definitions may surprise you.

When you are solving word problems, you need to have a deep understanding of math that goes beyond knowing when to apply a rule to a certain circumstance. You need to know why the rule works and how. Knowing these definitions will help.

The terms in appear in this glossary first in order of subject, from simplest to most advanced, and then appear again in alphabetical order for easy reference.

This glossary only covers the math concepts discussed in this book.

# Math Glossary - In Subject Order

**math**
Mathematics. The study of quantities and shapes using numbers and symbols.

**number**
Characters we use in our language to quickly describe how much of something there is. Examples of numbers include 7, 12, and -4,682.

**quantities**
How much of something there is. For example, if there are three apples in a basket, you would say that there is a quantity of 3 apples in the basket. Numbers describe quantities.

**symbols**
Something that stands for something else. For example, a statue is a symbol of the person it represents. A number on your computer screen that tells you how much money you have in your bank account is a symbol for the actual cash. In some math problems, we use letters as symbols for an unknown number.

**operation**
Any action that you take on a number or a set of numbers that changes it or causes it to stay the same. For example, if you add 2 to 3, you have just used an operation. The basic operations are adding, subtracting, multiplying, and dividing. They have symbols that can stand for them, instead of having to write the words out.

**add**
Addition. Combining two numbers or increasing one number by another number. Adding describes when you increase a quantity—for example, if you put 2 apples into a bag that already has three apples, you have added 3 apples to the bag. Adding is an operation.

**+**
This is called the plus symbol. The plus symbol represents the operation of addition. When you see 3 + 2, that means you are doing the operation of adding 2 to 3. You could represent putting two apples into a bag that already contains three apples with the symbols 3 + 2.

**plus**
The word that describes the operation of adding. When you are reading the symbol "+" aloud, you say "plus." 3 + 2 is read "three plus two."

**subtract**
Taking away from a number by another number. Subtracting describes when you decrease a quantity—for example, if you take away 2 apples from a bag that contains 5 apples, you have subtracted 2 apples from the bag. Subtracting is an operation.

**-**
This is called the minus symbol. The minus symbol represents the operation of subtraction. When you see 5 − 2, that means you are doing the operation of subtracting 2 from five. You could represent taking two apples from a bag that contains five apples with the symbols 5 − 2.

# Math Glossary

**minus**
The word that describes the operation of subtracting. When you are reading the symbol – aloud, you say "minus" 5 – 2 is read "five minus two."

**multiply**
Multiplication. The operation of adding repeatedly (adding multiple times). For example, if you add three apples into a bag four times, you could either do the operation of adding 3 four times, or you could do the operation of multiplying 3 and 4.

**x or * or •**
The x or * is used as the symbol of multiplication. We call it the times symbol. When you see 3 x 4, that means you are doing the operation of multiplying 3 and 4. You could represent the action of adding four sets of 3 apples to a bag as 3 x 4 (3 * 4). In lower level math, an x can be used as the symbol of multiplication, but for higher level math, you should use the * or •.

**times**
The word that describes the action of multiplying. When you are reading the symbol * or •, you say "times". 3 * 4 is read "three times four."

**divide**
Division. The operation of splitting a quantity into equal groups of quantities. For example, if you split 6 apples into two equal groups, that means that you are doing the operation of dividing 6 by 2.

**/**
The symbol that describes the operation of dividing. We call it the "divided by" symbol. When you see 6 / 2, that means that you are doing the operation of dividing 6 into 2. You could represent the action of splitting 6 apples into 2 equal groups as 6 / 2.

**into**
Another way to say "divided by." When you are reading 6 / 2, you can either say "six divided by two" or say "six into two." The words "into" are really short for "in to _____ equal parts."

**equals**
Being the same or identical in value. When we say that two things are equal in math, we mean that they have the same value. For example, 2 apples equals 2 apples. 2 apples do not equal 3 apples.

**=**
The symbol for "equals." When we write an "=" sign, we are saying that whatever is on the left of the sign is the same as whatever is on the right of the sign. For example, 2 = 2. Sometimes on the ACT you'll be asked a question such as: 2 + 3 = ? You are being asked what number is equal to 2 + 3.

**arithmetic**
The part of math that studies numbers using addition, subtraction, multiplication, and division.

**≈**
The symbol that stands for APPROXIMATELY EQUAL TO. This is used when we are rounding a number. Approximately means that a number is close but not exactly the same as another number. For example, 6.8247757 ≈ 6.82

**set**
A group of numbers or values.  For example, the set of five test scores in the math class might be 92, 94, 95, 96, and 98.

**sum**
The end result of addition.  The sum of 3 + 2 is 5.

**average**
The number obtained by adding up all the numbers in a set and dividing that sum by the number of quantities in that set.  For example, the average of five test scores: 92, 94, 95, 96 and 98 would be found by adding them all together (92 + 94 + 95 + 96 + 98) and then dividing that sum by 5.

**mean**
Another word for average.  Also sometimes called arithmetic mean.

**outcome**
Something that happens as the result of an action.  For example, the outcome of a coin flip can either be heads or tails.

**desired outcome**
The outcome that we want to have happen or are measuring for.  For example, if a question asks us what are the chances of flipping a coin and having it land on heads, our desired outcome is heads.

**possible outcome**
Any outcome that is possible when an action is taken.  For example, if a question asks us what the chances are of flipping a coin and having it land on heads, our possible outcomes are tails and heads.  When counting possible outcomes, you count them individually even if they are the same.  For example, if you are rolling a die with six sides, four colored red and two colored blue, there are six possible outcomes: red, red, red, red, blue and blue.  It would be incorrect to say that there are only two possible outcomes.

**probability**
A measurement of how confident one may be about whether or not an event will occur, measured on a scale of 0 (impossible) to 1 (completely certain).  We also define probability as the number of desired outcomes divided by the total number of possible outcomes.

**combination**
A possible grouping of different things.  For example, if there are red, blue and green shirts, as well as red, blue and green shorts, then one possible combination of clothing would be a red shirt and blue shorts.  Some math problems ask you to find how many different combinations are possible.

**chances**
Another word for probability.  "What are the chances of this happening?" and "What is the probability of this happening?" are both asking the same question: you're being asked to express in a number between 0 and 1 how confident we are about whether or not an event will occur.  This can be expressed as a decimal (for example, .5), as a percentage (50%), as a fraction (1/2), or as a ratio (1:1).

# Math Glossary

**ratio**
A ratio compares one number to another number. The colon (:) is the symbol for a ratio. Typically when you are dealing with probability, a ratio shows the probability of a desired outcome happening vs. the probability of a desired outcome not happening. For example, if there is one desired outcome, and one undesired outcome, then the ratio is 1:1. You read this as "one to one."

**odds**
Another word for probability. However, when the word "odds" is used you are typically being asked to express the probability as a ratio. For example, the odds of flipping heads on a two-sided coin is 1:1.

**fraction**
A part of a whole number. The top part of a fraction shows you how much of something you have, and the bottom shows you how many parts are equal to 1. For example, the fraction 5/4 tells you that there are five parts, and every four parts is equal to one. So you have a little more than one of something if you have 5/4.

**algebra**
The part of math that uses symbols to represent unknown numbers in order to solve problems and demonstrate relationships between numbers. If I don't know how fast a train is going, I could use algebra to figure it out.

**equation**
A mathematical expression that states that one set of numbers and symbols is equal to another set of numbers and symbols. For example, 2 + 3 = 5 is an equation.

**variable**
A letter that is used as a symbol for an unknown or changing number. It's called a variable because it can vary from one problem to the next.

**x, y, a, b**
All of these are examples of variables that can be used in equations. Any letter can be used as a variable.

**constant**
Any number that is set and can't change from equation to equation is a constant. That means that it can't change or be different. 9 will always be 9. This is different than a variable. The variable x in one problem may be a symbol for 5 and in the next problem be a symbol for 8.

**formula**
A formula is an equation that expresses a relationship or describes a way to arrive at an answer. To use a formula, you often plug in numbers in the place of the variables in the formula. For example, the formula for the area of a square is: s * s = a, where s is the length of the side and a is the area. This is used by plugging in the side length of whatever square you are measuring.

**geometry**
The part of mathematics dealing with the measurement and relationship of points, lines, angles, surfaces, and solids.

**point**
An exact location. In geometry, a point is often placed on a graph and compared to other points.

### line
A figure formed by a point moving along a fixed direction and the opposite direction. A line always has the same slope and continues on and on indefinitely.

### line segment
The part of a line starting at one point and ending at another point.

### length
The distance from one point to another point on a shape. Typically the length is the measurement of the longer side of a shape.

### width
The distance from one point to another point on a shape. Typically the width is the shorter of the two measurements of a shape.

### axis
One of two lines on a graph that serve as a reference when solving geometry problems.

### x-axis
A horizontal line on a graph that is used as a reference to figure out where a point is.

### y-axis
A vertical line on a graph that is used as a reference to figure out where a point is.

### coordinate
A set of two numbers that describe where a point is. The first number describes where the point is on the x-axis. The second number describes where the point is on the y-axis. For example (3,2) describes a point that is over the number 3 on the x-axis and next to the number 2 on the y-axis.

### slope
Slope describes how steeply a line is moving from left to right. A slope of 4 means that for every 1 x on the line, y increases by 4. So a line with slope 4 passing through the point (1,1) would also pass through the point (2,5) and (3,9).

### slope formula
The slope formula describes how you can figure out the slope of a line. For any two sets of coordinates $(x_1,y_1)$ $(x_2,y_2)$, the slope of the line between them is $(y_2 - y_1) / (x_2 - x_1)$. In other words, the slope is equal to the change in y divided by the change in x. Use the slope formula to determine the slope of any line.

### y-intercept
The point on a line that crosses the Y axis on a graph. The y intercept is always the y coordinate on the line when x = 0.

### y = mx + b
The equation of a straight line (a linear equation), in "slope-intercept" form. In this form, you can easily identify the slope and the y-intercept of any line. Some math problems require you to simplify a more complicated equation into slope-intercept form and then identify the parts. X and Y refer to coordinates on the graph. M is the slope. B is the y-intercept.

# Math Glossary

**m**
The slope of a line in a linear equation in slope-intercept form. See y = mx + b.

**b**
The y-intercept of a line when an equation is in slope-intercept form. See y = mx + b.

**circle**
A shape made by drawing a curve that is always the same distance from its center.

**radius**
The distance from the center of a circle to its curve.

**diameter**
The distance from one side of a circle through the center to the other side. The diameter is always double the radius.

**perimeter**
The total distance around the edges of a shape.

**binomial**
A math expression with two numbers and a + or -. For example, 5 + 2 is a binomial. So is x – 7.

**FOIL**
A method of simplifying the process of multiplying two binomials. FOIL stands for FIRST, OUTSIDE, INSIDE, LAST. In multiplying 2 binomials, for example (x + 3)(x + 2), you multiply the first terms together, then the outside, then the inside, then the last terms. You add all of these together to get your answer.

**sequence**
A series of numbers that have a definite pattern, one to the next, and have a definite operation or series of operations conducted between one number in the series and the next.

**pattern**
A series of numbers that follow a rule in changing one to the next.

**arithmetic sequence**
A sequence where the difference between any two numbers in the series is a constant, unchanging number. For example, in the arithmetic sequence 3, 5, 7, 9…the constant unchanging number is 2.

**geometric sequence**
A sequence where each number in the series is found by multiplying the previous one by a fixed number. For example, in the geometric sequence 2, 4, 8, 16… the fixed number is 2.

**intersect**
Where two lines cross.

**angle**
The space between two intersecting lines, usually measured in degrees (°). The space on all sides of two intersecting lines = 360°.

**degrees**
Describes how open or closed an angle is, from 0 degrees (completely closed) to 360 degrees (completely open). A point has 360 degrees around it. If two lines closed off 25% of the space around the point, those lines would form a 360 * 25% = 90 degree angle.

**°**
The symbol for degrees, a unit of measure for angles.

**triangle**
A shape with three sides.

**square**
A shape with four equal sides.

**rectangle**
A four-sided shape with two sets of sides with equal length and four right angles (90° angles).

**parallelogram**
A 4-sided shape with 2 sets of equal sides.

**right triangle**
A triangle with a right angle (90° angle).

**area**
The amount of space inside a shape. There are many formulas for figuring out area, depending on what shape you are calculating.

**Pythagorean theorem**
A formula for calculating the length of the sides of a right triangle. On the right triangle ABC, $a^2 + b^2 = c^2$.

**²**
This is read aloud "squared." It tells you to multiply a number by itself. For example, $5^2 = 5 * 5 = 25$. $X^2 = x * x$.

**in²**
A unit of measure that describes an area one inch long by one inch wide. It is read "square inch." If there is more than one square inch, in² is read aloud "square inches."

**parallel**
We say that two lines are parallel if they have the same slope and therefore will never intersect. If 2 lines never intersect and have the same slope, they are parallel. 2 line segments can only be parallel if they have the same slope. Just because 2 line segments don't intersect doesn't mean that they are parallel.

**internal angle**
The angle inside the shape.

**external angle**
The angle on the other side of an internal angle. The angle outside the shape.

# Math Glossary

**rate**
How quickly or how slowly something happens. Usually this is expressed with 2 units of measure and a "per" in between. For example, "miles per hour" or "miles per gallon" or "dollars per hour."

**solve**
To find the answer for something.

**simplify**
To turn an equation or number into a simpler format. For example, 10/4 = 5/2. 5/2 is the simplified format of 10/4.

# Math Glossary - In Alphabetical Order

**+**
This is called the plus symbol. The plus symbol represents the operation of addition. When you see 3 + 2, that means you are doing the operation of adding 2 to 3. You could represent putting two apples into a bag that already contains three apples with the symbols 3 + 2.

**-**
This is called the minus symbol. The minus symbol represents the operation of subtraction. When you see 5 – 2, that means you are doing the operation of subtracting 2 from five. You could represent taking two apples from a bag that contains five apples with the symbols 5 – 2.

**x or *or •**
The x or * is used as the symbol of multiplication. We call it the "times" symbol. When you see 3 x 4, that means you are doing the operation of multiplying 3 and 4. You could represent the action of adding four sets of 3 apples to a bag as 3 x 4 or (3 * 4). In lower level math, an x can be used as the symbol of multiplication, but for higher level math, you should use the * or •.

**/**
The symbol that describes the operation of dividing. We call it the "divided by" symbol. When you see 6 / 2, that means that you are doing the operation of dividing 6 into 2. You could represent the action of splitting 6 apples into 2 equal groups as 6 / 2.

**=**
The symbol for equals. When we write an "=" sign, we are saying that whatever is on the left of the sign is the same as whatever is on the right of the sign. For example, 2 = 2. Sometimes on the ACT you'll be asked a question such as: 2 + 3 = ? You are being asked what number is equal to 2 + 3.

**≈**
The symbol that stands for APPROXIMATELY EQUAL TO. This is used when we are rounding a number. Approximately means that a number is close but not exactly the same as another number. For example, 6.8247757 ≈ 6.82

**°**
The symbol for degrees, a unit of measure for angles.

**2**
This is read aloud "squared." It tells you to multiply a number by itself. For example, $5^2 = 5 * 5 = 25$. $X^2 = x * x$.

**add**
Addition. Combining two numbers or increasing one number by another number. Adding describes when you increase a quantity—for example, if you put 2 apples into a bag that already has three apples, you have added 3 apples to the bag. Adding is an operation.

**algebra**
The part of math that uses symbols to represent unknown numbers in order to solve problems and demonstrate relationships between numbers. If I don't know how fast a train is going, I could use algebra to figure it out.

# Math Glossary

**angle**
The space between two intersecting lines, usually measured in degrees (°). The space on all sides of two intersecting lines = 360°.

**area**
The amount of space inside a shape. There are many formulas for figuring out area, depending on what shape you are calculating.

**arithmetic**
The part of math that studies numbers using addition, subtraction, multiplication, and division.

**arithmetic sequence**
A sequence where the difference between any two numbers in the series is a constant, unchanging number. For example, in the arithmetic sequence 3, 5, 7, 9…the constant unchanging number is 2.

**average**
The number obtained by adding up all the numbers in a set and dividing that sum by the number of quantities in that set. For example, the average of five test scores: 92, 94, 95, 96 and 98 would be found by adding them all together (92 + 94 + 95 + 96 + 98) and then dividing that sum by 5.

**axis**
One of two lines on a graph that serve as a reference when solving geometry problems.

**b**
The y-intercept of a line when an equation is in slope-intercept form. See $y = mx + b$.

**binomial**
A math expression with two numbers and a + or -. For example, 5 + 2 is a binomial. So is x – 7.

**chances**
Another word for probability. "What are the chances of this happening?" and "What is the probability of this happening?" are both asking the same question: you're being asked to express in a number between 0 and 1 how confident we are about whether or not an event will occur. This can be expressed as a decimal (for example, .5), as a percentage (50%), as a fraction (1/2), or as a ratio (1:1).

**circle**
A shape made by drawing a curve that is always the same distance from its center.

**combination**
A possible grouping of different things. For example, if there are red, blue and green shirts, as well as red, blue and green shorts, then one possible combination of clothing would be a red shirt and blue shorts. Some math problems ask you to find how many different combinations are possible.

**constant**
Any number that is set and can't change from equation to equation is a constant. That means that it can't change or be different. 9 will always be 9. This is different than a variable. The variable x in one problem may be a symbol for 5 and in the next problem be a symbol for 8.

**coordinate**
A set of two numbers that describe where a point is. The first number describes where the point is on the x-axis. The second number describes where the point is on the y-axis. For example (3,2) describes a point that is over the number 3 on the x-axis and next to the number 2 on the y-axis.

**degrees**
Describes how open or closed an angle is, from 0 degrees (completely closed) to 360 degrees (completely open). A point has 360 degrees around it. If two lines closed off 25% of the space around the point, those lines would form a 360 * 25% = 90 degree angle.

**desired outcome**
The outcome that we want to have happen or are measuring for. For example, if a question asks us what are the chances of flipping a coin and having it land on heads, our desired outcome is heads.

**diameter**
The distance from one side of a circle through the center to the other side. The diameter is always double the radius.

**divide**
Division. The operation of splitting a quantity into equal groups of quantities. For example, if you split 6 apples into two equal groups, that means that you are doing the operation of dividing 6 by 2.

**equation**
A mathematical expression that states that one set of numbers and symbols is equal to another set of numbers and symbols. For example, 2 + 3 = 5 is an equation.

**external angle**
The angle on the other side of an internal angle. The angle outside the shape.

**equals**
Being the same or identical in value. When we say two that things are equal in math, we mean that they have the same value. For example, 2 apples equals 2 apples. 2 apples do not equal 3 apples.

**FOIL**
A method of simplifying the process of multiplying two binomials. FOIL stands for FIRST, OUTSIDE, INSIDE, LAST. In multiplying 2 binomials, for example (x + 3)(x + 2), you multiply the first terms together, then the outside, then the inside, then the last terms. You add all of these together to get your answer.

**formula**
A formula is an equation that expresses a relationship or describes a way to arrive at an answer. To use a formula, you often plug in numbers in the place of the variables in the formula. For example, the formula for the area of a square is: s * s = a, where s is the length of the side and a is the area. This is used by plugging in the side length of whatever square you are measuring.

**fraction**
A part of a whole number. The top part of a fraction shows you how much of something you have, and the bottom shows you how many parts are equal to 1. For example, the fraction 5/4 tells you that there are five parts, and every four parts is equal to one. So you have a little more than one of something if you have 5/4.

# Math Glossary

**geometry**
The part of mathematics dealing with the measurement and relationship of points, lines, angles, surfaces and solids.

**geometric sequence**
A sequence where each number in the series is found by multiplying the previous one by a fixed number. For example, in the geometric sequence 2, 4, 8, 16… the fixed number is 2.

**into**
Another way to say "divided by." When you are reading 6 / 2, you can either say "six divided by two" or say "six in to two." The words "into" are really short for "in to ____ equal parts."

**in²**
A unit of measure that describes an area one inch long by one inch wide. It is read "square inch." If there is more than one square inch, in² is read aloud "square inches."

**internal angle**
The angle inside the shape.

**intersect**
Where two lines cross.

**length**
The distance from one point to another point on a shape. Typically the length is the measurement of the longer side of a shape.

**line**
A figure formed by a point moving along a fixed direction and the opposite direction. A line always has the same slope and continues on and on indefinitely.

**line segment**
The part of a line starting at one point and ending at another point.

**m**
The slope of a line in a linear equation in slope-intercept form. See $y = mx + b$.

**math**
Mathematics. The study of quantities and shapes using numbers and symbols.

**mean**
Another word for average. Also sometimes called arithmetic mean.

**minus**
The word that describes the operation of subtracting. When you are reading the symbol "–" aloud, you say "minus" 5 – 2 is read "five minus two."

**multiply**
Multiplication. The operation of adding repeatedly (adding multiple times). For example, if you add three apples into a bag four times, you could either do the operation of adding 3 four times, or you could do the operation of multiplying 3 and 4.

**number**
Characters we use in our language to quickly describe how much of something there is. Examples of numbers include 7, 12, and -4,682.

**odds**
Another word for probability. However, when the word "odds" is used you are typically being asked to express the probability as a ratio. For example, the odds of flipping heads on a two-sided coin is 1:1.

**operation**
Any action that you take on a number or a set of numbers that changes it or causes it to stay the same. For example, if you add 2 to 3, you have just used an operation. The basic operations are adding, subtracting, multiplying, and dividing. They have symbols that can stand for them, instead of having to write the words out.

**outcome**
Something that happens as the result of an action. For example, the outcome of a coin flip can either be heads or tails.

**parallel**
We say that two lines are parallel if they have the same slope and therefore will never intersect. If 2 lines never intersect and have the same slope, they are parallel. 2 line segments can only be parallel if they have the same slope. Just because 2 line segments don't intersect doesn't mean that they are parallel.

**parallelogram**
A 4-sided shape with 2 sets of equal sides.

**pattern**
A series of numbers that follow a rule in changing one to the next.

**perimeter**
The total distance around the edges of a shape.

**plus**
The word that describes the operation of adding. When you are reading the symbol "+" aloud, you say "plus." 3 + 2 is read "three plus two."

**point**
An exact location. In geometry, a point is often placed on a graph and compared to other points.

## Math Glossary

**possible outcome**
Any outcome that is possible when an action is taken. For example, if a question asks us what the chances are of flipping a coin and having it land on heads, our possible outcomes are tails and heads. When you are counting possible outcomes, you count them individually even if they are the same. For example, if you are rolling a die with six sides, four colored red and two colored blue, there are six possible outcomes: red, red, red, red, blue and blue. It would be incorrect to say that there are only two possible outcomes.

**probability**
A measurement of how confident one may be about whether or not an event will occur, measured on a scale of 0 (impossible) to 1 (completely certain). We also define probability as the number of desired outcomes divided by the total number of possible outcomes.

**Pythagorean theorem**
A formula for calculating the length of the sides of a right triangle. On the right triangle ABC, $a^2 + b^2 = c^2$.

**quantities**
How much of something there is. For example, if there are three apples in a basket, you would say that there is a quantity of 3 apples in the basket. Numbers describe quantities.

**radius**
The distance from the center of a circle to its curve.

**rate**
How quickly or how slowly something happens. Usually this is expressed with 2 units of measure and a "per" in between. For example, "miles per hour" or "miles per gallon" or "dollars per hour."

**ratio**
A ratio compares one number to another number. The colon (:) is the symbol for a ratio. Typically when you are dealing with probability, a ratio shows the probability of a desired outcome happening vs. the probability of a desired outcome not happening. For example, if there is one desired outcome, and one undesired outcome, then the ratio is 1:1. You read this as "one to one."

**rectangle**
A four-sided shape with two sets of sides with equal length and four right angles (90° angles).

**right triangle**
A triangle with a right angle (90° angle).

**sequence**
A series of numbers that have a definite pattern, one to the next, and have a definite operation or series of operations conducted between one number in the series and the next.

**set**
A group of numbers or values. For example, the set of five test scores in the math class might be 92, 94, 95, 96, and 98.

**simplify**
To turn an equation or number into a simpler format. For example, 10/4 = 5/2. 5/2 is the simplified format of 10/4.

**slope**
Slope describes how steeply a line is moving from left to right. A slope of 4 means that for every 1 x on the line, y increases by 4. So a line with slope 4 passing through the point (1,1) would also pass through the point (2,5) and (3,9).

**slope formula**
The slope formula describes how you can figure out the slope of a line. For any two sets of coordinates $(x_1,y_1)$ $(x_2,y_2)$, the slope of the line between them is $(y_2 - y_1) / (x_2 - x_1)$. In other words, the slope is equal to the change in y divided by the change in x. Use the slope formula to determine the slope of any line.

**solve**
To find the answer for something.

**square**
A shape with four equal sides.

**subtract**
Taking away from a number by another number. Subtracting describes when you decrease a quantity—for example, if you take away 2 apples from a bag that contains 5 apples, you have subtracted 2 apples from the bag. Subtracting is an operation.

**sum**
The end result of addition. The sum of 3 + 2 is 5.

**symbols**
Something that stands for something else. For example, a statue is a symbol of the person it represents. A number on your computer screen that tells you how much money you have in your bank account is a symbol for the actual cash. In some math problems, we use letters as symbols for an unknown number.

**times**
The word that describes the action of multiplying. When you are reading the symbol * or •, you say "times." 3 * 4 is read "three times four."

**triangle**
A shape with three sides.

**variable**
A letter that is used as a symbol for an unknown or changing number. It's called a variable because it can vary from one problem to the next.

**width**
The distance from one point to another point on a shape. Typically the width is the shorter of the two measurements of a shape.

**x, y, a, b**
All of these are examples of variables that can be used in equations. Any letter can be used as a variable.

**x-axis**
A horizontal line on a graph that is used as a reference to figure out where a point is.

**y-axis**
A vertical line on a graph that is used as a reference to figure out where a point is.

**y-intercept**
The point on a line that crosses the Y axis on a graph. The y intercept is always the y coordinate on the line when x = 0.

**y = mx + b**
The equation of a straight line (linear equation), in "slope-intercept" form. In this form, you can easily identify the slope and the y-intercept of any line. Some math problems require you to simplify a more complicated equation into slope-intercept form and then identify the parts. X and Y refer to coordinates on the graph. M is the slope. B is the y-intercept.

# About the Author

Craig Gehring has helped thousands of students work toward their higher educational dreams since 2003, his junior year in high school when he earned perfect scores on both the ACT and the SAT. That year, parents started calling the school and asking for Craig to tutor their children. Ten years later, he has written the books—literally—on mastering the ACT and leads an effort to improve preparation for standardized tests. His *ACT Mastery* program averages more than a three point improvement in only six weeks, four times better than the national test prep average.

Contact Craig by email, on his blog, or on Facebook:

craig@MasteryPrep.com
www.MasteryPrep.com
http://www.facebook.com/CraigGehringACT

# Further Study

For more information, and to find an ACT prep course in your area or online, visit www.ACTMastery.com

Classroom discounts available upon request.

Other Craig Gehring Titles:

*SAT ACT Mastery*
*ACT English Mastery, Level 1*
*ACT Reading Mastery, Level 1*
*ACT Science Mastery, Level 1*
*ACT Writing Mastery, Level 1*

Made in the USA
Middletown, DE
02 February 2015